Health Insurance Plans: Promise and Performance

HEALTH, MEDICINE, AND SOCIETY: A WILEY-INTERSCIENCE SERIES

DAVID MECHANIC, Editor

Evaluating Treatment Environments: A Social Ecological Approach
by **Rudolf H. Moos**

Human Subjects in Medical Experimentation: A Sociological Study of the Conduct and Regulation of Clinical Research
by **Bradford H. Gray**

Child Health and the Community
by **Robert J. Haggerty, Klaus J. Roghmann,** and **Ivan B. Pless**

Health Insurance Plans: Promise and Performance
by **Robert W. Hetherington, Carl E. Hopkins,** and **Milton I. Roemer**

The End of Medicine
by **Rick Carlson**

Humanizing Health Care
edited by **Jan Howard** and **Anselm Strauss**

ROBERT W. HETHERINGTON, Ph.D.
CARL E. HOPKINS, Ph.D.
MILTON I. ROEMER, M.D.

Health Insurance Plans: Promise and Performance

with the assistance of

Arthur Gerst
Eleanor Parsons
Clayton Stouffer
Carolyn Aydin
Donald M. Long
Marilyn Miller

A WILEY-INTERSCIENCE PUBLICATION

JOHN WILEY & SONS, New York • London • Sydney • Toronto

Library of Congress Cataloging in Publication Data:

Hetherington, Robert W. 1936–
Health insurance plans.
(Health, medicine, and society)
"A Wiley-Interscience publication."

Includes index.
1. Insurance, Health—United States. 2. Medical care—United States. I. Hopkins, Carl E., 1912– joint author. II. Roemer, Milton Irwin, 1916– joint author. III. Title.

HD7102.U4H45 368 3'8'00973 74-30014
ISBN 0-471-38230-2

Printed in the United States of America
10 9 8 7 6 5 4 3 2 1

Preface

AMERICAN HEALTH SERVICE organization is often described as pluralistic, and for no sector is this description more apt than for health insurance plans. Unlike most European countries, we have no national health care system but a galaxy of autonomous, often competing, health programs. Although this diversity creates serious problems of inequity in the receipt of services by population groups, it does provide fertile ground for social research that can compare the consequences of different systems of health care financing and organization.

The research reported in this book is based on the comparative analysis of the main types of health insurance plan operating in the United States. Although the principal work was launched in 1965, its beginnings must be traced to exploratory studies of the California health insurance scene begun by Milton Roemer in 1962. Because it is applied research, an investigation of problems in the work-a-day world, its execution required countless contacts with the organizations and individuals under study. The relationships that ensued, as every social researcher knows, are often delicate and time consuming. Human beings are not so readily "handled" as laboratory mice.

The first important statistical outputs of our investigations therefore did not emerge until about 1971 and preliminary analyses, until 1972. This was just at the time when national debates on statutory health insurance were reaching a high pitch and, on invitation of committees from both houses of the U.S. Congress, before which we testified, we were urged to report our findings. Even though, as explained, the analyses were not yet completed, we complied with these requests. Thus in 1972 we published a preliminary report of our findings, which were presented according to the three main plan types rather than for the six separate health insurance plans reported on in this book (Roemer, et al., 1972).

The perceptive reader will discover some apparent, but not real, discrepancies between the findings reported in the 1972 monograph and those in this volume; for example, data on health expenditures appear in the earlier report by family units, while here they are presented more meaningfully on a per capita basis. Percentage distributions of consumer opinions about their health insurance plans differ slightly because, after further study, we found it advisable to use a somewhat modified scheme of scaling the responses. Rates of hospital admission were more reliable when based on our medical record data than on our questionnaire responses, as in the preliminary report. Nevertheless, the basic relations among the three plan types are consistent across the preliminary and final reports.

It is evident from this book that there are important differences *within* plan types. Two examples of each plan type do not constitute a large sample, of course, and 10 or 20 of each would have been better. Financial constraints set these limits, but even these small samples serve to remind us of the need for caution in making generalizations about health organizations. Yet we may point out that this is the first American research that has reported on the findings of even two cases of each of the three main types of health insurance plan. Other research has been confined to single examples of each plan type.

In the course of this research several working papers were produced which helped to shed light on the phenomena being studied. A number of them were published in professional journals, and in 1970 we assembled 23 of them in a processed volume issued by the UCLA School of Public Health (Roemer, et al., 1970); a second printing of this collection was made in 1972.

The crucial data, on which most of the statistical analyses in this volume are based, apply to the years 1967 through 1969. Some may ask if these findings are still valid for 1974 or 1975. We believe they are. Changes in the operation of health insurance plans occur every year, but the basic principles of the three types of plan and the six specific organizations we have analyzed have remained relatively constant. There is also no reason to think that any major changes have occurred in the composition of the populations covered by each of the plans in relation to one another over these years. The major change of the 1960s, the enactment of the federal Medicare law which covers aged persons (65 years plus), took place in 1965, before our data were gathered. We are confident, therefore, that the basic comparative findings reported in this book remain valid today.

We have taken pains to state this because of the enactment in December 1973 of federal legislation to promote "health maintenance organizations" (HMOs), a pattern of health insurance quite similar to what we call "group practice plans." We believe that the findings reported—both those comparing the group practice plan type with the other two types and those comparing one group practice plan with the other—can furnish information of use to policy makers under the HMO law and, indeed, under national health insurance legislation that may well be enacted in the near future.

One *caveat,* however, should be kept in mind. The performance of a health insurance plan, or any other organized entity, may be expected to differ in a social environment in which it represents a minority phenomenon (like the prepaid group practice plans today) from its probable performance in a future setting in which it will become more common and closer to the national norm. Minority status suffers handicaps, in a sense, of social deviance, which affect the behavior of all the actors in the system—doctors, patients and plan personnel. At the same time this minority status may have certain assets—a missionary spirit, for example, in its advocates—which may not characterize the same social pattern when it attains a more commonplace and "respectable" position. Predictions of the performance of future HMOs, after a period of statutory encouragement and growth, must therefore be made with caution. Much also depends on the general influence of social and political forces in the years ahead.

In the performance of this research contributions were made by many people beyond those recorded on the title page. For their work in the early exploratory stages our appreciation goes to Richard Sasuly, Martin Horowitz, Monroe Epstein, Addie Lou Klotz, Donald M. DuBois, Lorraine Rogson, Bryan Gerstel, Jessica Buxbaum, and Shirley W. Rich. The contributions of other research personnel during the seven years of data collection, processing, and analysis must also be gratefully acknowledged. Among the mainstays during these busy times were Gail McKee, Valerie Thorsness, Sharon Harris, Laurel Chelsom, George Mancini, and Debbie Scott. Much appreciation is also due to Sharyn Holloway, project secretary for the entire period, for the thousands of pages of typing and retyping she did.

This book has been set in type using a photocomposition computer program designed and developed by David Packard at UCLA Campus Computing Network. This is the first book of this type to be produced and typeset using this computer program. The book was composed for the most part at a computer console, editing and paging done using the computer's text-editor, and photoready copy produced on the videocomp at the Los Angeles Times. We are indebted for help at various stages from many persons, among whom are David Packard, Victor Tolomei, Howard Golden, Chon Vinson, Fred Hoffman, Annette Lightell and Kerrick Foster.

Without financial support, principally from the U.S. Department of Health, Education and Welfare, this research could not have been carried out. In chronological order, we wish to acknowledge, with much appreciation, awards made to the University of California, Los Angeles: (1) California State Department of Public Health (California Standard Agreement No. 608) in 1963; U.S. Department of H.E.W., Public Health Service (HEW-PHS Contract No. 108-64-25) in June 1964; (3) U.S. Department of H.E.W., Public Health Service (a major five-year "program grant" on Patterns of Medical Care Organization—Comparative Studies, CH 00102-01 to 05) in January 1965; (4) Renewal of the above grant (9 P01 HS-00274-06) in January 1970; and (5) second renewal (2 P01 HS-00274-07) in January 1971.

For computing work we are grateful for the services of the UCLA Campus Computing Network and also the Health Sciences Computing Facility. For field interviews we appreciated the assistance of the UCLA Survey Research Center and the National Opinion Research Center.

Most of all, we wish to acknowledge the cooperation of the health insurance plans, their staffs, their associated doctors, and their thousands of members whose responses to our many questions made this study possible. We would be remiss if we failed to recognize the whole-hearted cooperation of the two commercial insurance companies and the two prepaid group practice plans. The lesser cooperation of the two provider-sponsored plans compelled us to collect the necessary data by a methodology that was more laborious and costly and thus delayed the completion of the study.

A great deal more data were collected in this research than have been analyzed and presented in this book. The constraints of time, funding, and competing demands—well known to health service researchers—are responsible; for example analyses of the use of and expenditures for drugs or dental care or opinions of insurance plan members about issues beyond financial coverage and medical care received have not been presented, although the raw data are available. Multivariate analyses of the combined effects of the numerous independent variables remain to be made.

We trust, nevertheless, that the findings reported here, and perhaps their interpretations, will be useful to policy makers in grappling with the complex problems of designing improved health insurance programs for the people of America.

Milton I. Roemer, *Principal Investigator*
Carl E. Hopkins, *Co-Principal Investigator*
Robert W. Hetherington, *Project Director*

School of Public Health
University of California, Los Angeles
January, 1975

REFERENCES

Roemer, Milton I., Hetherington, R.W., Hopkins, C.E., Gerst, A.E., Parsons, E., and Long, Donald M. *Health insurance effects: services, expenditures, and attitudes under three types of plan,* Ann Arbor: University of Michigan, School of Public Health, Bureau of Public Health Economics, Research Series No. 16, 1972.

Roemer, M. I., DuBois, D.M., and Rich, Shirley W. *Health insurance plans: studies in organizational diversity,* Los Angeles: University of California School of Public Health, processed, 1970.

Contents

Health Insurance Plans: Promise and Performance

I

The Approach

THIS IS AN ERA of public accountability. In the health insurance field it is also an era of debate about the form national health insurance might take. This study is relevant to both issues. For the former it provides an in-depth look at how well each of the major types of health insurance plan now operating in the United States serves the public. Such data are generally lacking on a comprehensive scale so that people spend large amounts of money on health insurance without adequate performance indicators. For the latter the study adds information to the debate over national health insurance. The comparison of representatives of leading contenders documents advantages and disadvantages for the consideration of policy makers.

Our study, Patterns of Medical Care Organization (POMCO), was begun in 1965 and completed in 1972. It was designed to compare the performance of three major types of health insurance plan in America today:

Commercial insurance company plans: these plans offer choice of physician with payment to the subscriber for some or all of his medical bills.

Provider-sponsored plans: choice of physician with payment to member physicians and hospitals for some or all medical services used by the subscriber.

Prepaid group-practice plans: one of the Health Maintenance Organization (HMO) models in which physicians practice in a group, on a salary; the plan usually provides rather complete benefits to subscribers.

Two representatives of each type of plan were chosen (one large and one small) from the Los Angeles metropolitan area. These plans are referred to in the study as

(1) large commercial plan,
(2) small commercial plan,
(3) hospital-sponsored plan,
(4) physician-sponsored plan,
(5) large group practice plan,
(6) small group practice plan.

Interest in the performance of the group practice plans has recently been heightened by the President's health strategy message of February 1971 in which Health Maintenance Organizations were promoted as one solution to the problems of the U.S. health care delivery system.

The six plans in the study were compared on four effects:

Quantity of physician and hospital services used.

Quality of services provided in terms of range of technical services given (preventive, diagnostic, and therapeutic).

Consumer expenses, including premiums paid and out-of-pocket expenses.

Consumer satisfaction with financial coverage and medical care received.

Data on these effects or outputs are vital to the planning of any national health insurance scheme. To get this information we studied representative samples of consumers in each plan and in addition gathered data from plan officials, physicians, and medical records.

The study of health delivery and financing systems is not new. Controversy has raged in the literature for some time over such issues as the advantages and disadvantages of group practice, fee-for-service versus salaried physicians, preventive medicine, the relative emphasis on ambulatory as opposed to in-patient treatment, control of unnecessary use of services by deterrent fees and coinsurance, and regulation of quality of care.[1] The reasons for much disagreement over these issues are ideological rather than factual. Representatives of the conservative persuasion, for instance, could usually be counted on to defend free-enterprise, competitive medical practice, regardless of the evidence attesting to its shortcomings. Liberals, on the other hand, are predictably fond of reciting this evidence and ignoring or explaining away criticisms of newer forms of delivery and financing of health care, such as prepaid group practice and government-supported systems. In this study we have tried to present an objective account of the facts regarding the central issues. In all cases the data are presented as completely as space allows so that the reader is given the chance to accept or reject our conclusions and interpretations.

Certain large issues have occupied the attention of previous major investigations similar to ours. Since everybody is in favor of economy, one of these large issues is the promotion of preventive and ambulatory services in place of costly hospital services. A study in 1958 by Densen and his colleagues provided data for the argument that prepaid group practice plans with salaried physicians lead to lower use of hospital services than the free-choice open market alternative. All other things being relatively equal, this would be a good thing. In 1961 Anderson and Sheatsley did another study and came to similar conclusions, and supportive data were found subsequently by Perrott (1966 and 1971) and in 1971 by the Medical Advisory Council to the California Public Employees Retirement System. Evidence from a study by the Columbia University School of Public Health and Administrative Medicine in 1962, however, indicated essentially no difference in hospital use between prepaid group practice and the fee-for-service pattern. Although this does not adequately represent much work done on this question, it is evident that data suggest a savings on hospital use by prepaid group practice

---

[1] This is not an exhaustive exploration of the literature. Many other studies deal with the same concepts and problems—namely the influence that method of organization and financing services have on medical care. Freidson (1961), for instance, has provided data relevant to this study on the attitudes of consumers in prepaid group and solo practices, and the influences of these types of delivery systems on the physician's role. Freidson dealt with accessibility to care among these types, recognizing the limitations of group organization which are documented in this book. A review of the recent evidence of performance under the Health Maintenance Organization (HMO) mode is provided in Roemer and Shonick (1973).

plans, but the desirability of such savings awaits the demonstration that they are not at the expense of subscribers who in fact *require* hospitalization. We have more to say on this issue later.

In regard to use of medical services outside the hospital, there is a long history of concern by the medical profession and by insurance companies that comprehensive benefits which include these services lead to frivolous use. Because of the relative scarcity of physicians, it is feared that overuse by those with low need will leave insufficient time to care properly for those with more serious needs. This is no simple question, since use of ambulatory (out-of-hospital) services might logically be inversely related to use of in-patient services; hence increases in the former could be seen as desirable. The core of the question concerns the definition of "frivolous" use of services. Previous studies have not dealt extensively with this question in the ambulatory setting. Evidence from previous studies, again not conclusive, supports the idea that prepaid group practice plans with relatively comprehensive benefits (i.e., covering ambulatory as well as in-hospital services) tend to have higher physician-visit rates (Columbia University study, 1962; Perrott, 1971; California PERS, 1971; Peterson, 1971). The Anderson and Sheatsley study (1961) found somewhat lower rates of doctor visits under the prepaid group practice pattern. We will examine our data with these questions in mind: which health insurance plans have higher rates of physician services and is there evidence that comprehensive benefits for these services encourage unnecessary use? As important (or perhaps more important) is the question about the effect of deterrent fees and coinsurance on use of physician services: do they prevent those who need care from seeing a physician?

Quality of medical care has occupied the interest of evaluators for some time. At this point it carries with it a certain aura or mystique that makes objective study difficult. Physicians tend to feel, as all professionals do, that the quality of their work can be judged only by peers. It is no easy task, however, to find two physicians who would agree on standards and criteria and who would come up with similar evaluations independently. The ability of the profession to monitor quality of care within its own ranks has been brought into question with the current establishment of Professional Standards Review Organizations (PSRO) all over the country. The task of these organizations is to monitor quality of care within government-financed programs, and they will undoubtedly play a large part in any national scheme adopted. The PSRO model relies heavily on use of information from medical records and their translation into standard computerized data.

Previous studies of quality of care have employed the medical audit process, and a few have looked at outcomes such as perinatal mortality to measure quality of care. Generally speaking, evaluations can concentrate on *structure, process,* or *outcome* . Structure refers to the qualifications of doctors providing the care and adequacy of facilities available; process refers to medical procedures performed and outcome means the effect of structure and process on the health of the patient.

The issue of quality of medical care raises two important questions. First, can aspects of quality be assessed in a satisfactory manner from medical records information? Second, what is the influence of different delivery and financing systems on quality? Some information in other studies suggests that we should expect to find more preventive medicine practiced in prepaid group practice plans. It is plausible that the group practice setting may be conducive to quality care because of constant opportunity for peer review and consultation.

Expenditures for medical care by the consumer is of vital interest in a time of rapidly increasing prices. Under which system of delivery and financing does the patient pay the most for care received? An answer to this question cannot afford to ignore the question of quality of care. Two types of consumer expenditure must be considered: the amount he pays in the form of an insurance premium and the money he pays out-of-pocket for services not covered by his insurance. Anderson and Sheatsley in 1961 found that consumers in a prepaid group practice plan paid less on the average than consumers in fee-for-service plans. The Columbia University study in 1962 confirmed this finding, and lower expenditures by prepaid group practice consumers were found again in 1971 in the study of the California Public Employees Retirement System. Critics of this evidence suspect that one explanation for lower expenditures is *out-of-plan* use—that is, purchase of medical services from private physicians and hospitals by consumers in the group practice plans. Such out-of-plan use might not be adequately reported (or not at all) in estimates of consumer expenditures in these plans. Another issue which has not been adequately dealt with in previous studies is that of expenditure per unit of service received. It is possible that lower average consumer expenditures may be achieved by reduction of the quality of services. This, of course, brings us back to a consideration of adequacy of services provided. All of these questions will occupy our interest when we discuss the data on consumer expenditures.

Finally there is the opinion of the consumer to consider. Other research has concluded that consumers tend to be "satisfied" with their health plans. Consumers attended by fee-for-service physicians tend to be more satisfied with medical care received, whereas those in prepaid group practice plans are more satisfied with financial coverage. But what are the bases on which these opinions were formed? Does consumer satisfaction with medical care in fact rise and fall with fluctuations in the quality of care he receives, or does it depend more on predisposing attitudes and values, or perhaps on characteristics of physicians seen and seriousness of illness experienced? As for opinions of financial coverage, how do they vary with claims experience? That is, do consumers with much illness experience (and therefore claims experience) become more sensitive to comprehensiveness of benefits? Do those with little or no need tend to be disgruntled with financial coverage regardless of its comprehensiveness? How does accurate knowledge of one's benefits affect opinion? These questions (and others) will lead us through an examination of the data on consumer satisfaction.

The major issues that guide this study and that have guided previous studies are concerned with variations from one health insurance plan to another, in use of services, quality of those services, consumer expenditures, and consumer satisfaction.

THEORETICAL FRAMEWORK

The research design included both dimensions of performance and dimensions of plan structure and function. Dimensions of performance were easily settled because most researchers agree that use of services, quality of care, cost, and customer satisfaction are crucial aspects of health insurance. The results or outcomes of health care in each plan would, of course, also be a crucial measure, but it could not be explored in this study. Dimensions of plan structure and function were more difficult because they have not been systematically developed in other studies. This involved searching for some of the key concepts that apply to all health insurance plans and that, if measured across these plans, would lead to greater understanding of the variations in performance.

Early in the study two of these concepts were identified (Sasuly and Roemer, 1966). The first concept, *sponsorship,* was defined as the type of people or organization responsible for founding the plan. Sponsors of health plans were thought of as three types: commercial insurance companies, providers of service, and consumer or employer groups. The second concept was the *type of practice* of physicians who provide medical care to subscribers in the plan. Type of practice could be dichotomized into predominantly individual or predominantly group practice. Cross-classification of these two dimensions provided a six-cell typology of health insurance plans.

	Commercial life insurance	Providers of service	Consumer groups
Individual practice	(1)	(2)	(3)
Group practice	(4)	(5)	(6)

Placing any health plan in an appropriate cell directs attention to some of the most controversial issues in the medical care field, such as the implications of the profit motive for control of costs and provision of service, the possible conflict between self-interest and self-regulation in the "provider-sponsored" plans, or the gains or losses in all performance areas in the group-practice plans. Information on these and other issues can be generated by comparing the performance of plans in the six cells.

A comprehensive study would explore the performance of all types of plan, but practical limitations led us to concentrate on the plans of major national interest. These were identified as plans with commercial sponsorship and predominantly individual medical practice (about 55% of the national market), provider sponsorship with predominantly solo practice (about 40%), and consumer or employer sponsorship with group practice (about 5%).[2]

Sponsorship and *type of practice* provided a convenient and meaningful typology for classifying health plans, but an expanded conceptual scheme was needed which would integrate other key concepts also related to performance.

[2] Consumer- or employer-sponsored group practice plans (sometimes referred to as "independents") do not have a large share of the national market but are regarded as extremely important alternatives to the predominant national plans. Indeed, some would claim that the predominant types of plan do not differ significantly from one another in structure and performance, and the only meaningful comparisons are to be found between the group practice plans and all other plans.

A SOCIAL SYSTEM

A social system is an organization of components which are interdependent and which develop orderly and systematic interactions with one another (Loomis, 1960). The nature of each component and the amount and type of interaction differentiate one social system from another. If we think of each health plan as a social system, each would be made up of three components:

— *The health insuring agency* which underwrites the program of insurance and processes the claims, sets eligibility terms, determines premiums, etc.
— *The consumers* who, in this study, are the subscribers to health insurance plans through group contracts based on their employment.
— *The providers* who are the physicians and other medical professionals who provide services to consumers.

These components interact with one another according to formal rules peculiar to each plan and with role-expectations derived from participation in the larger system. Interactions may involve, for instance, enrollment, provision of medical care, billing, provision of insurance, payment of premiums, and response to complaints.

The Health Insuring Agency

The functions of each component define the manner in which it will relate to other components in the system; for instance, the main function of a health insuring agency is to produce and sell insurance. The mechanism created to perform this function is the formal organization, which is itself a social system. It has the unique distinction, however, of being created for a particular and specified purpose (Stinchcombe, 1965). "Deliberate creation" implies that the organization is designed to perform its functions in the best possible way. The degree to which the design is successful is a measure of the effectiveness of the organization (Etzioni, 1961).

The health insuring agency may be studied in terms common to all organizations in society. Although there are endless possibilities for organization design, they may be incorporated into a general model that describes organizational structure in terms of three levels: institutional, managerial, and technical (Parsons, 1960).

The institutional level is represented by the board of directors, which involves a consideration of *sponsorship.* The board of directors is usually composed of the founders or representatives of their interests. The potential influence of a board of directors on its organization is immense, for it decides organizational goals which in turn define the legal nature of the organization.

The goals of an organization are desired future states toward which the organization strives (Parsons, 1937). They largely reflect the values and beliefs of the directors; for instance, if the board were composed primarily of industrialists and bankers, the organization would probably have different goals from those of a board composed of physicians or union representatives. Because these people represent different segments of the population, the values that become implemented as goals tend to reflect their individual concerns.

All organizations pursue many goals simultaneously, and goal setting is a dynamic process. At the most general level, however, it is possible to recognize that organizations emphasize either profit or service in performing their functions. The difference in emphasis is recognized by society, and, depending on whether an organization is classified as profit or nonprofit, a different set of legal sanctions is applied.

The model thus directs our attention to the study of three aspects of the institutional level of the organization: the composition of the board of directors, emphasis on profit or service as the organizational goal, and the legal sanctions applied to the organization.

The management level has the responsibility of translating the goals of the board into operational realities and to design the process by which the organization will be sustained.

Regardless of whether the principal emphasis is on profit or service, all organizations must survive financially. Financial viability is the basic problem management must resolve. This is accomplished by placing controls on the organization's cost of production. In the instance of a health insuring agency the "product" is a benefit package that contains those medical services for which the insuring agency agrees to assume some degree of fiscal responsibility for its customers. The cost of the product to the organization is contributed to by prices charged by the providers of service, amounts of insured services used by the consumers, and efficiency of the payment procedure.

Control of the price charged by providers is accomplished if the plan establishes medical facilities and persuades physicians to practice there for a salary. Under such an arrangement levels of expenditure for professional service and facilities can be predicted and controlled. The organization may also give the provider a vested interest in the success of the organization by arranging profit sharing so that the provider receives a dividend if he successfully avoids excessive use of costly services (e.g., hospitalization). Another control method is the establishment of a fee schedule by which provider charges may be monitored in order to set rates on which to base payments. Both methods require cooperation from the providers that is often difficult to arrange.

Control of the consumer is much easier and insuring agencies have devised a variety of ingenious ways to accomplish it. Consumer utilization rates are controlled by limiting the items included in the benefit package, the organization's fiscal liability for these items, and the kinds of people who are eligible to buy the product. Limits on the benefit package items are reflected in various, more or less descriptive titles such as "surgical," "major medical," "regular medical," and "comprehensive" (Somers and Somers, 1961), which indicate a range of products that management may choose to market. Limits on fiscal liability for items included in the benefit package take the form of deductibles, coinsurance, and ceilings. *Deductibles* require the consumer to pay an initial portion of charges before the organization's fiscal responsibility takes effect. *Coinsurance* requires the consumer to pay a percentage of all charges. *Ceilings* limit the total amount the organization will pay in any circumstances on behalf of one consumer in one year. *Eligibility requirements* exclude people with certain characteristics indicative of high risk, such as those who are likely to use a large amount of medical services (e.g., older persons, chronically ill persons, women of child-bearing age, people in dangerous occupations) (Shepherd and Webster, 1957).

The efficiency of the payment procedure determines the amount added by the organization to the price of the product (premium) to cover administrative costs and perhaps profits. The payment procedure involves an interaction between the organization and the consumer or provider. This is a transaction by which the organization "exchanges funds," taking in premiums and paying out insured services. Management's major function in this exchange is to design an administrative structure to handle the necessary operations within the framework of the company's goals. A majority of these "necessary operations" is directed toward establishing eligibility of consumers and legitimacy of the providers and services. They must be defined as appropriate before payment will be made.

In order to reduce the cost of these claims procedures, management may choose to streamline or eliminate some of them. In the extreme case the entire administration may be delegated to the purchaser, provided he is a group purchaser and has an administrative structure into which the procedures could be built. Under this system the insuring agency simply becomes a risk underwriter. Delegation of functions to groups outside the organization, such as union-management trust funds, may improve efficiency and reduce costs because it assigns activities to those with knowledge and experience and takes advantage of existing structures (March and Simon, 1958). When procedures are not delegated outside the organization, control over activities increases but is hampered by a lack of knowledge and information. This occurs especially if the procedures require professional expertise.

The technical level is responsible for production, which in this case is the delivery of the benefit package. Operating within the guidelines established by the board of directors and management, technical level personnel define practical alternatives within the more general policy. Management then is responsible for choosing among these alternatives in order to realize the goals of the board of directors (Parsons, 1958).

The technical level in health insuring organizations often includes professional experts (actuaries), whose function is to define the organization's product. Actuarial determinations are largely concerned with definition of risk which guides rate setting. "Risk" refers to the probability of resource expenditures by the organization as the result of people using insured medical services.

The technical level is also responsible for the disposal of the product, but marketing procedures are not included in this study.

The Consumers

The consumer component of the health plan social system has no formal organization. In this study the consumer component is a population composed of occupational groups whose major functions relate to their employing organizations and whose participation in the health plan social system is usually a "fringe benefit" of employment. It is not legally permissible for groups to form specifically for the purpose of purchasing health insurance (Somers and Somers, 1961). The concept of "fringe benefit" usually implies that the price of the product is shared in some manner by employer and employee, although ultimately the employer's contribution is merely in lieu of wages.

The degree of access to the health insurance products for consumers in this study was dependent on their employment situation. For some the groups provide alternative products from which the employee may choose, whereas for others no alternatives are provided. Consequently, the characteristics of the consumer component of any given health plan social system are a complex mixture of self-selection (in which the consumer is free to choose the product he feels best meets his needs assignment, in which the consumer has no choice except whether or not to buy the health insurance package offered), and situations of limited self-selection (in which a narrow range of alternative products is offered).

These consumer choices are of considerable interest to a health insuring agency because they determine the most important characteristic of the consumer component: *risk.* The reason for its importance is related to the organization's goals. If the primary goal of a health insuring agency is profit, then risk may be minimized by the various means discussed earlier. If the organization is service-oriented, other cost control methods are needed. Financial stability cannot be legitimately achieved by minimizing risk because this would exclude the very people most in need of service. The *raison d'etre* of the organization would then be undermined.

We regard risk-defining consumer characteristics as vital to an understanding of the performance of any health plan social system. They are obviously directly related to extent of use of medical services and by use to expenditures and consumer satisfaction. From the consumer perspective risk may be translated into the concepts of *need* and *demand.*

Need refers to objective evaluation that health care services should or should not be obtained. The medical care system relies primarily on consumer initiative in arranging for initial (although not usually subsequent) provider-patient contacts. Therefore social definitions of illness, values, and attitudes with respect to seeking medical care and command of economic resources (including health insurance), which facilitate the access to health care services, become important factors in translating *need* into *use*. The latter factors, which underlie a readiness to consume health care services, both initial and subsequent, may be sociologically defined as *demand* for services.

The Providers

The third category within the social system constitutes the providers of care. For purposes of this study the central provider is the physician, with other health workers considered in terms of their contribution to his performance. As in the consumer component, we are interested in those characteristics that are expected to influence plan performance. Differences in provider characteristics from one system to another may be expected because of the methods of selecting and organizing physicians.

When selecting physicians, the health insuring agency may or may not exert influence on the selection of the physician. If it does not, then the provider component is defined entirely by the consumer's selection of physicians from the community practitioners. Such "free choice of physician" has long been argued by private medicine as a vital element in establishing a good doctor-patient relationship and thereby promoting high quality medical care. On the other hand, the health insuring agency (or its delegated authority) may preselect a panel of physicians according to specified criteria. The consumer is then required to seek insured medical services only from designated physicians. The patient is usually allowed free choice among these physicians, but his alternatives have been reduced. Whether because of exigency or preference, he may decide to accept any physician who is available when the need arises. There are thus marked contrasts in the definition of the provider from one health plan social system to another. We expect these contrasting methods to result in different physician populations. Of course, there are practical limits to the degree of selectivity available to the health insuring agency, such as the supply of well-trained physicians willing to work in a group situation.

Method of organizing physicians brings us to a reemphasis of the importance of type of practice. Where the provider component takes on the relatively formal structure of a large group practice there is a clear boundary dividing physician members and nonmembers, with a greater amount of patterned interaction among the members. Consequently, there is pressure toward convergence of values, beliefs, and behaviors (Merton, 1957). This greater patterned interaction among physicians has been cited by proponents of group practice as a major advantage because it involves constant peer review and increased access to consultation. The convergence of behaviors theoretically should raise levels of performance.

Thus combinations of the method of defining and the method of organizing providers in various health plan social systems will result in provider diversity that is relevant to quality of medical care. Our interest is mainly in comparing the performance of providers selected by health insuring agencies with that of providers selected by individual consumers.

The characteristics expected to influence physician performance are conceptualized along four dimensions:

Limiting — particulars within a physician's background which might limit his access to the best medical education, limit his perspectives, or remove him from contemporary practices.

Qualifying — the physician's training.

Facilitating — (a) structural: conditions of practice, including number of ancillary personnel; (b) behavioral: practices related to a physician's relationships with his colleagues and his profession.

Motivational — attitudes, values, and beliefs.

In summary, the objective of this research is to seek an understanding of the variations in the health plans' performance by examining characteristics of the three components of the social system and their interactions. This objective is reflected in the schematic summary of the conceptual scheme presented in Figure 1-1.

It may be helpful to discuss the approach we have taken to each of the three components in the conceptual scheme. The greatest interest is in the consequences of different ways of organizing the insuring agency component. Formal organizations are designed by people to attain goals and as such they are subject to change to meet those goals or to meet different goals. Such change lies at the heart of public policy decision making regarding methods of financing and delivering of health services. Consequently, emphasis is on the effect of different health insuring agencies on the behaviors and attitudes of consumers and providers measured by use, quality, expenditures, and consumer satisfaction; for instance, with respect to use of medical services, what are the experiences of consumers with similar need and demand characteristics under different health insuring agencies? Characteristics of consumers and providers are obviously important to an understanding of such outputs, but the relevant social policy issue is the change in output that appears to be due to differences in such organizational characteristics as profit or service motivation, various methods of cost control, degree of influence on provider organization, and comprehensiveness of benefit packages.

METHOD

The information needed for the study had to be procured from people who were in the organization of each selected insurance agency, from subscribers to each plan, and from the physicians who treated the subscribers. For this purpose questionnaires and interview schedules were designed and pretested.

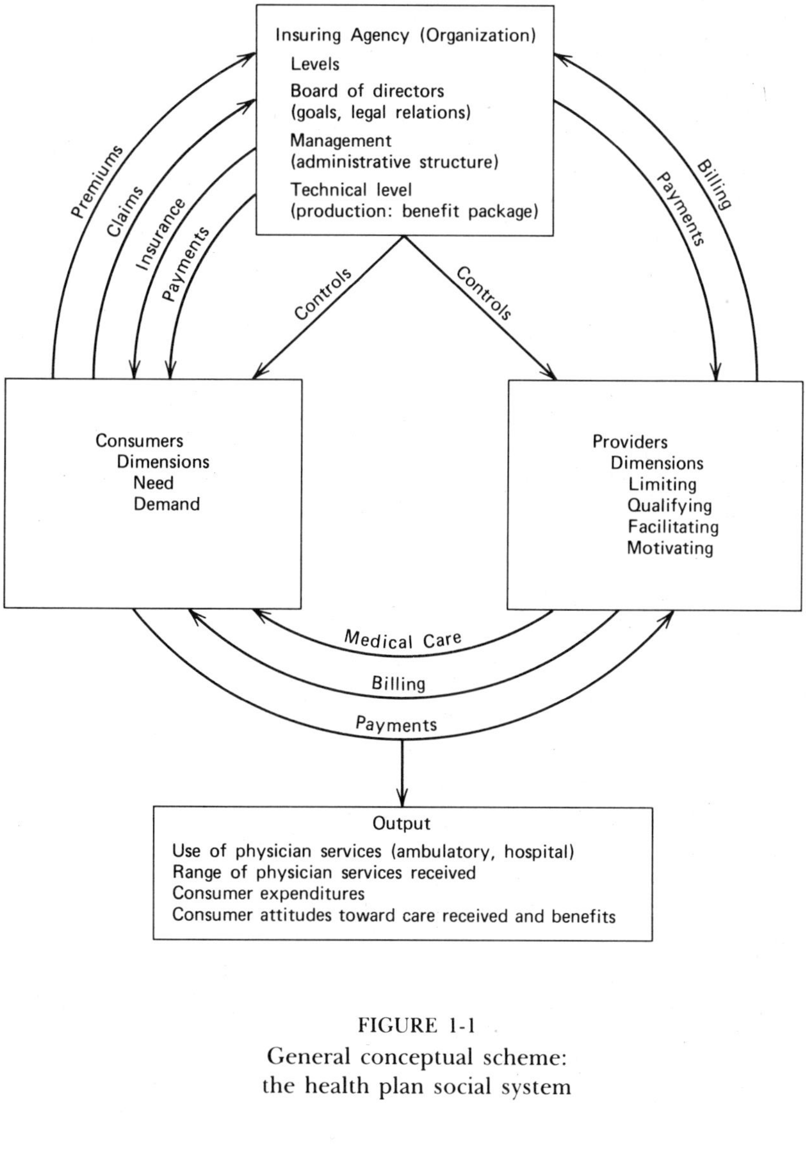

FIGURE 1-1
General conceptual scheme:
the health plan social system

The insuring agencies received questionnaires that were designed for management and supervisory personnel. We were interested in their perceptions of organizational goals and the manner in which their activities and training contributed to attaining these goals. Information from other knowledgeable persons regarding structure and procedures was also solicited. The history, goals, and legal environment of each agency were taken from sources such as company constitutions and other written materials.

With the help of a voluntary agency, questionnaires and interview techniques were developed and tested. The subsequent research was based on these experiences. One result of the test case was the decision that legal training was required to understand and interpret laws regulating the operation of health insuring agencies. A final-year law student specializing in corporate law at UCLA was subsequently added to the research staff.

Information sought from the consumers included subjective information that could be gained through questionnaires and interviews and objective information such as background and medical history that could be found in medical records and claim forms. A questionnaire was written and then pretested on employees of the Federal Aviation Agency in Los Angeles who were enrolled in three health insurance plans that resembled the commercial, provider, and consumer-sponsored types we wished to study. The questionnaire was designed to gather data on organization, physician, and consumer characteristics, as well as medical care use, family medical expenses, and attitudes toward the plans. Questions were also included to provide an indication of the consumers' medical need and demand.

In order to gain access to medical records and claims, which are confidential sources of information, a legal release form was required. This form was designed in cooperation with the UCLA School of Law.

The physician pretest was conducted on a sample of doctors who provided medical service to members of a small consumer-sponsored health insurance plan. Through the pretest we made sure that the questions asked were meaningful to practicing physicians. Another concern had been to get physicians to complete a lengthy questionnaire, but the pretest assured us that the subjects were of interest to them and that we could expect a good response rate.

Selecting the Samples

The insuring agencies selected for this study were those that represented the commercial-solo, provider-solo, and consumer-group types we wished to compare. One large and one small plan of each of these types were sought for replication and representation across plan sizes. The plans selected were those having meritorious reputation and a range of group enrollment contracts in Los Angeles County. The plan headquarters did not have to be located in the county.

The study design involved interviewing members of the board of directors, key executives, and administrators as well as distributing questionnaires to supervisors, managers, and other top officials within each selected plan. The time and the release of confidential information inherent in this design impeded the plans we had selected from participating. Two of the four commercial-solo insuring agencies approached finally agreed to cooperate. As the study progressed, however, each one qualified its involvement and placed limitations on the information to be released. The provider-sponsored agencies both declined to participate and the information about these plans was collected without their assistance. The group-sponsored plans initially agreed to cooperate. Later one plan refused interviews with members of its board of directors and the other did not disclose certain financial information.

In the end, however, six plans were chosen. These plans are called large commercial and small commercial (size ratio is 3:1), hospital-sponsored and physician-sponsored (size ratio is 2:1), and large group practice and small group practice (size ratio is 6:1).

Six to eight people in each cooperating plan were interviewed. Whenever possible, one person was a member of the board of directors and the others were key executives in the organization. Questionnaires were sent to managers in charge of group contracts. The cooperating plans also assigned staff members to assist us with the interviews and research from other sources. Selecting consumers was more complicated.

The desired number of families responding from each plan was set at 600, which would yield enough infrequent events, such as hospitalizations, to determine the patterns of overall medical care. Because the provider-sponsored plans were not cooperating with the study and time and money were short, we decided to aim for 300 families in these plans. Our goal was to include people in each plan who would be representative of subscribers to group contracts in the six plans.

Consumers defined as eligible for our study were those under 65 years of age living in Los Angeles County. The age limit was introduced because people 65 years of age and older were covered by the government's Medicare program. Once we had chosen the participants, we then went back to choose a smaller but representative group for medical-record and insurance-claim analysis.

Questionnaires were sent to each selected family, and release forms for medical and claim records were sent to every fourth family. The response to the questionnaire was 50%, much as we expected. The response to the medical and claim record releases was lower. In order to avoid a bias caused by certain persons being more willing than others to cooperate, we arranged to interview those families who decided not to respond. From the nonrespondents a group was also chosen for the medical and claim records study. A comparison of the consumers who responded and those who did not is given in Appendix A.

Two possible sources of bias in the consumer study were the method of choosing participants and nonresponse. The attempt to have equal numbers of consumers in each contract size group created bias because the enrollments in these contracts were not equal. People not responding to the questionnaire may cause a study to have a "middle-class" bias, since nonrespondents tend to come from other social strata. To allow for these biases a weighting procedure was used to alter the sample composition of the whole population. This involved estimating the probable behavior of the total population regarding response to the questionnaire. The physicians asked to participate in the study included any doctor who had served a family member in the medical record study. Names of physicians were taken from the authorization form signed by people in the medical and claim records study. Names of consulting physicians or other doctors seen were taken from hospital and medical records. In this way we came as close as possible to communicating with all the physicians caring for people in our study. Only medical doctors were included, so there were psychiatrists, but no psychologists, ophthalmologists, but no optometrists. The physicians in the sample are representative of doctors serving people in the six study plans.

The physician response rate was high. For physicians not responding to the questionnaire information was taken from the Los Angeles County Medical Association, California Board of Medical Examiners, and other medical organization sources. Biases due to nonresponse could then be reported, but in this case we did not weight the results to compensate for them.

Collecting and Organizing the Information

The negotiations with the insuring agencies we hoped would cooperate met with varying degrees of success. Two companies refused to be included, and companies agreeing to participate did so at different times. The first health insurance agency began working with us in 1967, but the limited cooperation we obtained from another was not cleared until 1969. Part of the difficulty in securing information on finances and certain administrative methods was caused by the competitive market situation. Our promise not to release the indentities of the insurance companies was not satisfactory because plan descriptions are unique to each type.

The refusal to participate, either entirely or in part, made cross-agency comparisons problematic. Emphasis was therefore placed on basic concepts such as sponsorship, goals, legal environment, administrative structure, and product, insofar as these could be described from interviews and printed materials. The questionnaire information was uneven from one plan to another, thus limiting its usefulness.

In the consumer study more than 11,000 contacts were made. When enough questionnaires had been returned, the information was coded, processed, and checked for possible coding errors.

For those people who authorized release of medical records and claims information photocopies of medical and claim records were made. All care received by a patient from a single provider on one day and all laboratory or radiology work ordered during that contact regardless of when it was performed, was termed "medical care bit" (MCB). This unit of care provided a basis from which calculations and analysis could be conducted.

The information gathered from the insurance personnel, the consumers, and providers was coded into six datasets. The sizes of the samples available for analysis were 159 organizational personnel, 3130 families answering only the questionnaire, 805 families in the medical record and claim study, 1309 physicians, and 11,379 medical care bits.

The entire process to this point took six years to complete, from late 1965 to 1971.

ANALYTIC APPROACH

Our major concern is variations in performance among the health insuring agencies; that is, relating features in the health insuring agency structure to the consumer experiences on four output measures. Such an analysis must be accomplished descriptively because the sample contains only six different health insuring agencies, an insufficient number for statistical generalization. A different analytic approach to the conceptual scheme would have been to sample many health insuring agencies and then measure the relationship between organizational structure (e.g., goals) and outputs (e.g., consumer expenditures). This was not the approach adopted because it would have necessitated greatly reducing the consumer sample for each plan in order to keep the study within manageable limits. Such a reduction would also render estimates of infrequently occurring, but vital, items unreliable (such as hospitalization). Moreover, in order to obtain a sufficient sample of various agency types, it would have been necessary to go beyond the Los Angeles County area to the nation as a whole, and this involves serious problems of comparability due to geographic differences. Finally, as we stated earlier, it was felt that the greatest interest from the viewpoint of public policy was in the major types of health insuring agency, and within the local area there were a limited number of examples of all these types to study.

Descriptive analysis has been referred to by Hyman (1955) as "precise measurement of one or more dependent variables in some defined population or sample of the population." In this study we are measuring the dependent variables (the "outputs") on six consumer populations defined by the health insuring agencies included in the study. We expect variations in the dependent variables from one plan to another, since previous research suggests such variation. Thus the research is not totally exploratory in nature but will rather confirm, clarify, or contradict findings of other studies. *The first analytic objective*, then, is to establish whether there are significant differences in the study samples on various measures of the dependent variables. It will be necessary to make careful note of the limitations of our data and their impact on conclusions drawn (i.e., sample size, confidence in the data-collection technique, and implications of different measures of the same dependent variable).

If we are reasonably confident that variations in the dependent variables have been demonstrated, then the task is to offer plausible explanations for these variations. Explanations will be sought in the characteristics of the three components of each health plan social system—the insuring agency, the providers, and the consumers. These components have been conceptualized earlier in terms of dimensions thought to have direct relevance for the dependent variables. Therefore measurement of the six plans in terms of these dimensions will provide logical expectations about performance, which can then be examined in light of the empirical variations found. This typological analysis examines the extent to which there is concomitant variation of the independent variables (characteristics of the components) and the dependent variables (output measures). Variations such as these, which are both logical and meaningful, form tentative explanations from which hypotheses may be derived for more rigorous testing. Thus *the second analytic objective* is to relate differences in characteristics of the social systems logically to differences in the dependent variables.

Insofar as these explanations involve the health insuring agency and the providers, they will be left at this level and will possibly stimulate further analysis by other researchers. The measurement of the impact of provider-consumer interactions is feasible by the identification of provider-consumer pairs, but this was beyond the scope of the present analysis.

The influence of consumer characteristics on the dependent variables will be subject to testing. Also, the influence of provider characteristics will be studied in relation to *quality of care* and *consumer attitudes*. This provides the *third analytic objective*, which is to determine the extent to which variations in the dependent variables from plan to plan can be explained by differences in the makeup of the consumer and physician components. This follows on the heels of the second objective. The technique of analysis by observing concomitant variations is limited, since with this technique it is frequently impossible to separate the consequences of two or more independent variables which apparently act in the same direction; for example, in regard to use of ambulatory medical services it is possible that a health plan will be characterized by both comprehensive benefit packages (implying little constraint on consumer use of services) and consumers with a relatively high incidence of chronic illness (a measure of high consumer need). It is logical to hypothesize that such a plan would exhibit a higher rate of consumption of ambulatory services, all other items being equal, than a plan with less comprehensive benefit packages and less chronic illness in its consumer population. But what is the relative importance of the two independent variables? From the perspective of social policy it is important to know the effect of varying the comprehensiveness of the benefit package on meeting the consumer's needs for medical services because characteristics of the health insuring agency (such as the benefit package) can be changed, but the health needs of the consumer population must be regarded as relatively fixed. We can approach this problem statistically by controlling for the consumer characteristics while allowing the insuring agency characteristics to vary. It is then possible to examine the effect of varying degrees of comprehensiveness of the benefit package on the use of ambulatory medical services by consumers with the same level of need measured by incidence of chronic illness. If plans with the more comprehensive benefit packages exhibit significantly higher use of ambulatory services by consumers with high need but do not change the behaviors of those with low need, we have then effectively separated the effects of the two independent variables.

The above example is a beginning of explanatory analysis involving more than one independent variable. Of course, multivariate techniques are available for dealing with the simultaneous effects and interactions of a large number of independent variables. This will hopefully be the subject of subsequent work.

A *fourth analytic objective* is to examine the similarities and differences in performance of "plan types," as established by the six-cell typology described earlier. In this task we calculate averages in proportion to the total memberships of the two plans in each of the three basic types. Such analyses enlarge sample sizes and address issues that are frequently posed on a national scale.

Results of the analysis begin in Chapter 2, with a presentation of characteristics of each health plan social system in terms of the concepts introduced in this chapter. Chapters 3 to 6 deal with the dependent variables in the order of use of medical services, quality of services, consumer expenditures, and consumer attitudes. Presentation of the data generally follow the analytic objectives:

- Chapters open with reviews of findings from other relevant studies and distributions of our data on the dependent variable by plan. Statistically significant differences are emphasized.
- The discussion that follows deals with the relationships between characteristics of the plans and variations in the dependent variables.
- Controls for consumer and physician characteristics are run.
- Data on the dependent variable are presented according to the three basic types of health insurance plan when this serves as a

useful summary device.
— Summary and conclusions.

Chapter 7 summarizes the major findings of the research and discusses implications for social policy decisions. Appendices give further details on our methodology, designed to inform and aid future research in health insurance plan performance.

CONCLUSION

The objective of the study is to evaluate the performance of the major types of health insurance plans in the United States today. These types are commercial, provider-sponsored, and consumer- or employer-sponsored plans. Two plans of each type were selected for study, one large and one small. Measures of performance are use by consumers, aspects of quality of care, consumer expenditures, and consumer satisfaction.

Each health plan is seen as a social system with three components: the health insuring agency, the providers of service, and the consumers. Each of these components interacts with the others, and it is the characteristics of the components and their interactions that produce different "outputs" in terms of use, quality of medical care, consumer expenditures, and satisfaction.

The research fieldwork consisted of interviews and questionnaires for personnel in the health insuring agencies, questionnaires mailed to people enrolled in group contracts with each of the health insuring agencies, questionnaires mailed to physicians who provided services over a 12-month period to a smaller subsample of consumers, photocopies of all medical (office and hospital) records for the subsample of consumers, and gathered information on benefit packages and claims from applicable health insuring agencies.

Data collected were coded and analyzed. Sample sizes available for analysis were, organization personnel, 159; consumer families, 3130; families in the medical care subsample, 805; number of medical care bits, 11,379; physicians, 1309.

The analytic objectives were to study variations in the dependent output variables by plan, to relate differences in plan characteristics to the output variables, to determine the extent to which variations in the dependent variables can be explained by consumer and physician characteristics, and to compare the behavior of the plan types.

REFERENCES

Anderson, Odin W. and Sheatsley, Paul B. "Comprehensive medical insurance: a study of costs, use and attitudes under two plans." Research series #9, Health Information Foundation, New York 1961 .

Association of Teachers of Preventive Medicine. *Newsletter,* 19 Winter 1972 , 2.

Columbia University School of Public Health and Administrative Medicine. "Family medical care under three types of health insurance." Foundation on Employee Health, Medical Care and Welfare, New York 1962 .

Etzioni, Amitai. *A comparative analysis of complex organizations.* New York: The Free Press, 1961, 71-88.

Freidson, Elliot. *Patients' View of Medical Practice.* New York: Russell Sage Foundation, 1961.

Hyman, Herbert. *Survey design and analysis: principles, cases, procedures.* New York: The Free Press of Glencoe, 1955, 68.

Loomis, Charles P. *Social systems: essays on their persistence and change.* Princeton, New Jersey: D. Van Nostrand Co., 1960, 3.

March, James G., and Simon, Herbert A. *Organizations.* New York: John Wiley and Sons, 1958, 40-44.

Medical Advisory Council to the Board of Administration of the Public Employees' Retirement System. "Final report on the survey of consumer experience under the state of California employees' hospital and medical care act." Sacramento, 1971. (Monograph)

Merton, Robert K. *Social theory and social structure.* New York: The Free Press, 1957, 284-288.

Parsons, Eleanor. "The group health insurance component of a large commercial carrier," in Milton I. Roemer et al., (editors). *Health Insurance Plans: Studies in Organizational Diversity.* University of California School of Public Health, Los Angeles (1970), 190-236. (Monograph)

Parsons, Talcott. *Structure and process in modern societies.* Glencoe, Illinois: The Free Press, 1960, Chapter 2.

—— "Some ingredients of a general theory of formal organization," in A. W. Halpin (editor). *Administrative theory in education.* Chicago: Midwest Administration Center, University of Chicago, 1958, 43.

—— "Suggestions for a sociological approach to the theory of organizations — I," *Administrative Science Quarterly,* 1, no. 1 June 1956 , 63-85.

—— *The social system.* Glencoe, Illinois: The Free Press, 1951, 24.

—— *The structure of social action.* New York: McGraw-Hill, 1937, 44.

Perrott, George S. *Federal employees health benefit program: enrollment and utilization of health services 1961-1968.* Washington, D.C.: Public Health Service, Health Services and Mental Health Administration, 1971. See also: George S. Perrott, "Federal employees health benefits program: utilization of hospital services." *American Journal of Public Health,* 56, no. 1 (January 1966), 57-64.

Peterson, Malcolm L. "The first year in Columbia: assessments of low hospitalization and high office use." *Johns Hopkins Medical Journal,* 128, no. 1 January 1971 , 15-23.

Peterson, Osler L., Andrews, Leon P., Spain, Robert S., and Greenberg, Bernard G. An analytical study of North Carolina general practice." *Journal of Medical Education*, 31, no. 12 December 1965 , 1-165.

Roemer, Milton I., and Shonick, William. "HMO performance: the recent evidence." *Milbank Memorial Fund Quarterly: Health and Society*, 51 (Summer 1973), 271-317.

Sasuly, Richard, and Roemer, Milton I. "Health insurance plans: a conceptualization from the California scene." *Journal of Health and Human Behavior*, 7, no. 1 (Spring 1966), 36-44.

Shepherd, Pearce, and Webster, Andrew C. *Selection of Risks*. The Society of Actuaries: 1957, 1-11.

Somers, Herman M., and Somers, Anne R. *Doctors, Patients and Health Insurance*. Washington, D.C.: The Brookings Institution, 1961. 249-254, 273.

Stinchcombe, Arthur L. "Social Structure and Organizations." in James G. March (editor). *Handbook of Organizations*. Chicago: Rand McNally and Company, 1965, 148.

II

The Plans

IN THIS CHAPTER we describe the six health plan social systems in terms of the concepts introduced in Chapter 1. The six systems have been given descriptive names:

— large commercial plan,
— small commercial plan,
— hospital-sponsored plan,
— physician-sponsored plan,
— large group practice plan,
— small group practice plan.

Each system is comprised of three components:

— the health insuring agency (organization),
— consumers,
— providers of service.

Each component of the system is conceptualized along dimensions thought to pinpoint aspects of the system which influence its "output" or performance. Performance is measured by

— amount of medical service used,
— aspects of quality of those services,
— consumer expenditures,
— consumer satisfaction.

We begin our description of the health plans with a discussion of the insuring agencies, then go on to the consumers and physicians. The agencies are seen as organizations with three levels (institutional, managerial, and technical) the overall function of which is to produce and sell health insurance. Consumers are discussed in terms of characteristics that influence the amount and kind of medical services they consume (need and demand). The description of providers of service deals with concepts such as qualifications and facilities which are related to competence and proficiency.

HEALTH INSURING AGENCIES

Board of Directors

The founders of an organization, or representatives of their interests, constitute the board of directors. This may be referred to as "sponsorship" of the organization. Our interest is in its definition of general policy and goals and the subsequent effect on the performance of the organization. General policy and goals reflect the perceived purpose of the organization, and perceptions of this purpose by board members are, at least in part, a function of their *social characteristics.* Boards of directors tend to be composed of people from many sections of society who bring various perspectives and personal purposes into the organization.

Goal setting allows society to define the organization legally. The board of directors decides the general goals of the organization and in a sense enters into an agreement with society to fulfill a certain need. This agreement or "contract" has *legal boundaries* that define what the organization may and may not do (Koontz, 1967). Federal, state, and local governments patrol these boundaries on behalf of the public interest.

Six boards: history and current composition

All health insuring agencies have the same function—to produce health insurance—but the founders of the various organizations came to the function in rather diverse fashions; for instance, the commercial plans are basically *life insurance* companies.

The large commercial company was first licensed to do business in 1906. Little is known about its original sponsorship. Most insurance companies with main offices in the West were started as a source of capital for businessmen in response to a reluctance of eastern insurance firms to accept California risk. Very likely this was the case for this company as well. In 1928 it began operations in Canada. Today business is transacted in 49 states and all provinces of Canada and in four offices overseas. It is the largest insurance company home-based in California. In 1930 a California-based diversified service company acquired complete ownership of this firm. Fifteen members of the business community, including five top officials of the organization, make up the board of directors. Representation is heavily weighted in the areas of finance and insurance.

Group health insurance was introduced in 1932. Currently the company writes a wide variety of ordinary life, group life, pension-trust, salary allotment life, individual and group annuities, and individual and group accident and health insurance.

The small commercial company is a stock company. Accordingly, its board of directors consists of representatives of the major stock owners.

Home-based in Sacramento, it was incorporated under California law in 1910, when it began operations with resources acquired by sale of shares of common stock. The organization was farmer-oriented and in part their original goal was to acquire a source of money for farm loans; California farmers and businessmen were generally dissatisfied with the eastern loan market. It grew in size by acquisition of and consolidation with other insurance companies. The date of inclusion of health insurance in the company's portfolio is unknown, although a company spokesman stated that some health insurance was being written when he joined the organization in 1935. The company also writes individual and group annuities, pension plans, group life insurance, and a wide variety of group and individual accident, health, and hospitalization coverage.

The governing board of 14 members is an "outside" board—only the president of the company serves on the board and works in the organization as well. Farming interests are still represented in slightly greater strength compared with other segments of the business and legal community.

Health insurance in California is dominated by the commercial plans (DuBois, 1970). Nationally, the commercial insurance companies have about 60% of the business (*Sourcebook of Health Insurance Data,* 1970). What interests have life insurance companies in health (or sickness) insurance? Answers vary, but the great majority (80%) of management, supervisory, and board personnel from the commercial companies responded that "health insurance helps sell life insurance." As a Director of the Health Insurance Association of America puts it, "such coverages had become a necessary part of a personal insurance program" (Follmann Jr., 1963). The inclusion of health insurance in life packages was begun by the smaller companies but quickly extended to the larger companies, with one after another entering the area in order to remain competitive. There was much public demand, and following World War II health insurance was well established because of the money available for purchasing and the right of labor unions to bargain for health and welfare benefits in lieu of wages (Munts, 1967).

In summary, two major points may be observed. First, the boards of directors of the two life insurance companies in our study are largely manned by representatives from the business and legal communities. Second, life insurance companies began offering health insurance coverage (especially on a group basis) as a method of increasing life insurance sales. Health insurance thus forms a relatively small portion of their total business.

The next two health plans in our study are the products of the providers of service: hospitals and physicians.

Discussion of the previous plans indicates that much of the activity in insuring for health began in the depression years (1929-1939). Origins of the hospital-sponsored plan follow this pattern, since it began in 1932 in Sacramento with several hospitals combining to sponsor one multihospital, community-wide plan. Reasons for the move are easily found: hospitals were suffering financially because of empty beds and the inability of people to pay their hospital bills. The plan has been and must continue to be approved by the American Hospital Association which develops standards for the plans.

As an instrument of the hospitals the board of directors might be expected to be weighted toward the hospitals' perspective. The current board is composed of 18 people, 11 of whom represent hospitals and the medical profession. Public representation, which has been expressed as a requisite by the parent body, features a trade union executive, a manufacturer, a utilities executive, several bankers, and a public relations expert.

Organized private medicine in California founded the physician-sponsored plan in 1939 as a defensive reaction against impending compulsory, state-sponsored health insurance. The state plan did not get started, but the physicians' plan did, thanks to original financial backing by the California Medical Association and subsequent backing by physicians who contracted with the plan to provide services at prorated fees. Early leadership was provided by a prominent physician who served as chairman of the nationally important *Committee on the Costs of Medical Care* and oriented the plan toward comprehensive benefits. Comprehensiveness was soon abandoned when the plan found it could not pay physicians at full fee because of financial difficulties associated with high use of services.

The board of directors of this plan is composed presently of 18 members elected by the Governing Council of the California Medical Association. Predictably, there is a preponderance of physicians—13 in all. The other members are business executives and bankers.

Historical beginnings of the large group practice plan reveal a somewhat different arrangement of influences. The plan as presently constituted began in 1943, but its beginnings were in evidence earlier. There was an obvious consumer need for medical care for construction workers isolated from regular community resources. The *isolation* feature predicated important characteristics of the forming system. Because there were no accessible medical resources, the new system was created from scratch and involved integration of facilities and employed personnel rather than private practice. Isolation also meant dependence on the industry it served. As the plan developed, it expanded after World War II to include other employment groups and is now available to all in the community through their places of work.

Although one physician played an important role in the development of the plan, the greatest impetus came from a financial windfall during World War II and the consequent financial backing for expansion of the medical personnel and facilities associated with it. Because of this association, ultimate authority for the health plan itself resides in a board of directors largely dominated by representatives of the industry. Currently the board is composed of 10 members, two of whom are physicians. One is the physician associated with the founding of the plan.

The founders of the small group practice plan were all physicians—but they were rebels. One of them had practiced medicine under a social health insurance program in another country. These physicians established the earliest of the six plans in this study in 1929 in response to requests for low-cost medical care from consumers in a Los Angeles-based enterprise. They were pioneers in the group practice and prepaid method of financing medical care. The local county medical association accused them of being unprofessional because of alleged advertising practices and dropped them from membership. The founders fought at the California Medical Association level and again at the national level with the American Medical Association before they won and were officially reinstated in the County Medical Association.

The origin of the small group practice plan was a combination of specified needs by consumers and their representatives (as in the large group plan) and an innovative conceptual approach of the physicians. The initiative for the organization was perhaps more on the part of consumers than of providers, but it was the particular way of approaching the problem of providing low-cost medical care to the consumers that really made the difference. The original physicians, and others who joined them through time, definitely carried the ball and made the plan work. Throughout the history of this plan there has been no question about who was in charge because the originating physicians have maintained their financial and organizational control. It began essentially as an expansion of an already existing group medical practice. Currently an executive committee of the

TABLE 2-1
Composition of the boards of directors, by occupational category

	Occupation				
Plan	All (N)	Industry	Other entrepreneurial	Health professionals	Consumer representatives
All plans	(79)	44 %	09 %	47 %	01 %
Large commercial	(13)	92	08	00	00
Small commercial	(13)	85	15	00	00
Hospital-sponsored	(17)	30	00	70	06
Physician-sponsored	(17)	18	00	82	00
Large group	(10)	40	40	20	00
Small group	(09)	00	00	100	00

physician partnership functions as the board of directors. It has nine members, all of whom are physicians. At the time of the study one of the physicians who joined the original group practice was still a member of the board.

By way of summary, then, we have discussed certain *social characteristics* of the people who fill roles as board members for the six plans in the study. Board composition by occupational identification of members is provided in Table 2-1. It is evident that rather different interests are involved in the boards of the six plans. What are the consequences of these differences for the goals of the organizations?

Goals

It should be recognized that for every organization there are two types of goal which descriptively might be termed *legitimating* and *motivating*. Legitimating goals are developed and enunciated in order to indicate that the product of the organization is valued as a resource in meeting the needs of a society (Parsons, 1956). Motivating goals have the organization as the beneficiary rather than society and are phrased in terms of returns to the organization of sufficient quantity and value to ensure the continued functioning of the organization and its components. Customarily public statements of policy and objectives stress legitimating goals over motivating goals.

Motivating goals may differ from the legitimating; when it is possible to measure them, they are usually the goals that receive the greatest amount of organizational attention in the form of allocation of resources, personnel, and rewards. Without a longitudinal or historical perspective it is often difficult to determine whether the legitimating and motivating goals are congruent. Our approach was to assess the degree of consensus about goals among organizational personnel, physicians who deliver the services insured by the plans, and the recipients or consumers of the services. This was based on the rationale that the opinions sustained from prolonged association of consumers and physicians with the plan, along with opinions of personnel formally associated with the organization, should provide a good idea of what the organization is in fact attempting to accomplish—that is, its motivating goals.

Thus organizational goals were ranked by the three different populations in our study: organization personnel, physicians, and consumers. For the organization, all managerial employees who had responsibility, either wholly or in part, for group health insurance and a sample of board members were asked to rank a list of eight goals in order of importance for the insuring agency in its health insurance function. By order of listing in the questionnaire the goals were service, profit, growth, welfare of plan employees (morale), efficiency, community relations, keeping government out of the health insurance field, and keeping government out of medicine. In the case of the hospital-sponsored and the physician-sponsored plans, however, the project was denied access to organization personnel.

Consumers were asked to rank the same goals for the plan under which they were insured. Physicians who treated patients insured by the six plans were asked to choose the organization they knew best of the six. They were also asked to rank the same list of goals as that given to the organization personnel and the consumers.

Results of the analysis of goal ranking are given in Table 2-2. Because the theoretical model designated the goals of *service* and *profit* as of primary interest, these two goals are reported in the table.

TABLE 2-2

Service and profit as goals of the organization, ranked by organization personnel, consumers, and physicians

		Goals ranked by			
Plan	Goal	All respondents (average rank)†	Organization personnel (position out of eight goals)	Consumers	Physicians
Large commercial	Service	2.60	3	1	1
	Profit	3.26	1	4	4
Small commercial	Service	2.80	3	1	-
	Profit	2.60	1	4	-
Hospital-sponsored	Service	2.90	-	1	1
	Profit	4.20	-	2	6
Physician-sponsored	Service	2.85	-	1	1
	Profit	4.55	-	3	8
Large group	Service	1.86	1	1	1
	Profit	5.00	6	5	5
Small group	Service	1.66	1	1	1
	Profit	4.23	3	5	4

†Equal weight to each of the three groups of respondents.

It appears that the consumers are, on the average, indiscriminate in ranking organizations on *service:* in all six plans service was ranked the most important goal by the consumers. This is somewhat misleading, since the table reports only on the position of that goal in relation to the other seven in the question. When one looks at the actual *average rank* given the service goal by consumers from plan to plan, variations are noted:

Large commercial	2.7
Small commercial	2.9
Hospital-sponsored	3.3
Physician-sponsored	3.4
Large group	2.7
Small group	2.1

It is clear from these figures that the consumers are most skeptical about the service goals of the two provider-sponsored plans and feel the small group plan is the most service-oriented. Still it is a fact that the consumers feel all six organizations have service as their primary goal. It may be, as discussed elsewhere (Hetherington, 1970), that this is a consequence of reluctance on the part of the public to accept a separation of legitimating and motivating goals on the part of organizations associated with physicians and health care. In other words, health plan organizations are ascribed the idealized goals of the medical profession; they are legitimized in the social system by their contribution to the maintenance of health. Any suggestion that such organizations are mainly profit-making institutions, much the same as commercial businesses, is not readily acceptable to a majority of the people.

Regarding the profit motive, personnel from both commercial organizations rank it as the most important goal. This is an interesting switch: the consumer feels that the organization is most concerned with service, but people in the organization feel it is primarily profit-oriented in its health insurance programs.

There is a major discrepancy in the ranking of profit for the two provider-sponsored organizations by consumers and physicians. Physicians who chose the hospital-sponsored plan as the one they knew most about ranked profit as the second least important goal; those commenting on the physician-sponsored plan ranked it least important of all. The consumers are considerably more skeptical in their assessment of the motives of these organizations. They rank profit as the second most important goal for the hospital-sponsored plan and third for the physician-sponsored. In the group practice plans there is apparently greater organizational emphasis on profit in the small group plan than in the large group plan, according to personnel respondents. Consumers in both plans rank profit equally far down the list, but personnel from the small group plan apparently are reflecting a more entrepreneurial attitude.

If we give each of the three respondent groups equal weight, and derive an overall assessment of the importance of these goals for the organizations under study, this result is obtained:

Service		Profit	
Small group	(1.66)	Small commercial	(2.60)
Large group	(1.86)	Large commercial	(3.26)
Large commercial	(2.60)	Hospital-sponsored	(4.20)
Small commercial	(2.80)	Small group	(4.23)
Physician-sponsored	(2.85)	Physician-sponsored	(4.55)
Hospital-sponsored	(2.90)	Large group	(5.00)

It is useful to compute a single score for each organization that would reflect the *relationship* between service and profit goals as assessed by our respondents. This is accomplished by dividing the average ranking for service by the average ranking for profit. The higher the resulting score, the more important the profit in comparison to service.

Profit index

Small commercial	1.10
Large commercial	0.80
Hospital-sponsored	0.69
Physician-sponsored	0.63
Small group	0.39
Large group	0.37

Ordered by their profit indices, the six plans fall roughly into the three types we have described earlier in terms of sponsorship, although the difference between the commercial and the nonprofit provider-sponsored types is not great. The large commercial plan's score is closer to the provider-sponsored plans than to the small commercial plan. The two consumer or employer-sponsored plans score nearly identically and are judged by the respondents to have a very low profit motive in relation to their service orientation.[1]

Another goal that provides some interest is that of keeping government out of health insurance. Plan personnel, consumers, and physicians concurred on the low priority given to this goal by the two group practice plans and the large commercial plan. This was not so for the provider-sponsored plans. Consumers ranked this goal sixth for these plans, whereas physicians ranked it fifth. We had no information from the plan personnel. Evidently physicians and consumers discern some emphasis placed by these plans on curtailing governmental influence in the health insurance field. This would be in keeping with the historical origins of the physican-sponsored plan.

This method for assessing an organization's motivating goals serves as a type proxy for the more rigorous method that we were unable to undertake because of the inaccessibility of comparable financial information across the plans. In some ways it is even better, since the assessments of the three groups of rankers should reflect considerable experience with the organization over a length of time and from rather different perspectives.

If the assessments of the importance of service and profit as goals of the insuring agencies reflect reality, then it should be possible to demonstrate these organizational orientations in an examination of *loss ratios:* the relationship of the price of the product (premium) to the amount spent for insured services received by the consumer and paid for by the plan. Of course, it is evident that since we are examining an organization's performance for only one 12-month period we might by chance pick anomalous years for some or all agencies in the study. There is the additional consideration that the difference between organization premium-income and benefit-payments is not all profit. Much of that margin is allotted to administrative expenses, a figure that is batted around with abandon in arguments pro and con for different types of health plan organization and about which we will have something to say later. What the organization decides to do with the remaining margin once administrative costs (salaries, taxes, debts, etc.) are taken care of gets at the heart of the definition of "profits."

---

[1] It should be noted that the indices for the provider-sponsored plans had no input from organization personnel and the large group plan had no input from members of its board. In all cases such input would be expected to *lower* the scores on the profit index, since legitimating goals in these organizations emphasize service. The degree to which this would affect the rankings is not clear, however, since our experience with personnel in other organizations indicated various amounts of disagreement on rankings of goals of the organization (E. Parsons, 1972).

We will regard the remainder as profit of sorts, whether it ends up in the pockets of stockholders, is held as "reserves" for future use, or is reinvested in expansion of the plan.

It should be clear, then, that an organization scoring high on the profit index will not necessarily realize large profits; for instance, a large margin between income and payments may be eaten up by an inefficient administration. Furthermore, in the commercial plans, which are frankly profit-motivated, policy makers may be quite willing to accept modest profits (or even losses) on their health insurance ventures in order to reap the rewards of associated life insurance sales which go arm-in-arm with the health insurance product.

With all these *caveats,* it is still enticing to look at loss-ratios across the plans. From the buyer's perspective he expects *on the average* to get back in services what he pays in premiums, minus a small amount for the risk bearing and the transaction expense. If this does not hold for a random sample of buyers (which will include some who get no services and some who get many), their demonstrated faith in the service orientation of the plans might be shaken.

Loss-ratios involve the proportion of premiums paid by the consumer which is paid out as benefits by the organization. Calculations for the ratio are based on a 12-month period for each consumer, except for those who were members of the organization for less than one year at the time of the study. Amount of payment by the organization was determined by a study of claims forms when they were available (the hospitalization portion of the small group practice, the hospital-sponsored plan, and the two commercials). For the large group plan, the physician services portion of the small group plan, and the physician-sponsored plan we calculated the value of the medical care received by application of conversion factors to the *California Relative Value Studies* units and hospital day rates for various types of accommodation in each hospital used. Conversion factors for the group plans were obtained from the organizations. Factors for the physician-sponsored plan were obtained from each physician who provided care. When information was lacking because of nonresponse, we applied a "usual and customary" rate for the physician's area of practice derived from other responses. Hospital rates were obtained from the hospital administrators at each hospital used. The proportion of the total value of care actually assumed by the latter three insuring agencies was derived from a study of the benefit packages. For the group plans there is no error involved. For the physician-sponsored plan, however, items included in the benefit package may not have had a claim actually filed and acted on. This will cause our estimates of plan payments for the physician-sponsored plan to be somewhat inflated and consequently make the plan look "better" than it is.

Table 2-3 presents the outcome of our calculations. Loss-ratios are calculated for all families, then for families with low total per person medical expenses, and finally for those with high expenses.

According to the average loss-ratios in Table 2-3, the health insurance industry represented by these six plans pays out $1.18 per

TABLE 2-3

Loss-ratios by plan and by total value of care received per family member

Percent of premium return in benefits	Plan						
	All plans	Large comm	Small comm	Hosp-spon	Phys-spon	Large group	Small group
All families							
None (%)	48.8	74.3	62.0	72.3	51.3	19.2	10.7
Up to 50%	22.0	9.0	10.0	8.5	23.4	44.2	38.6
50% - 100%	8.8	2.5	3.9	1.0	10.3	22.1	14.1
100% +	20.4	14.1	24.1	18.1	15.0	14.5	36.6
Mean	$1.18	$.54	$1.15	$.93	$2.48	$.60	$1.61
SD	$4.46	$1.46	$2.86	$2.53	$10.31	$1.33	$2.71
N	817	137	146	147	117	146	129
Families with annual care valued at $75 or less per covered member †							
None (%)	38.5	87.2	64.6	90.4	54.6	.3	1.9
Up to 50%	48.8	12.8	34.2	9.6	32.3	76.9	75.7
50% - 100%	11.2	...	1.2	...	12.2	22.0	14.0
100% +	2.2	...	...	...	.8	.8	8.4
Mean	$ .21	$ .04	$ .04	$ .02	$ .16	$ .34	$ .39
SD	$ .32	$ .11	$ .09	$ .07	$ .30	$ .24	$ .48
N	300	28	34	34	67	72	65
Families with annual care valued at more than $75 per covered member							
None (%)	17.7	26.8	20.6	41.6	2.1	.9	...
Up to 50%	12.3	20.3	5.3	14.5	20.5	17.4	1.8
50% - 100%	13.7	8.1	9.8	2.4	14.0	35.7	17.6
100% +	56.3	44.9	64.4	41.5	63.4	46.0	80.6
Mean	$3.16	$1.68	$3.04	$2.12	$10.40	$1.39	$3.53
SD	$7.15	$2.21	$4.02	$3.50	$19.81	$2.18	$3.44
N	284	43	55	64	27	44	53

†Families with no care during the study year are omitted here but not in the category "all families."

$1.00 taken in through premiums. Three of the health plans run in the black (large commercial, hospital-sponsored and large group) and three in the red, with the physician-sponsored plan paying out the most per premium dollar (but this figure is an overestimate because of the methodology described above). The large commercial and hospital-sponsored plans ranked second and third on the "profit index," and it is fitting that the figures should indicate that they actually do make a profit. The large group plan, however, ranked last on the index but shows a margin of 40 cents in "earnings" on the premium dollar.[2]

Averages are of limited value in estimating the true picture because they can be grossly distorted by extreme values. The standard deviations in Table 2-3 indicate the extent of this variation. Differences in means are not significant ($F=3.43$, not significant at $P=0.05$).

The distributions tell a somewhat different story. The majority of families in the commercial and provider-sponsored plans received *none* of their premium dollars back in benefits, whether because of lack of payment for services received or lack of services. In the large group plan 19% received no benefits; in the small group, 11%. Losses by the health plans (i.e., returning more in benefits than taken in through premiums) are observed for 20% of the families in all plans. In the small group plan 37% of the families are in this category, by far the highest percent of any plan.

For families that are high users of medical care (total value of more than $75 per covered member) net losses to the health plans are experienced by 56%. Again the highest percent is in the small group plan at 81%, with the lowest in the hospital-sponsored at nearly half that rate—42%.

Families who receive 50% or less of their premiums back in services during a year might be thought of as "high profit" from the perspective of the insuring agency. When the plans are ranked according to the percent of families falling into this "high profit" category, the following ranking occurs:

Large commercial	83.3 (most high profit families)
Hospital-sponsored	80.8
Physician-sponsored	74.7
Small commercial	72.0
Large group	63.4
Small group	49.3 (fewest high profit families)

[2] It should be noted that this plan, unlike the other five, finances the construction of its own hospitals.

Agreement between these rankings and those according to profit index is not total but similar patterns emerge. Again there is the scrambling of distinctions, if we speak of "plan types," between the commercials and the provider-sponsored plans.[3] As in the profit index, the large commercial plan is closer in score to the provider-sponsored plans than it is to the small commercial plan. In these rankings the two group plans have reversed their order. It is evident from the statistics in Table 2-3 that the small group plan tends to pay out rather heavily in terms of services rendered and lives up to its reputation among consumers reported earlier: it is the most service-oriented plan.[4]

Health insurance plans and the law [5]

Insuring organizations are subject to formal laws aimed at protecting society against unfair or antisocial methods of attaining their goals. Power to regulate the business of insurance has been primarily the province of the states, though by acts of Congress insurance is subject to minor controls imposed by the Internal Revenue Code, the Fair Labor Standards Act, the Equal Employment Opportunities Commission, and other federal agencies.

In California an insurance code and a code-enforcing insurance commission constitute the major regulatory forces, with the state attorney general also having some jurisdiction. Commercial carriers of health insurance are subject to the code and the commission. A special section of the insurance code exempts "nonprofit hospital service plans" from the burdens and restrictions imposed on commercial companies by the commission. The California Supreme Court has ruled that certain nonprofit group health plans were providers of *service* rather than of *indemnity*. They were therefore not insurers, hence could not be subject to control by the insurance code or the commission. Included in this category are the group pracice plans and

---

[3] On the other hand, if we recognize that both the commercial and provider-sponsored plans are patterned on open-market medical care dynamics, they cluster quite distinctly in a series separable from the basically different group practice plan type.

[4] Value of care received in the group plans is dependent on the unit conversion factor provided us by the plans. The factor provided by the small group plan was higher than that for the large group (i.e., for medicine it was $7 in the small group and $6 in the large group). These factors reflect cost of production of a unit of medical care. It would thus appear that organizational characteristics of the two plans result in rather different costs of production.

[5] Written in collaboration with Jeff Freedman, L.L.B.

the physician-sponsored plan.

In these three types of control it can be seen that the regulatory powers of the state increase as the profit orientation increases.

In summary, there is a confusing array of legal regulations and jurisdictions governing the form of corporate organization, the marketing of insurance contracts, and the definition of the product (benefit packages). The formal mechanisms for control of the commercial plans are more stringent than those for the nonprofit plans, but even when stringent legal controls are possible the laws are written under the influence of insurance and provider lobbies. These laws are written in vague terms and are not readily enforceable. Action on the laws is seldom taken. The level of effectiveness of the laws governing health insurance plans is far below the level of performance of well-established entities such as those in this study: within very wide boundaries they are essentially self-regulating.

Permeability

We may regard regulatory mechanisms as part of a *permeability* concept. "Permeability" encompasses all formal machinery set up by a society and any social system in the society in which the system may be influenced by relevant outside forces. Formal machinery set up by the society is law and presumably renders a social system such as a health plan *permeable* to (responsible to) the people. There are two obvious ways in which this may be set up: by requirements for representation on the board of directors and by establishment of grievance procedures. The organization itself may ensure permeability beyond legal requirements in many other ways.

Our discussion of the social characteristics and background of the six boards of directors demonstrated that there was almost no consumer representation. What is the effectiveness of the legal machinery just described in handling grievances? First of all, when asked what they would do if they had complaints about their health plans, only 6.7% of the consumer sample said that they would consult the state insurance commissioner or the attorney general. The most popular alternative chosen in response to this question was to approach the health plan itself (57.4%). When asked if they had actually made any complaints during their experience with one of the six health plans in the study, 17% said they had. We consider this a rather high level of complaint, given that most research on health insurance in the past has shown a reluctance of the great majority of consumers even to *express* dissatisfaction with their plans.

The highest rate of complaint was in the provider-sponsored plans.

In the hospital-sponsored plan 22% of the consumers had complaints and in the physician-sponsored, 24%. The lowest rate was in the large commercial plan: 14%.

We followed the complaint question with an inquiry into satisfaction with the outcome of complaints that had been made. We found

28.8% completely satisfied,
18.0% somewhat satisfied,
19.3% somewhat dissatisfied,
13.7% completely dissatisfied,
20.2% concluded that no action had been taken.

Collapsing the last three categories, we conclude that more than half (53.2%) of those making complaints expressed some degree of dissatisfaction with the action taken.

As with rate of complaint, dissatisfaction with action taken on the complaint was highest in the provider-sponsored plans. In the hospital-sponsored plan 68% were dissatisfied with the results. Figures for the other plans are physician-sponsored, 58%, small group, 50%, large commercial and large group, 34%, small commercial, 32%.

Of course, there is no guarantee that all complaints made by the consumer are legitimate. It was pointed out earlier that many complaints arise from consumer misunderstanding of the terms of the group contract with the insuring agency. But where does the responsibility lie for ensuring clear understanding? The law says it lies at least in part with the insuring agencies, which are required to define clear and complete contracts and to provide each consumer with certificates explaining the agency obligations. Our experience was that consumers and consumer representatives alike did not understand their benefits. After attempting to understand the benefit packages involved, we could see why. In many cases they defied comprehension by all but the most determined analyst.

Knowledge of contract benefits was measured by a question in the consumer questionnaire concerning nine benefit package items. The respondent was asked to indicate what he believed his benefits were for each item by checking complete, partial, none, or don't know. Since benefit packages are complex documents and there may be disagreement even among experts on the meaning of "complete" or "partial" in any given case, we are reporting here only the percent of people checking "don't know" for all nine items:

Physician-sponsored	58.6%	(least knowledgeable)
Hospital-sponsored	56.8	
Large commercial	42.1	
Small commercial	29.1	
Large group	14.1	
Small group	0.5	(most knowledgeable)

In each plan the number of items checked "don't know" is inversely related to education of the respondent. This relationship is highly significant ($p=0.001$ or less) in all plans except the small group ($p=0.05$) whose respondents appear to be relatively knowledgeable about their benefits.

If we regard these measures (satisfaction with complaint action and knowledge of benefits) as indicators of permeability, the provider-sponsored plans are least responsive to consumer influence. The interaction of the health insuring agency and the consumer component results in a majority of consumers who have no idea what the product is that they have purchased and cannot satisfactorily have their complaints about the plan resolved. Further, in studying the physician component, we found similar dissatisfactions on the part of the providers in regard to access to these organizations. Physicians were asked to rate one of the six plans they knew best on "effective representation of the medical profession." Only 4.8% of the physicians rated the hospital-sponsored plan as *excellent* on this item and 13.6% so rated the physician-sponsored plan. Even the commercial plans fared better (15.6%), which may relate to their lack of any rigorous review of medical claims and therefore respect for the independence of the medical profession.

Managerial Level

Management's task in the system is to operationalize the goals of the board of directors. This is accomplished by the definition of an administrative structure designed to produce and deliver the product and at the same time realize the organization's goals. We have concentrated on the profit and service goals of the study plans.

As we discussed in the first chapter, management is mainly interested in *controls* over the costs of producing the product. If the organization is service-oriented, more effective cost controls will allow expanded services or lower prices to the consumer. If the organization is profit-oriented, lowered production costs lead to greater earnings.

Costs of production arise from provider charges, consumer use of services, and administrative costs. It appears that one of the first questions management must answer is, where shall we concentrate our controls—on the providers or on the consumers? This is one of the first questions because it has obvious implications for the functions of the administrative structure and its costs. It is theoretically undesirable for organizations with service goals to emphasize controls over consumers, since service to the consumer must be maximized.[6] When service is a lower priority goal, controls over consumer behavior may be consistent with attaining greater profits.

Now our interest is in how management in each organization acts to control the three sources of costs of production.

Costs due to physician charges

The health insuring agencies with the highest scores on the profit index are those that place minimal emphasis on control of provider charges. They also attempt no controls over the provider on amount and type of service provided, although claims may be reviewed if they appear unusual and frequently the physician or hospital providing service is consulted. If no settlement can be made informally, it may theoretically be referred to the County Medical Association. Under this system there is minimal "third-party" interference in the doctor-patient relationship. As we discussed earlier, the entire exchange of medical services for funds may be exclusively between the doctor and his patient. Since charges for medical services have, in this the most widespread type of insurance, been left to marketplace controls, they have skyrocketed.

Beginning with the physician-sponsored plan, slight controls over physician charges emerge. This plan has contractual relationships with most of the physicians in the state, but not with all. Since there is no limitation on the consumer in regard to the physician or group of physicians he must visit, he may or may not choose a member under contract. The contract between the plan and member physicians customarily involves an agreement to accept payment from the insuring agency as payment in full for consumers with incomes below $8000 a year. "Payment in full" is currently based on an assessment by the insuring agency of the provider's "usual and customary fee" established by repeated billings over the years, and the going rate for

[6] The plan can argue that by controlling frivolous or unneeded service demands they are able to provide more *necessary* service. The problem is: how many consumers can distinguish the necessary from the unnecessary?

the locality of practice. The fee is based on a conversion factor for the California Relative Value Study units. The physician-sponsored plan pays all physicians on this basis, whether or not they have chosen to engage in a contract. For member physicians the monetary exchange is between physician and insuring agency, without involvement of consumers. For nonmember physicians there are normally no fiscal transactions between provider and insuring agency unless the consumer formally assigns benefits to the provider.

Controls over physician charges are thus minimal. In the instance of lower income people there is control, but there is considerable leeway for the unscrupulous physician to avoid the agreement and attempt to collect further income beyond payments by the insuring agency. For nonparticipating doctors there is no control, but from the perspective of the insuring agency the use of usual and customary fee levels is moderately effective, because it limits the agency's fiscal liability to a certain rate per unit of service provided. The rate, however, is still in the hands of the physicians, and it is up to them to determine what the market will bear because it is ultimately the doctors who determine what is "usual and customary." Beyond this the insuring agency has the problem of having its costs tied to the amount of service provided—a problem avoided in the salary systems described later. Under this system an increase in the amount of service increases a physician's income. In addition, there is leeway for physicians even to claim for services not provided. This system places considerable reliance on the integrity of the professionals, which in large measure is a good bet, but one involving certain risks. Controls over hospitals, of course, are nonexistent in this plan, as in the commercial plans.

The hospital-sponsored plan negotiates contracts with hospitals, and the plan itself cannot function unless a majority of the hospitals in the area are member institutions. Rates charged by the hospitals are negotiated between the insuring agency and hospital representatives. The method of arriving at appropriate rates varies, but one should not deduce from the arrangement that the hospital plan in any significant way *controls* charges by the hospitals except for exclusion of certain hospital costs such as teaching or research activities. Hospitals for the most part regard themselves as autonomous institutions and the hospital-sponsored plan as a payment mechanism only. Consequently, the costs to the hospital-sponsored plan tend to reflect rather than control hospital charges. Control over physician charges in this plan is nil. The plan does tend, however, to follow the physician-sponsored plan in determining appropriateness of physician charges through usual and customary fees. Monetary exchanges occur between hospitals and the plan without consumer involvement, but the plan does not pay physicians directly.

We have seen that the large group practice plan achieves the lowest score on the profit index, a measure of perceived importance of profit over service goals. In addition, this organization is classified legally as a nonprofit corporation and as such is subject to almost no legal controls. It seems evident that this is the best example of a service health plan of the six organizations in the study. In structuring the administration to achieve the service goal, control over physician costs has been emphasized to a greater degree than in any other plan.

In the large group practice plan there is no fee-for-service arrangement. Physicians are paid salaries in accordance with their training and experience. The physicians are a tightly organized, closed group which behaves in many ways like a formal organization: there is a board of directors that represents the partnership of doctors (partnership status is attainable by a new doctor after three years of service on a vote of the partners) and a line of authority running through the overall medical director to area medical directors in each of six administrative areas. The physician group is in full charge of its own affairs, distributing income among members, making promotions, and monitoring quality of care through peer review and supervision by chiefs of service.

Of course, the physician group is dependent on other entities for income and for working facilities. Clinics are owned by the plan itself, whereas hospitals are owned and operated by a separate nonprofit corporation which enters into contractual relationships with the insuring agency.

Monetary flow between the health insuring agency and the providers is thus simplified and controlled by annual contracts. The formula used to determine the amount of payment due under these contracts is a capitation amount for each person enrolled and eligible for services. The contracts call for a physician to practice only within the group and to provide services only to eligible members. Hospitals are, in principle, open to the community (especially for emergencies), but in practice they are used almost exclusively by eligible consumers from the plan.

All physicians are on salary. At the year end surplus income, built into the system by the plan as a hedge against high use of expensive hospital services or unusual drain on other resources, is distributed 50-50 to the hospital corporation and the medical partnership. Partners in the medical group get equal shares of this excess. In the mid 1960s the annual distribution is said to have been around $2400 per partner. This partner's bonus is often referred to as "incentive pay." It is viewed within the group as an incentive to conserve hospital resources. "High use" of hospital facilities should not be confused with efficient use. The insuring agency is interested in restraining hospitalization to keep it within their rather low bed-population ratio (under two beds per 1000 members, or about half the statewide average). Efficient administration should result in high bed occupancy (it tends to exceed 90% in the 1970s) because empty beds mean maintaining facilities that are not needed.

The small group plan has a somewhat different setup. It is operated much more in the fashion of a traditional partnership of physicians, with the important difference that a health insuring function is included. Unlike the large group, the insuring function is overseen directly by the physicians rather than influenced by contractual relationships between the insuring agency and the provider group. Control of physician costs is by the same mechanism: all physicians are paid by salary, reflecting training and experience. The physician group is composed of a partnership that hires additional salaried physicians to provide services to consumers. Physicians are not limited, however, to care for plan patients only, but may in addition conduct fee-for-service practices while using plan facilities. Physicians are eligible to become partners after two years of service on a vote by existing partners and may purchase one percent of the group ownership. Participation in the decisions of the group is on the basis of percent ownership, and this may increase only with the passage of time and when other partners leave or die. Thus control is effectively in the hands of senior partners. Margins between income and expenses are shared by partners as personal profit at the end of each year. No estimate was available of the extent of this additional income to each partner.

Facilities for clinic practices are rented by the partnership rather than owned outright as in the large group. The plan owns no hospitals; it uses selected community hospitals in the same manner as physicians outside the plan. Throughout the years physicians associated with the small group have generally admitted patients at one particular hospital, but recently there has been difficulty getting patients admitted. By definition the plan has no control over hospital charges or policies, and there is no agreement between the plan and any hospital. Hospital portions of the benefit package marketed by the small group are underwritten by a local insurance company that has close historical ties with the small group plan.

The topic of controlling charges by physicians and hospitals immediately raises political issues and values, neither of which we wish to deal with here. It seems reasonable, however, that the stress in a fee-for-service system with increasingly comprehensive health insurance benefits is toward higher fees and increased services (inflation). On the other hand, in a system in which a physician's income is dependent on his training, experience, and efficient use of resources the inflationary stress is partly held in check (Roemer, 1962). The control is not total, of course, since physicians under salaried systems may gauge the adequacy of their incomes in terms of the earning power of physicians in the community at large.

An idea of relative cost due to physician charges is provided by the CRVS conversion factors[7] reported by the physicians responding to our questionnaire. We have reported elsewhere that the conversion factors used by the large and small group plans for medicine are $6 and $7, respectively, and we believe that the differences in the factors are due to different administrative organization *vis-a-vis* physicians in the two plans. Physicians providing services to consumers in the other plans reported these factors for medicine: large commercial, $7.43, small commercial, $7.44, hospital-sponsored, $7.79, physician-sponsored, $7.20. Standard deviations around these averages tended to be about $1.00. The maximum conversion factor reported for medicine was $11.00.

Costs due to consumption of insured services

If management's decision is to emphasize controls over consumer behavior rather than provider behavior, the vehicle of control is the *benefit package.* By decreasing the number of items in the package and by placing limits on fiscal liabilities associated with each item the insuring agency can reduce its costs. Further limitations may be introduced by designating consumers with certain characteristics ineligible to buy the product.

Because the responsibility for defining the product of the organization (benefit package) lies with the actuaries, a discussion of benefit packages in the six study plans will be given in the section on the technical level.

---

[7] Applied to the 1964 edition of the California Relative Value Study. This edition applied to almost all medical care in this study. The 1969 version was released just at the end of the research, and some physicians reported factors in terms of the 1969 version. These were converted to equivalent 1964 factors.

Costs due to administration

Administrative systems vary according to various management decisions which we have discussed above. In general, two extreme variations of the pattern of interactions among components of the health insurance social system have evolved. These are illustrated in Figure 2-1.

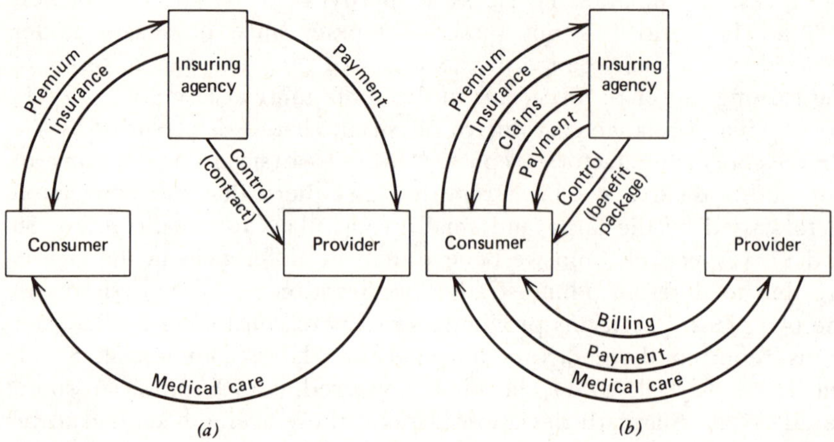

FIGURE 2-1
Administrative types in
health insurance social systems

Type *(a)* administration emphasizes control of providers and is best realized in the large group plan. Interactions among components are minimized, reduced to their simplest elements. The administrative type is approached by the small group plan, but controls over physicians are weaker and insurance involving hospital care involves Type *(b)* administration.

Type *(b)* administration emphasizes control over consumers through the vehicle of the benefit package. The commercial companies exhibit this interaction pattern. It is considerably more complex than Type *(a)*, and there is more room for error. Errors that can occur in this system are failure to submit claims, failure to complete the payment chain from the insuring agency through the consumer to the provider, and filing of fraudulent claims. The provider-sponsored plans exhibit elements of both administrative types but are basically Type *(b)*, since the thrust of their effective cost control is over consumer behavior and neither plan totally avoids the claims procedure.

Besides being error-prone, Type *(b)* administration appears to be more expensive. Processing claims, checking eligibility, calculating coinsurance levels, checking medical procedures and prices, and making thousands of payments all add to its administrative complexity. It is difficult to assess administrative costs across plans, since figures released voluntarily by the plans do not necessarily reflect comparable processes and we were unable to obtain financial information in the form we wished across all plans. Our information on administrative costs came primarily from interviews with plan officials in four of the study plans, plus information contained in annual reports and other written sources. Thus it is not "hard data," but takes the form of estimated proportions of premium income. The data obtained are listed below.

	Estimates of proportion of premium income used for administration
Large commercial	5%
Small commercial	9%
Hospital-sponsored	9%
Physician-sponsored	10%
Large group	3%
Small group	No estimate [8]

These figures are for 1968. The lower administrative cost of the large commercial plan is possibly due to the delegation of administrative authority to certain enrollment groups (Pickerell, 1961).

Technical Level

Comprehensiveness of the product

The function of the technical level is the production and sale of the benefit package. We deal with the production aspect.

The nature of our sampling procedure causes us to include a wide

[8] In addition to the reluctance of plan officials to release this estimate and the lack of written estimates, there is difficulty here in estimating the portion of administration performed by the associated commercial life insurance company that handles hospital claims. Because of the mixed nature of the organization, we assume that the administrative portion is higher than the large group plan, but there is no way of estimating how much higher.

variety of benefit packages which represent the range of products offered by each health insuring agency. It is difficult to assess the full range of the products from one agency to the next. For the group plans the problem is not so great because they tend to offer very few benefit packages. The other plans, however, tailor their products according to the requests and financial resources of the consumer groups. One commercial plan official said that with the ingredients available they could make up 21,800 different insurance packages.

We offer three methods of assessing the relative comprehensiveness of benefit packages in the six plans. First, each plan is assessed and discussed in terms of the extent of benefits for eight health service items. Second, comprehensiveness is measured by the proportion of total family medical expenses met by the study plan. Third, evaluations by consumers and physicians of the adequacy of benefits are presented.

Content of the benefit packages

Table 2-4 provides information on the extent of inclusion of eight items in the benefit packages of consumers in our samples. Each item is coded as *complete* (no controls on consumers), *nearly complete* (few deterrents on consumer use), *limited* (major limitations on consumer use), and *none* (item was not included at all). The "limited" designation covers a wide range of possibilities.

Table 2-4 shows that for the first item, *routine physical examinations* (i.e., preventive examinations) there are generally no benefits in the commercial and provider-sponsored plans. The exception is the large commercial plan in which 18.5% of the consumers have complete benefits for these examinations. These consumers represent an atypical portion of the sample, having the choice of a combined plan in which the large commercial company handled the hospital portion of the benefit package and underwrote the medical portion which was provided by a small group practice under contract to a labor-management trust fund. The remainder of the sample resembles the small commercial and provider-sponsored plans in providing no benefits. Nearly three-quarters of the consumers in the large group practice plan have complete benefits for routine examinations. The remainder have "nearly complete" benefits, which means that a $2.00 charge is made for each visit (a small fraction of the actual cost). All consumers in the small group practice plan have "nearly complete" benefits for routine physical examinations. In this plan there is a charge of $1.25 for dependents in the most comprehensive packages (but none for the primary subscriber) and $2.00 for subscriber and dependents in other packages.

TABLE 2-4
Extent of selected benefits
in benefit packages

Benefit	Extent of benefit	Plan: Large comm	Small comm	Hosp-spon	Phys-spon	Large group	Small group
Routine physical examination	Complete	18.5	0	0	0	72.6	0
	Nearly comp	0	0	0	0	27.4	100.0
	Limited	0	0	0	0	0	0
	None	81.5	100.0	100.0	100.0	0	0
Doctor's office visits	Complete	18.5	0	0	0	72.6	0
	Nearly comp	0	0	0	0	27.4	100.0
	Limited	80.3	99.6	25.6	65.6	0	0
	None	1.3	0.4	74.4	34.4	0	0
Doctor's services in the hospital	Complete	18.5	0	0	0	100.0	30.9
	Nearly comp	30	40	60	60	0	69.1
	Limited	51.5	60	40	40	0	0
	None	0	0	0	0	0	0
General hospital services	Complete	0	0	0	32.0	2.9	0
	Nearly comp	50	50	50	34.0	48.6	46.8
	Limited	50	50	50	34.0	48.5	0
	None	0	0	0	0	0	53.2
Doctor's care for normal maternity	Complete	18.5	0	0	0	13.3	17.1
	Nearly comp	0	0	0	0	36.7	50
	Limited	80.7	6.9	65.3	65.3	50	32.9
	None	1.0	93.1	34.7	34.7	0	0
Doctor's home calls	Complete	7.5	0	0	0	0	0
	Nearly comp	0	0	0	0	0	0
	Limited	91.3	99.6	25.6	65.6	100.0	100.0
	None	1.3	0.4	74.4	34.4	0	0
Psychiatric services	Complete	0	0	0	0	0	0
	Nearly comp	0	0	0	0	0	0
	Limited	33.4	28.6	48.6	12.9	22.4	0
	None	66.6	71.4	51.4	87.1	77.6	100.0
Vision examinations	Complete	18.5	0	0	0	72.6	0
	Nearly comp	0	0	0	0	27.4	100.0
	Limited	0	0	0	0	0	0
	None	81.5	100.0	100.0	100.0	0	0
Average %	None	29	46	53	49	10	19
(N)		576	683	334	272	618	657

For *doctor's office visits* (i.e., visits because of illness) the great majority of consumers in the commercial plans and both provider-sponsored plans have only limited benefits. This generally means that a substantial deductible must be satisfied, usually $100 per member or $250 per family, beyond which the plan will pay 80% of the charges up to a maximum for the year. The nearly complete benefits in the group practice plans mean the availability of ambulatory services with payment by the consumer (in some enrollment groups) of a small deterrent fee. The percent of consumers with no benefits for doctor's office visits under the provider-sponsored plans (especially the hospital-sponsored plan) shows the concentration here on in-hospital benefits.

The tabulation of benefit packages involving *doctor's services in the hospital* was not easy for all four provider-sponsored plans. Except for the atypical subsample in the large commercial plan linked to a prepaid group practice (mentioned above), all consumers in these plans are subject to a variety of ceilings and copayments; for instance, the benefit package bought by the largest enrollment group of the large commercial plan pays only $1 per day for in-patient doctor services or $300 for six months, whichever is reached first. Similarly, one of the largest enrollment groups in the small commercial plan offered a $5 payment per doctor call in the hospital up to a maximum of $155 in the "basic plan" and, beyond that, 80% of covered services following a $100 deductible in the "major medical expense" plan. For surgical services a fee schedule is set up to define the commercial carrier's maximum liability for each procedure, the highest fee being $750 in the large plan. In the small commercial plan the surgical fee schedules were generally lower. Moreover, the surgeon in both indemnity plans was free to charge the patient more than the scheduled allowance (and for higher income patients these supplemental charges are often considerable).

In-hospital doctor's services in the provider-sponsored plans were somewhat more liberal. In the hospital-sponsored plan a large enrollment group allowed $15.50 in its benefit package for the first hospital day of physician visits, up to $6 for the second to 20th days, and up to $5 for the 21st to 120th days, with an overall maximum of $629.50 per hospitalization. The physician-sponsored plan in its best packages (which feature combined benefits with the hospital-sponsored plan) pays "usual or customary" fees to physicians for in-patient care up to a maximum annual number of days (120 to 180) per hospitalization. For surgical services the hospital-sponsored plan used the CRVS as a basis for its fee schedule, with varying values ($4 to $6) per unit, in addition to maximum liabilities per year. The physician-sponsored plan followed the same principle of paying "usual or customary" fees for surgical as for nonsurgical services.

In the large group practice plan in-hospital doctor services, whether medical or surgical, were covered completely. In the small group plan the same comprehensive in-patient doctor's services—whether medical or surgical—were usually (though not always) provided for the primary enrollee. For dependents in this plan, however, for a majority of the benefit packages extra fees of \$15 to \$25 were charged for surgical procedures, depending on their complexity.

For *general hospital services* (i.e., the hospital bill, distinguished from the doctor's fee) all benefit packages in both commercial plans had certain limitations. Their diversity was so great in our sample that the extent of benefits was difficult to classify, and in Table 2-4 the percentages offered are only approximations. To be considered "complete," the provision for this benefit had to allow 365 days of hospitalization per year at the full hospital charges. Under the large commercial plan typical limitations on room and board benefits were "\$22 per day up to \$682 per disability," or "up to 85% of the daily rate for 70 days," or "up to \$18 per day for the first 20 days, plus \$20 per day for the next 80 days," or "not to exceed \$14 per day up to 31 days per disability." Other limitations were customarily imposed on in-patient diagnostic tests, operating room use, drugs, etc. In both commercial plans these hospitalization benefits were customarily accompanied by a "major medical expense" or "supplemental" package involving deductibles, copayments, and ceilings.

In the hospital-sponsored plan almost the same arrangements prevailed. None provided full 365-day benefits, with the number of days of protection varying from 21 to 180 and the percent of total costs paid after stated time period being 50 to 80%. Some supplementary benefit packages, which took effect after basic benefits and a \$200 deductible were met, paid 80% up to a maximum ceiling of \$10,000. Under the physician-sponsored plan it may be noted in Table 2-4 that complete 365-day benefits applied to about 32% of the enrollees; these packages were sold in conjunction with the hospital-sponsored plan. The "nearly complete" and "limited" benefits were similar to those in the other provider-sponsored plan.

In the group practice plans, unlike physician's care, hospitalization benefits were rarely complete (in the sense defined above). Packages of the large group plan were generally limited to 30 to 125 days at full charges, beyond which 50% copayment is required. Only a few packages (with 2.9% of enrollees) have unlimited hospital benefits. In the small group practice plan those enrollees with "nearly complete" hospitalization benefits are insured by a commercial life insurance company closely linked with the plan, and the limitations are similar to those of the commercial and provider-sponsored plans. The high percentage of enrollees with no hospitalization benefits under this plan may perhaps be a bit misleading; these persons have only medical and surgical benefits with the small group practice plan, but hospitalization insurance is typically obtained from another company unrelated to it.

The analysis of these benefits for general hospital services, as noted above, was not easy to classify into our four categories of extent. It must be remembered that more than 90% of hospitalizations are for less than 30 days so that a benefit package of 30 to 70 days, paying full charges, can be considered "nearly complete." Even considering the hospital days at risk, rather than the admissions, patients remaining in the hospital for fewer than 30 days account for the vast majority of total hospital use. Because the Medicare law of 1965 has removed aged persons (with long-stay conditions) from the responsibility of all six of the voluntary insurance plans studied, the proportion of hospital *days* covered, for example, by a 30- or 70-day package is close to the high proportion of *admissions* protected by such packages.

As for *doctor's care for normal maternity* under the large commercial plan, physician costs are completely covered for the 18.5% of the sample belonging to the atypically associated prepaid group practice by the labor-management trust fund. The great bulk of enrollees in this plan have limited maternity benefits, whereas only a handful (1.0%) have none. By contrast, in the small commercial plan, only a very small percentage of enrollees have even limited maternity benefits and 93.1% have none at all. In both commercial plans "limited benefits" for normal maternity care involve a ceiling of $100 for hospital charges and an additional lump sum of $75 to $100 for the obstetrical fees—amounts that were much below the usual costs at the time.

In the two provider-sponsored plans quite similar restrictions applied to normal maternity cases. Large enrollment groups might be entitled to "full service benefits" (i.e., payment of total charges) for hospitalization but only $90 toward physician obstetrical fees. About one-third of the enrollees had no maternity care protection. Moreover, any of these benefits were payable only after a nine-month waiting period.

The group practice plans, including prenatal and postpartum

services, were clearly more liberal for maternity care. About 13% in the large group plan and 17% in the small one had complete protection. The majority of enrollees in our sample, however, had restrictions on maternity benefits. In the large group plan the most common package levied a charge on the patient of $100 if childbirth occurred 10 or more months after joining the plan and $175 if sooner. In the small group practice plan there was usually a $50 charge (relatively small) for any childbirth. (The hospitalization portion of maternity costs in the small group plan was subject to more severe limitations similar to those described above for the commercial plans, but the percentages in Table 2-4 refer only to benefits for physician services.)

Doctor's home calls in both the commercial and provider-sponsored plans were generally included under "supplementary" benefits, subject to the type of limitations described earlier for doctor's office visits. The 7.5% of enrollees in the large commercial plan with complete home-call benefits were in certain subgroups that used the associated special group practice, whereas other subgroups paid a $3 charge for home calls. In both group practice plans home calls are provided but with a $5 charge. It may be noted in passing that general experience under health insurance indicates a very low demand for home calls when there is easy access, without financial deterrents, to doctor's office visits.

As for *psychiatric services* (mainly ambulatory psychiatric care), the majority of enrollees in all six plans have no benefits. In the commercial and provider-sponsored plans, for those having "limited" benefits, there is usually a requirement of hospitalization for at least 24 hours. If ambulatory treatment is provided, maximum amounts (such as $20) per visit are usually specified, and there are typically deductibles plus a maximum number of visits. For 22.4% of enrollees in the large group practice plan there were complete benefits for inpatient psychiatric services and up to 10 visits per year for ambulatory psychiatric services. No psychiatric benefits at all were offered in the small group practice plan.

Finally, for *vision examinations* (refractions for eyeglasses) benefits were generally excluded in both commercial and provider-sponsored plans—except for the special group in the large commercial plan enrolled with the group practice. In the large group practice plan complete refractive services were available to the majority of enrollees without charge and for 27.4% they were available with a $2 charge. In the small group plan the consumer pays $1.25 to $2.00 for any refraction, although in some packages these fees apply only to dependents.

As a brief summary of the comprehensiveness of benefits for the eight types of services analyzed in Table 2-4, the six plans may be ordered by an average of percentages of enrollees having no benefits (high control over consumer use).

Consumer constraint index

Large group	10 (least controls)
Small group	19
Large commercial	26
Small commercial	46
Physician-sponsored	49
Hospital-sponsored	53 (most controls)

Perhaps more significant in terms of overall medical care needs are the relative *emphases* in benefits offered by the three plan types. All offered hospital benefits which in dollars probably covered more than one-half or three-quarters of the costs. The commercial plans, with their indemnification principles, various deductibles, copayments, and cost ceilings, were more restricted than the provider-sponsored plans which usually (though not always) provided full service benefits for in-patient hospitalization.

Much greater differentials characterize physicians' care. For in-patients the commercial plans applied fee schedule indemnification, beyond which the doctor was free to make extra charges. The provider-sponsored plans more often paid full service benefits, although higher income patients could be levied with extra charges. The group practice plans offered complete or nearly complete in-patient doctor services.

For ambulatory doctor's care—the crucial sector of comprehensive health service—the differentials were greatest. Only in the group practice plans were these completely or nearly completely (i.e., a nominal charge of $1 or $2) available. In both of the other plan types ambulatory doctor's services were usually offered only after substantial deductibles (such as $100 per person per year) and in a "major medical expense" supplementary policy.

As for other items of health service contributing to comprehensive care—routine physical examinations, maternity service, vision examinations—the differentials between the open-market and the group practice plans were generally in the same direction. Only for psychiatric services were all three types of plan deficient to about the same degree. Except for the last, the cluster of benefits in the group practice plans may be epitomized as much more strongly oriented toward preventive medicine than in either of the two open-market plan types.

Portion of family expenses paid by plan

The second measure we employed of the comprehensiveness of the benefit packages assessed the portion of each family's total medical bills for one year that was paid for by the health insurance plan. The reader should be careful to note that we are reporting portions of total bills paid by *one plan* in the study for each consumer. We are not reporting portions paid by all insurance plans, and it is possible that consumers had additional benefits paid by other plans we are not studying. In this assessment only care provided to *covered* family members was considered in the total. Methods of calculating value of care have already been reported in reference to Table 2-3.

Table 2-5 presents the results of this calculation. It is evident that the group practice plans pay a much larger portion of total expenses than the other plans. One must be careful when interpreting the figure assigned to the physician-sponsored plan, because this figure represents the care for which the plan was *liable* in the event that all applicable medical care was claimed. The difference between the group plans and the others shrinks a bit when the value of total care per family member rises higher than $76 per year, but there is still a considerable differential. For low-consumption families the differences are huge. This is the effect of deductibles.

Consumer and physician evaluations

In both the consumer and physician questionnaire surveys the respondents were asked to evaluate the adequacy of financial benefits in each of the six plans. The results of the consumer questionnaire are represented and thoroughly analyzed in Chapter 6. It suffices here to note that consumers were asked to express their satisfaction with financial benefits, and were provided with a scale running from "very satisfied" to "very dissatisfied."

Those responding as "very satisfied" were large commercial, 40.8%, small commercial, 26.2%, hospital-sponsored, 29.4%, physician-sponsored, 25.5%, large group, 71.1%, and small group, 33.8%.

In the physician survey doctors were asked to evaluate one of the six plans which they felt they *knew most about.* The question asked was: "How would you evaluate the plan (you know most about) on adequacy of coverage of the most usual policy sold by the plan?"

TABLE 2-5

Portion of family medical bills paid by plan and by total value of care per covered family member

Percent of family's total bills paid	Plan						
	All plans	Large comm	Small comm	Hosp-spon	Phys-spon	Large group	Small group
All families with care							
None (%)	28.3	50.7	37.5	58.5	39.7	.5	.5
Up to 33%	9.1	9.4	11.3	11.8	11.8	6.1	5.6
34-66%	14.2	24.5	22.1	13.6	22.4	2.7	8.4
67-100%	48.4	15.4	29.1	16.0	26.2	91.7	85.4
Mean	.52	.24	.36	.22	.37	.88	.80
SD	.41	.30	.34	.31	.39	.25	.41
N	584	71	89	98	94	116	117
Families with annual care valued at $75 or less per covered member							
None (%)	38.3	87.2	64.6	90.4	54.6	.3	1.9
Up to 33%	8.0	5.0	17.4	6.5	11.7	6.9	2.8
34-66%	6.6	2.8	15.6	3.1	14.6	2.2	1.9
67-100%	47.1	5.1	2.4	...	19.1	90.6	94.4
Mean	.48	.06	.12	.03	.27	.88	.87
SD	.45	.18	.23	.09	39	.26	.18
N	300	28	34	34	67	72	65
Families with annual care valued at more than $75 per covered member							
None (%)	17.7	26.8	20.6	41.6	2.1	.9	...
Up to 33%	10.1	12.3	7.5	14.6	12.0	.8	9.1
34-66%	22.3	38.7	26.2	19.3	41.9	4.7	16.6
67-100%	49.8	22.2	45.8	24.5	44.0	93.6	74.3
Mean	.55	.36	.51	.32	.62	.88	.70
SD	.35	.31	.32	.34	.26	.23	.25
N	284	43	55	64	27	44	53

Response was requested in one of four categories: excellent, good, fair and poor.

Most of the community of physicians selected one of the provider-sponsored plans to evaluate, and, consequently, responses were combined for the commercial plans (total N=33). Those responding in the first category ("excellent") were commercials, 18.2%, hospital-sponsored, 2.5%, physician-sponsored, 7.4%, large group, 67.3%, and small group, 42.9%.

An overall evaluation index may be derived from these figures by averaging the percent of consumers and physicians who checked the "very satisfied" and "excellent" alternatives. For the two commercial plans the same figure is used for the physician evaluation. The index gives equal weight to consumer and physician evaluation.

Plans ranked according to the consumer-physician evaluation index

Large group	69.2 %
Small group	38.3
Large commercial	29.5
Small commercial	22.2
Physician-sponsored	16.4
Hospital-sponsored	16.0

Price of the product

The majority of plans in our study used experience rating as a method of determining the premiums charged in relation to the benefits offered. The most common factor taken into account by actuaries is the size of the family: plans in our study generally charged higher premiums for persons with more dependents. For plans that experience rated beyond this, age and sex distribution of the consumer group were the most important determinants. Older people and women of child-bearing age are known to use more medical and hospital services, and therefore groups with high proportions of women or older persons are charged higher premiums. The commercial plans and the provider-sponsored plans used age and sex as determinants but also took into account the cost of medical services in the geographical location, occupation, loss ratio of former years, size of employer group, amount of employer contribution, and whether the group was one that had been previously insured by another company (known in the industry as a "takeover"). When takeover groups are large, past use experience is generally the only criterion used.

In discussing the concept of "community rating" with an official from the large commercial plan, an interviewer was told, "Life isn't fair. Therefore why should you demand fairness from it? Who says everybody should have the same rate?" In any case, the possibility seemed out of the question for this company because the state would be required to regulate the rates if community rating was used by commercial carriers. In the present system the law provides that commercial insurers may set rates in accordance with "sound underwriting principles."

The hospital-sponsored plan had a long history of using a modified community rating system but gradually had to resort to experience rating because of competition from commercial carriers which siphoned off the low-risk groups by offering them lower premiums by virtue of their more favorable experience.

The one plan in our study not fitting this pattern was the large group practice plan, which used the community rating system rather than experience rating. By this method premiums are consistent from one consumer group to the next, regardless of risk factors.

The small group plan uses age and sex factors in determining price for the portion of the premium paid for the services of a physician. Premiums for hospital services are determined by the commercial insurance company in the manner described above.

The price of the product also reflects competition in the marketplace. For plans in our study effective competition takes place only among the provider-sponsored and commercial companies. The group plans, after experiencing great surges in membership, have closed their doors at least temporarily to new groups. Internal growth of existing enrollment groups (new employees in an enrolled firm, childbirths, etc.) has been about 10% per year in the large group plan. These group plans have limited facilities and personnel, and in each case the physician component of the plan insists on controlling the doctor-population ratio at about one physician for 1000 people. Increasing services to a greater population also means an increase in facilities and doctors (and other personnel). The large group plan has entered on an expansion program, but the program is not necessarily limited to existing locations. The small group plan is contemplating drastic revisions in its structure, one of which is the construction of its own hospital facilities. Federal legislation on a program of national health insurance for all people could alter the picture considerably, especially if the health maintenance organization (HMO) concept is encouraged.

Meanwhile the group plans have essentially "dropped out" of the competitive market, except in terms of maintaining their present level. Their presence in the area, however, still sets a standard of performance that the other plans have to try to meet.

Price is also affected by the tax structure within which each plan must operate. The commercial companies experience a considerably larger tax bite than the nonprofit companies. Their reliance on life insurance sales to back up the health insurance program has not been entirely lost on the nonprofit health plans.

The provider-sponsored and the small group plans are affiliated with life insurance companies so that combination health and life insurance policies can be sold. The only plan that has no combination health-life insurance benefit package for sale is the large group practice plan.

Health insurance plans are also selective in the occupational groups they will insure. If they accept an occupational classification that is considered dangerous, they insist that the group be large in the hope of offsetting high use. The large commercial plan generally does not exclude individuals because of job category; if they will accept the group, they are willing to take all employees in it. In the small commercial carrier, which tends to concentrate on smaller groups, there are more restrictions. In high risk occupations such as aeronautics or explosives, if the group contains three to 12 employees, only the executive and clerical employees are insured. In other small groups in less dangerous occupations, if 50% of the employees have worked for the employer two years or more and the employer pays 100% of the premium, they will insure the whole group. This includes groups usually considered high risk, such as dry-cleaning establishments, garages, and laundries.

Exclusions can be of another kind. None of the plans will treat alcoholism, drug addiction, occupational injuries or illness, or conditions caused by war or aggression. For the small commercial plan, in the smaller contract size, major medical benefits are available only for employees free of medical treatment for 90 days or insured for 12 months. For the large group plan, as noted above, enrollment is closed to all new membership groups. For the small group plan close screening is done to exclude even moderately risky occupations such as doctors' offices or restaurants.

Table 2-6 presents the results of premium calculations by the plans based on factors we have discussed. Premiums are presented by size of family, since most plans vary premiums according to the number of people in the family covered.

Highest premium rates on the average are found in the physician-sponsored plan. This is influenced to some degree by combined benefit packages with the hospital-sponsored plan which tend to be expensive. The large group plan's overall average is not far behind the physician-sponsored plan. The premium average for the small group practice plan is the lowest, influenced by packages that do not include hospitalization benefits. These packages are written in combination with hospital insurance by other companies that are not part of this study; thus the premium input was not included. Correspondingly, medical care received under the hospital portion of these packages was, of course, not a liability of the small group plan.

TABLE 2-6
Amount of annual premium† by plan by number in family covered

Family size	Plan						
	All plans	Large comm	Small comm	Hosp-spon	Phys-spon	Large group	Small group
All families							
Mean($)	245.11	235.57	226.38	247.64	293.38	282.06	217.20
SD($)	125.50	160.67	103.32	129.32	170.10	86.69	103.70
N	3,107	575	682	335	272	618	653
One member covered							
Mean($)	152.42	116.31	116.29	147.92	230.46	161.57	130.79
SD($)	102.90	108.73	46.07	65.35	210.14	63.91	57.85
N	1,006	206	221	149	111	131	189
Two members covered							
Mean($)	271.60	312.38	247.70	299.96	314.02	277.64	226.69
SD($)	142.11	302.33	69.66	105.04	105.35	49.37	82.71
N	637	100	105	64	64	150	155
Three or more members covered							
Mean($)	297.30	259.97	290.23	343.77	352.06	330.75	265.44
SD($)	91.19	78.67	72.06	110.66	123.94	55.62	101.85
N	1,463	270	332	121	97	337	307

†Total premiums for those in the study year less than 12 months were converted to 12-month equivalents.

If the three measures of comprehensiveness of the benefit package are valid, it is then possible to combine them in order to arrive at an overall index of comprehensiveness. This is done by ranking the plans in each of the three indices reported (consumer constraints, portion of family expenses paid, consumer-physician evaluations) and summing the ranks on each plan. With such an overall index, we are then able to observe the correspondence in plan rankings between comprehensiveness of the package and average price of the package.

From these figures it appears that, in relation to other major plans in the market, the small group plan is priced too low, given the level of comprehensiveness in its benefit packages, whereas both the provider-sponsored plans are too expensive for what they offer. The small group plan is the second most comprehensive but is least expensive on the average. The physician-sponsored plan, on the other hand, is second to last in comprehensiveness but is the most expensive. It should be noted that the composite index includes a rank assigned to the physician-sponsored plan based on fiscal liability rather than actual benefits paid. In reality, its ranking should be lower.

Comprehensiveness of benefit packages		Average price of benefit packages	
Large group	3 (most comprehensive)	Physician-sponsored	1 (most expensive)
Small group	6	Large group	2
Large commercial	12	Hospital-sponsored	3
Small commercial	12	Large commercial	4
Physician-sponsored	13	Small commercial	5
Hospital sponsored	17 (least comprehensive)	Small group	6 (least expensive)

CONSUMERS

Differences in composition of the consumer component, which significantly bias the distribution of "risks" across plans, may independently influence the effect of the plans on use and consumer costs and satisfaction. The risk status of consumers is derived from an insuring agency's actuarial conclusions regarding the use probabilities associated with the consumer groups. The variance in use (i.e., risk) from one consumer group to another is contingent on the distribution of certain risk-defining consumer characteristics.

These risk-defining consumer characteristics may be subsumed under two major concepts: *need* and *demand.* Need is an objective evaluation of whether or not health care should be obtained. The social factors that facilitate the access and underlie a readiness to engage health care services are sociologically defined as demand for services.

Use is conceptualized as the culmination of objective health status (need) and consumer discretion regarding the use of services (demand) acting on one another.

Consumer Health Care Needs

Indicators of need included in the study are subscriber age, average age of family members, women of child-bearing age, family size, number of family members who are chronically ill, and the number of family members having acute illness during a three-month period. Table 2-7 presents the distributions of the need indicators across the six study plans.

TABLE 2-7
Selected risk-defining consumer characteristics by plan: need

Characteristics	Plan					
	Large comm	Small comm	Hosp-spon	Phys-spon	Large group	Small group
Age of respondent						
47-65 (%)	32.8	35.7	44.1	32.0	39.6	46.3
Mean	41.6	41.5	42.6	37.7	42.5	45.1
SD	10.6	11.4	13.3	11.7	11.8	10.5
Average age of family members						
40 + (%)	42.4	38.5	43.8	43.5	44.0	60.0
Mean	31.8	31.5	34.8	32.7	33.6	36.6
SD	13.5	14.8	16.7	14.1	15.0	14.9
Family size						
3 + (%)	57.1	61.0	43.0	40.5	57.7	51.6
Mean	3.22	3.20	2.75	2.72	3.22	3.09
SD	1.86	1.60	1.14	1.55	1.70	1.73
Families with chronic illness						
(%)	36.5	40.2	52.2	37.2	61.8	53.6
Families with short-term illness						
(%)	16.3	19.5	27.5	16.5	26.5	18.7
Families with women of child-bearing age						
(%)	63.2	53.7	26.6	35.3	57.4	50.2
(N)	576	683	334	271	618	657

Analysis of consumer age and average age of family members reveals that the commercial plans and the physician-sponsored plan have fewer consumers in the middle-aged bracket and few older families. The small group plan has the most middle-aged and older consumers. The large group plan and the hospital-sponsored plan have age patterns in between these extremes. Since need increases with age, the group plans and hospital-sponsored plan have consumer populations that exhibit more need for health care services on the basis of age composition.

Consumer populations insured under the provider-sponsored plans are composed of smaller families than those of the remaining plans. Larger familes are found in the large commercial and the large group plans.

Each subscriber in the sample was presented with a list of 27 of the most frequent chronic illnesses and asked which family members, if any, suffered from these illnesses. The number of family members who experienced at least one chronic illness during the preceding 12-month period was thus identified.

The distributions and means of families with chronically ill members by plan are in Table 2-7. Families with chronically ill members, and therefore having a high need for health care, were most frequently enrolled in one of the group practice plans. The hospital-sponsored plan had the third largest proportion of families with chronically ill members. The large commercial plan included fewer families with chronically ill members than all others.

The percent of family members having a short-term illness within the three-month period preceding participation in our study is also reported across plans in Table 2-7. The large group plan and the hospital-sponsored plan demonstrated higher need levels, with nearly 30% of the covered families experiencing one or more acute illnesses. The remaining plans, including the small group plan, had about 20% of their covered families experiencing acute illnesses during the three-month period.

The proportion of women of child-bearing age in each of our six consumer populations shows that the provider-sponsored plans have enrolled fewer women in this bracket than the other plans. The commercial carriers tend to include slightly more women of child-bearing age than the group plans on the whole. Women of child-bearing age tend to use more health services because of their pregnancy, maternity, and postnatal child-care needs. In this respect the commercial plans have increased risks over those of other plan types.

Consumer Demand

Attitudes and skills that underlie readiness to engage health care services are differentially distributed among the various social strata of society. Demand increases as family income, education, and occupational status increase. Ethnic classes, which to some extent cut across income and educational lines, may be the source of cultural variation with consequences for demand.

Indicators of demand include annual income, education of the head of household, occupation of the head of household, ethnic background, perceptions of the influence of insurance on family use, symptom sensitivity, and doctor complaints. Although socioeconomic factors are not direct indicators of attitudes toward seeking professional care, previous research has documented that such orientations are distributed according to a person's socioeconomic status.

Time and space do not permit us to explore the psychosocial aspects of demand for medical care, but their importance must be stressed. Perception of symptoms and manner of seeking care are broad topics that we touch lightly in the discussion of symptom sensitivity. Why people react differently to the same symptoms is based on complex social, psychological, and cultural forces, among which self-esteem may play a basic role (Mechanic, 1974).

Table 2-8 reports percent distributions and averages on four indicators of social status for each of the plans. Annual family income includes reported gross earnings from all sources. Responses were forced into several precoded income categories. The group plans and the small commercial plan included more middle and high income subscribers. The large commercial plan enrolled the most persons with lower incomes.

On education the small group plan has the most highly educated consumers, and the small commercial plan has the smallest percent of college-educated consumers. The other plans are roughly equivalent. Average score on the Hollingshead occupational scale (range 1—7 with highest=1) is 3.8 and 3.7, respectively, for the small group and small commercial plans, with 73.4% of the consumers in the small commercial plan in either professional or white-collar occupations.

The large group plan subscribers included the largest proportion of persons with eastern and southern European backgrounds as well as the largest proportion of nonwhite persons. The small group plan and hospital-sponsored plan had the smallest proportion of ethnic minority subscribers.

We assume that those plans with greater proportions of middle and high socioeconomic status subscribers absorb greater risk because of the greater demand for health care services generally associated with high social status. Ethnic status is also correlated with socioeconomic status and may thus demonstrate demand patterns that increase in intensity with increasing assimilation into the American "mainstream." Ethnic classes persisting as cultural entities, however, may vary independently of their social class positions in their cultural response to health and illness problems. Prediction of demand solely on the basis of "social distance" theory would fall far short of reality.

Negative attitudes toward physicians may have consequences for demand in the form of greater reluctance to engage in the doctor-patient relationship. Previous investigations in this subject area have consistently reported that the principal source of patient complaint is a perceived lack of personal interest on the physician's part;

TABLE 2-8
Selected risk-defining consumer characteristics by plan: demand

Characteristics	Plan					
	Large comm	Small comm	Hosp-spon	Phys-spon	Large group	Small group
Family annual income						
$11,000+ (%)	28.1	49.4	38.7	37.8	48.2	48.3
Mean	$9,493	$13,111	$11,157	$10,704	$11,265	$11,561
SD	$6,600	$9,058	$9,633	$5,963	$5,054	$6,045
Education of head of household						
College (%)	25.1	16.4	22.6	25.8	24.9	28.4
Mean	12.4	12.8	12.9	12.9	12.8	13.5
SD	3.6	2.7	3.6	3.7	3.4	2.7
Occupation of head of household						
Upper†(%)	44.3	73.4	41.5	48.2	57.0	58.2
Mean††	4.4	3.7	4.4	4.1	4.1	3.8
SD	1.7	1.4	1.7	1.9	1.8	1.6
Ethnicity						
White American	51.1	55.2	51.8	41.7	37.0	59.9
High status European	17.5	21.1	25.4	23.0	18.4	25.9
Low status European	9.9	9.2	8.9	8.8	17.5	6.9
Minorities	21.5	14.5	13.9	26.5	27.1	7.2
Complaint: doctors keep patients waiting (%)	42.4	36.1	46.6	39.6	51.6	39.4
Complaint: doctors too concerned about money (%)	21.0	23.5	26.9	31.8	13.1	21.3
Complaint: doctors resent home visits (%)	33.7	42.7	37.3	32.5	29.3	36.3
Complaint: lack of individual attention from doctor (%)	27.8	31.4	25.6	27.3	27.7	45.7
Complaint: doctors make you feel visits aren't necessary (%)	10.6	6.9	7.4	12.1	25.8	18.1
Opinion: see doctors more often because of insurance (%)	11.1	17.9	9.8	10.5	44.5	32.9
Symptom sensitivity						
Hypersensitive (%)	54.8	59.3	55.9	53.0	62.5	56.7
(N)	576	683	334	271	618	657

†Professional and white-collar workers
††Low score reflects high occupational status

for instance, a respondent commenting on his group plan said, "They (doctors) are cold, aloof and borderline incompetent. Very little longitudinal concern; fix it now so you can be dismissed. If I can't treat it, stall so it will cure itself." A belief held widely by professionals and laymen alike is that entrepreneurial types of practice encourage physicians to demonstrate personal interest in their patients to a greater extent than do bureaucratic group practice settings. As one patient commented, "In the outpatient clinic, I feel patients are treated like animals. Your private doctors are great in their offices."

In Table 2-8 several attitudes toward physicians and physicians' behavior are measured. All of these items are related to the issue of the degree to which patients' personal (not necessarily medical) needs are considered by the provider of services.

Complaints about long office waits are prevalent under all types of plan, although most evident in the large group plan. Profit motives are considerably more frequently attributed to physicians in entrepreneurial contexts. Physicians are perceived to be more willing to make home visits under the large group plan, yet complaints directed at insufficient individual attention afforded by physicians are more frequent in this plan. Such complaints in the large group plan are about as frequent as in the indemnity plans in which solo practice and free choice of physicians predominate. Subscribers to the group plans, however, are more inclined to view their contacts with physicians with embarrassment; a substantial minority of these subscribers reported that their physicians give them the impression that their visits were unnecessary. Negative attitudes toward physicians appear to be somewhat more frequent in the group plans. The perception that individual attention is inadequate, however, is widespread and affected one-third of all subscribers, regardless of plan or type of practice.

Each subscriber in our survey was queried: Do you think having health insurance benefits for doctor's care makes any difference in the number of times you or your family go to see a doctor? Possible responses were (a) yes, we see doctors more frequently; (b) no difference; and (c) yes, we see doctors less frequently. Table 2-8 illustrates the impact of comprehensive insurance benefits on demand perceived by consumers themselves. The group plans provide greater benefits for doctors' services in and out of the hospital than are provided under the commercial carriers or provider-sponsored plans and are several times more likely to have been perceived by their subscribers as encouraging more frequent use.

Attitudes about the urgency of seeking professional care with respect to range of symptoms varying in seriousness, as objectively determined by a panel of physician judges, were scaled and applied as a measure of *symptom sensitivity* (Hetherington and Hopkins,1969). Because symptom-sensitivity[8] is defined in terms of inclination to seek professional health care services, increased symptom sensitivity should lead to increased demand.

The highest percent of "hypersensitive" consumers was found in the large group plan, and the highest number of "insensitive" consumers in the large commercial plan.

In summary, to obtain an overall measurement of the need and demand factors in the six study plans each plan was ranked from one through six, according to its score on the indicators presented. Percent figures were used in all cases. A rank of one was defined to mean that the plan scored the *lowest* on the need and demand indicator being considered so that when ranks were summed over the indicators a higher score would be indicative of higher need or demand; for instance, the scoring on the first indicator of need, according to the percent of respondents in the sample between the ages of 47 and 65 (see Table 2-7), produced these rankings: physician-sponsored=1, large commercial=2, small commercial=3, and so on. The same procedure was followed for the demand indicators, except for "complaints about doctors." Obviously a high percent of people with negative attitudes toward physicians is suggestive of low demand; for instance, assigned ranks for the first listed complaint were large group=1, hospital-sponsored=2, large commercial=3, and so on.

---

[8] The consumer questionnaire contained a question that asked the respondent to check symptoms from a list of 11 which he thought warranted a visit to his doctor. The 11 symptoms had been judged on seriousness by a panel of community physicians, on a five-point scale, with scores assigned to each symptom equal to the average of the weights given by members of the panel. The symptoms, in order of presentation in the questionnaire, were allergy, unexplained weight loss, insomnia, blood in the urine, "nerves," general fatigue, unexplained weight gain, persistent joint and muscle pains, gaseousness, pain in the chest, and frequent sore throats. The results of the consumer survey were Guttman-scaled, using the physician panel ordering as the criterion. Of the 11 symptoms, eight were scalable. In order of increasing seriousness they were insomnia, "nerves," general fatigue, persistent joint and muscle pains, unexplained weight loss, pain in the chest, and blood in the urine. Consumers checking symptoms considered relatively minor by the physician panel were termed "hypersensitive"; those failing to check symtoms considered serious by the panel were "insensitive"; those agreeing with the panel were "sensitive." Degrees of increasing sensitivity are reflected in total scores assigned to each consumer.

We used six indicators of need and 12 indicators of demand[9] in constructing the following scores. Scores are sums of rankings.

Ranking of plans according to sums of rankings on indicators of

Need		Demand	
Large group	30 (highest need)	Small group	51 (highest demand)
Small group	26	Small commercial	48
Hospital-sponsored	22	Large group	45
Small commercial	21	Physician-sponsored	37
Large Commercial	16	Hospital-sponsored	36
Physician-sponsored	11	Large commercial	35

PHYSICIANS

Physician characteristics have an important potential influence on all four output measures in this study. We are mainly concerned with their influence on quality of care provided and the degree of satisfaction of the consumer with his medical care.

The conceptual scheme in Chapter 1 placed physician characteristics in a four-part conceptual scheme. The components of the scheme were factors that influence physician performance. These factors were called *limiting, qualifying, facilitating,* and *motivating.*

The distinctions among physician characteristics that are relevant to this study are those that are influenced by the structure of the health insuring agency. Two of the six study plans select physicians as part of the provider group from which subscribers are allowed to choose if they wish to receive insured services (small and large group plans). Thus the typology is described across the two group plans and

[9] Under ethnicity, percents of "white American" and "high status European" were considered indicative of high demand.

TABLE 2-9
Characteristics of physicians by plan categories

	Plan		
	Comm-+ prov-spon	Large group	Small group
Limiting factors			
Age 60+ (%)	12	5	26
Qualifying factors			
Neither board certified nor eligible (%)	33	24	41
General practitioners (%)	31	24	28
No continuing education in 12 months (%)	43	49	62
Facilitating factors (structural)			
Physician-paramedical ratio	4.0	3.4	1.5
Hours needed for emergency blood-sugar (av)	2.8	2.2	3.1
Hospital occupancy average (%)	77	84	77
Facilitating factors (behavioral)			
Patients/hour (office)	4.2	3.6	3.1
Consultations in last week	12.8	16.7	12.5
Regularly scheduled medical meetings/month	5.3	8.7	4.2
CRVS conversion factor (medicine)	$7.40	$6.00	$7.00
Motivating factors			
Opinion: all people should have annual exam (% agree)	67	36	65
Number of complaints about patients (range=0-7)	3.3	4.4	3.9
Keep systematic and complete medical records (%)	52	59	54
(N)†	721	320	133

†Out-of-plan physicians in small and large group plans are omitted

across providers used by subscribers to health plans that have no restrictions on physicians.

It should be remembered that the sample of physicians is not random but a population of physicians used during a 12-month period by a random sample of consumers.

Results of the analysis of physician characteristics are presented in Table 2-9. Generally only indicators providing statistically significant differences are reported ($p < 0.05$ using the chi-square test).

Limiting factors

These variables are meant to reflect restriction of opportunity or of "life chances" because of the circumstances of the physician's background. Measures tested were age, years since M.D., father's socioeconomic status, location of medical school attended, and applicants per position for the school attended. The small group physicians were by far the oldest physicians of the three groups tested, the large group physicians, the youngest. Average age in the small group was 48.5, in the large group 42.0; 50% of the physicians in the large group were under 40 years of age.

Other physician variables conceptualized as limiting do not provide significant differences between plans. The general belief that the group plans recruit heavily from foreign countries is not borne out by these data. There is a tendency for the small group plan to have more physicians trained in Europe and Asia, but the percent of difference (12% in the small group compared with about 7% in all other plans) is not significant. Social mobility of physicians is interesting, if only to demonstrate lack of significant differences among plans. Again it is suspected that the group plans provide a convenient vehicle for physicians of limited means (i.e., from lower socioeconomic backgrounds) because no investment is required to begin practice. The data indicate that the average SES score [10] across the plans is about 18, with very little variation and almost identical standard deviations. A score of 18 means that the average physician came from a family at the upper end of social class II. Although the backgrounds of physicians are consistently upper class, there is considerable variation

---

[10] Under the Hollingshead Two-Factor Index of Social Position a score indicative of position in the social class structure is derived from a weighted combination of occupation and education. The two factors are ordered on a seven-point scale and combined by multiplying the scale score for occupation by seven, the scale score for education by four, and summing the result. Resulting scores range from 11 through 77; lower scores mean higher social class (i.e., scores 11-17=Class I).

by plan in the socioeconomic status of consumers. The interaction of physician and consumer will to some degree be affected by the *difference* in class backgrounds. Difficulties of communication and rapport (doctor-patient relationship) should be expected in those plans with a predominance of consumers from the lower classes—that is, the large commercial and hospital-sponsored plans.

Qualifying factors

This concept involves activities by the physician to qualify himself for practice beyond the attainment of the M.D. degree and internship, which are required by the system. Thus, although the limiting factors deal to a large extent with factors related to ascribed or required characteristics, the qualifying factors deal with options that the physician is free to choose for himself.

Variables tested under this concept were board status, specialty (as reported by the physician), formal courses in continuing medical education, and professional journals read.

There is significantly less use of certified physicians in the small group plan than in the other plans and less use of physicians who are neither certified nor eligible in the large group plan. Additionally, use of specialists is highest in the large group plan, predominantly in use of pediatricians, and markedly *lower* in use of surgeons. Group practice physicians receive less formal continuing medical education than others, although this is probably compensated for by in-house training programs. Reading of professional journals is not significantly different among the plans.

Facilitating factors

This concept involves a structural and a behavioral component. The structural component is meant to reflect those aspects of the physician's practice that allow him, or encourage him, to provide good medical care. Variables tested under this concept were number of paramedical people available to aid the physician, access to laboratory tests as indicated by hours required to obtain an emergency blood-sugar determination, and type of hospitals used (average bed size, accreditation, occupancy rates). Under the behavioral component we have in mind the actions of physicians in relation to patients and colleagues—actions that are relevant to his practice of medicine. Variables tested were patients seen in office practice per hour, consultations with and by other physicians in the preceding week, number of regularly scheduled medical meetings attended per month, and conversion factors used in determining charges to patients.

In consideration of structural facilitating factors, the large group physicians have an advantage over the small group physicians in support from paramedical personnel and over all other physicians in their access to laboratory facilities under emergency conditions.

Hospitals under the large group plan are more efficiently used than in other plans, with an occupancy rate of 84%. This has obvious implications for cost to the plan, since the large group plan is apparently capable of tying provision of hospital beds closely to need.

Behaviorally, the small group physicians see fewer patients per hour than any other physicians, and the large group physicians interact with one another more than others on medical problems.

Evidence is that the physicians from the large group practice plan tend to compensate for their lower participation in formal courses in continuing medical education by a higher rate of interaction among colleagues. This is not so in the small group plan.

Motivating factors

This set of indicators is meant to tap the intervening influence of physician attitudes toward medical care and patients, the influence that can theoretically destroy any relationship between the other factors discussed and the medical care actually provided; for example, the medical student with the best in medical education has to be *motivated* to apply his achieved knowledge and skills if the medical care he provides is to reflect his training. Motivation is a complex issue, and the indicators provided reflect only selected aspects of this concept.

Variables tested under this concept were attitude toward necessity of the annual medical examination for all people, agreement with each of seven frequent physician complaints about patients, and attitude toward medical records.

The data reveal that the large group practice physicians have largely lost faith in the annual preventive checkup for all people, in spite of their performing more of them—see Chapter 4—or perhaps because of them. In addition, they are more negative toward patients; small group physicians are less negative and other physicians least negative in terms of the complaints about patients listed. Particularly to be noted is that the most frequent complaint (made by 71%) of large group physicians is that patients see doctors unnecessarily.

In the small group plan the most frequent complaint is that patients do not make appointments ahead of time; 59% make this complaint; the second most frequent is that patients see doctors unnecessarily. In the other plans physicians are mainly concerned with payment of bills (46%), followed closely by failure to make appointments (45%), and seeing doctors unnecessarily (44%). All differences by plan are statistically significant.

Because some of our analysis depended on extent of information in medical records (especially in Chapter 4), we tried to obtain an estimate of the differences among physicians in their tendencies toward complete record keeping. We asked about use of social, psychological, and economic data in patient care, and the detail with which it was usually recorded in medical records. This kind of data, it was felt, was less likely to be recorded than the more traditional type of information one finds in medical records and would be a sensitive indicator of overall record-keeping habits. We also asked about the attitudes of physicians toward systematic and complete record keeping as a determinant of quality of care. Presumably, if the physician feels that this is an important determinant and wishes to provide quality care, he will keep good records. It is interesting to note paranthetically that record keeping was the second most frequently checked (62%) determinant of quality care of the alternatives offered (the most frequent was opportunity to consult with other doctors: 85%). The percents recorded in Table 2-9 indicate physicians who have positive answers on both items: that is, they feel that record keeping is an important determinant of quality care and they use and report socioeconomic information in the medical records. The differences among plans is *not significant.* Similarly, almost identical percents across plans are obtained for other combinations of answers to both questions; that is, one positive and one negative or both negative. We conclude that the differences in record keeping are not significantly influenced by health plans.

CONCLUSION

The statistics presented in Chapter 2 describe the structure and function of six health plan social systems in terms of their health insuring agency, consumer, and provider components.

The health insuring agency is composed of three levels: institutional (board of directors), managerial, and technical.

The composition of the board of directors represents the character of the agency; for instance, the commercial companies were founded as life insurance companies, whose boards represented industry and legal interests. The established medical profession founded the provider-sponsored plans and boards are dominated by physician and hospital representatives. Group plans began with the innovative response of a few physicians to the health needs of certain employer and consumer groups.

Organization personnel, consumers, and physicians were asked their opinions of the agencies' goals. The commercial plans were ranked highest on importance of profit in relation to service; the group plans were ranked lowest and the provider-sponsored plans in between. The division between the large commercial plan and the provider plans is not clear. On a measure of *loss ratios* (amount of premium dollar returned to consumer in benefits) the group plans had the lowest percent of families to whom 50% or less of the premium dollar was returned in benefits. The large commercial had the highest percent, but the distinction between the commercial and provider plans did not follow types. Dollar figures for loss ratios were of limited usefulness because of small Ns and large variances. These figures revealed three plans operating "in the black": large commercial, hospital-sponsored, and large group.

Commercial and hospital-sponsored plans fall under the legal jurisdiction of the insurance commissioner, but the latter plan is subject to much more lenient regulation under its status as "nonprofit hospital service plan." The remaining three plans are regulated by the office of the attorney general. The stiffest laws apply to the commercial plans but are written vaguely. Physician-sponsored and group plans are largely self-regulated. The extent to which organizations are responsive to public influence, either through laws or other mechanisms, is termed *permeability*. On measures of consumer satisfaction with action on complaints, consumer knowledge of benefits, and physician satisfaction with effective representation in the plans the provider-sponsored plans were least permeable.

Physicians in the group plans are largely on salary, although those in the small group plan may also have private practices. In the physician-sponsored plan agreement between plan and member physicians calls on them to accept plan payment as payment in full for consumers below a certain income level. Not all physicians are members. Other plans exert only indirect influence on physician charges. Conversion factors for medicine in the six plans showed the highest charges in the commercial and hospital-sponsored plans; physician-sponsored was next, then small group, and finally large group. Control over hospital charges is exerted only in the large group and hospital-sponsored plans.

Types of administration described are control over the provider and control over the consumer. The former is illustrated by the large group practice plan which is the most efficient. Control over consumers is emphasized in the commercial plans. Provider plans have characteristics of both. Estimates of portion of premium dollar used for administration show the provider and small commercial plans to be highest, the large group, lowest.

The provider-sponsored plans incorporate the most controls over consumer use of medical services as measured by eight items. Group plans have the fewest controls (i.e., benefits are most comprehensive). The large commercial plan scored closer to the group plans than to the others because of the inclusion of packages involving a comprehensive welfare fund "medical center plan."

The group plans pay a much higher overall percent of family medical expenses than other plans. A combination of consumer and physician evaluations shows that most respondents feel that the group plans sell the most comprehensive benefit packages on the whole and the provider-sponsored plans sell the least comprehensive product.

Benefit packages are most expensive in the physician-sponsored and large group plans. They are least expensive in the small group plan, but they include several packages written without financial liability for hospitalization on its part. A comparison of comprehensiveness and average price indicates that the provider-sponsored plans are overpriced, the small group plan underpriced.

Description of consumers is in terms of propensity to use medical services or "risk." Risk involves the concepts of *need* and *demand.* Need is measured on the bases of age, family size, incidence of chronic illness, incidence of short-term illness, and percent of women in the child-bearing years. The group plans have consumers with highest need and the physician-sponsored with the lowest. Demand indicators are income, education, occupation, ethnicity, negativity toward doctors, perceived influence of health insurance on use of medical services, and symptom-sensitivity. Highest demand is found in the small group plan and the lowest in the large commercial plan.

Physicians are described on four dimensions that compare large commercial, large group, small group, and all other physicians consulted by those in the consumer sample. *Limiting factors* are measured according to age, years since M.D., father's SES status, location of medical school attended, and applicants per position for school attended. Small group physicians are older, whereas large group physicians are younger than those in other plans.

Qualifying factors are board status, specialty, continuing medical education (formal courses), and professional journals read. Use of specialists is highest in the large group plan, but surgeons are used much less frequently. Use of certified physicians is lowest in the small group plan. Group practice physicians receive less formal continuing medical education than others.

Facilitating factors include a structural component and a behavioral component. The structural component is the doctor/paramedical ratio, access to the laboratory in emergencies, and characteristics of hospitals used. Paramedical ratio is lowest in the small group plan. Fastest return on emergency laboratory orders and highest hospital occupancy rate is found in the large group plan. The behavioral component is measured by patients seen in the office per hour, consultation rate, meetings among physicians, and conversion factors. Small group physicians see fewer patients per hour and large group physicians interact on medical problems more than all others.

Motivating factors include attitudes toward preventive examination, negativity toward patients, and attitude toward medical record keeping. Significantly fewer large group physicians agree with the necessity for all people to have an annual examination; they are also negative toward patients. Their most frequent complaint concerned unnecessary visits. No significant differences were found in attitude and reported behavior in record keeping.

REFERENCES

DuBois, Donald M. "The constellation of health plans in California," in Roemer, Milton I., DuBois, Donald M., and Rich, Shirley W. (editors). *Health insurance plans: studies in organizational diversity,* University of California School of Public Health, Los Angeles (1970), 61-62. (Monograph) Also found in California Medical Association, Bureau of Research and Planning. *Socioeconomic Report,* San Francisco May 1972, 2.

Follman, J.F., Jr. *Medical care and health insurance: A study in social progress.* Homewood, Illinois: Richard D. Irwin, 1963, 112.

Health Insurance Institute. *Sourcebook of health insurance data,* New York: 1970, 15-20, 30-40.

Hetherington, Robert W. "Health plans as organizations: a conceptual approach." in Roemer, Milton I., DuBois, Donald M., and Rich, Shirley W. (editors). *Health insurance plans: studies in organizational diversity,* University of California School of Public Health, Los Angeles 1970 , 127-141.

Hetherington, Robert W, and Hopkins, Carl E. "Symptom sensitivity: its social and cultural correlates." *Health Services Research,* 4, no. 1 Spring, 1969 , 63-75.

Koontz, Harold. *The board of directors and effective management.* New York: McGraw-Hill Book Company, 1967, 19-32.

Mechanic, David. *Politics, medicine, and social science.* New York: John Wiley & Sons, 1974, 123-139.

Munts, Raymond. *Bargaining for health: labor unions, health insurance, and medical care.* Madison, Wisconsin: The University of Wisconsin Press, 1967, 9-12.

Parsons, Eleanor M. *Structure, process and values in organizational goal consensus,* unpublished Ph.D. thesis (sociology), University of California, Los Angeles, 1972.

Parsons, Talcott. "Suggestions for a sociological approach to the theory of organizations—I, " *Administrative Science Quarterly,* 1, no. 1 (June 1956), 63-85.

Pickerell, Jesse F. *Group health insurance.* Homewood, Illinois: published for the S.S. Huebner Foundation for Insurance Education, University of Pennsylvania, by R.D. Irwin, 1961.

Roemer, Milton I. "On paying the doctor and the implications of different methods." *Journal of Health and Human Behavior,* 3, no. 1 Spring 1962 , 4-14.

III

Use of Services

USE OF MEDICAL SERVICES is of primary importance to our study because the measures of quality of service, medical care costs, and patient attitudes are to some degree dependent on the volume of services consumed. For instance, with limited medical personnel in the country it is obvious that high quality care cannot be maintained if doctors' time and facilities are overburdened. Expenditures are related to the amount of medical care people receive and to the amount that is covered by insurance benefits. Consumer attitudes toward health plans are influenced by the comprehensiveness of the insurance benefits during times of high consumption of services when personal budgets are strained.

This topic is extremely controversial in the medical care field. There is the question of adequacy: can Americans get the medical care they need? Is there discrimination against people of limited means so that, on the average, they receive fewer medical services than others? What is the effect of various consumer constraints on use of services: do they effectively curb "unnecessary" use, or do they interfere with use of services in time of real need? There is also the question of mode of delivery of services: is it possible to reduce the expense of medical care by encouraging use of ambulatory rather than hospital services?

These and other questions related to public and private policy are explored in the data presented in this chapter. We report on four measures of use:

— doctor visits in office and home,
— volume of physician services delivered,
— rate of hospital admission,
— length of hospital stay.

The analysis is guided by objectives to determine whether there are significant differences among the systems on use, relate characteristics of the three components of each social system to these variations, determine the extent to which the differences are due to consumer characteristics, and examine the use according to plan types if this seems appropriate and useful.

PREVIOUS RESEARCH

Before the data are presented previous research centered on the same output variables should be considered. The findings will help to place our results in perspective, even though these previous studies have not dealt, as ours has, with representative samples of major types of insurance within one geographic area.

The first study that is relevant to this research compared hospital use rates of the Health Insurance Plan of Greater New York (H.I.P.) with the New York Blue Shield plan (Densen, 1958). Populations under both plans were insured for hospitalization by the same Blue Cross plan. The comparison is of interest, even though the figures from this research are outdated, because *group practice* and *provider-sponsored* plans (by our terminology) are compared.

Physician care under H.I.P. was provided by a network of approximately 30 group practice clinics and was fairly comprehensive. The H.I.P. doctors were salaried, whereas the Blue Shield physicians worked in the free-choice open market in which physician care insurance coverage was limited to in-hospital services.

The H.I.P. sample consisted of 57,000 New York City government workers or dependents, the Blue Shield sample of 53,000 workers in private employment-groups of 1000 or more, chosen to match the city workers along socioeconomic lines. Data were obtained from the Blue Cross files for both samples.

The basic findings of this study were that the rates of hospital use—both in terms of admissions and aggregate days of hospital care per 1000 persons per year—were significantly lower under the H.I.P. pattern of medical practice. For hospital admissions the differential was about 20% and for hospital days, about 15%. H.I.P. hospitalization rates were especially lower for most elective surgical operations (though not all diagnostic categories) and they persisted for all age groups. No analyses were reported concerning use according to socioeconomic characteristics of persons, nor was use of ambulatory services examined.

This important study did much to establish the idea that prepaid group practice with salaried doctors leads to lower use of costly hospital services than solo practice with fee- for-service payments. The remaining debate is to what degree this result is caused by

—the preventive orientation and comprehensive scope of ambulatory services in group-practice clinics compared with conventional private practice,
—the incentives associated with salaried compared with fee-for-service payment of doctors, or
—the lesser accessibility (for various complex reasons) of hospital beds to H.I.P. group practice doctors compared with other doctors.

Conceivably all three factors and others may influence use of hospital services under the group practice plans (Greenberg and Rodburg, 1971).

Another study compared the H.I.P. experience with the Group Health Insurance Plan (G.H.I., rather than Blue Shield) (Anderson and Sheatsley, 1961). G.H.I. was another plan in New York City that offered free choice of private doctors who were paid on a fee-for-service basis. The scope of benefits, however, broader than that under Blue Shield, included virtually complete office and home care as well as in-hospital services of the doctor. The range of insured benefits under G.H.I. was more equivalent to those of H.I.P., although the differences in mode of payment and accessibility to hospital beds between the two sets of doctors (as well as the dynamics of group practice versus solo practice) remain.

This study was based on much smaller but matched samples of plan members: about 450 persons in each plan chosen from three unions—garment workers, machinists, and office employees. The findings with respect to hospitalization (derived from the records of the Blue Cross Plan which covered both populations) were essentially the same as in the Densen study: lower rates under H.I.P. for both hospital admissions and hospital days. Based on household interviews of the two samples, data were collected also on ambulatory services of doctors. Excluding in-hospital surgical and obstetrical services, there were 6.0 doctor visits per person per year under G.H.I., compared with 5.5 under H.I.P. In other words, the prepaid group practice pattern's lower use of hospitals did not seem attributable to a greater rate of out-of-hospital ambulatory services, since the latter were also slightly lower.

The first *major* American research comparing use under three types of health insurance plan was reported in 1962 (Columbia University School of Public Health and Administrative Medicine).

This study set out to examine the experiences of samples of families of machine workers who were members of the International Association of Machinists (I.A.M.) union. They belonged to three different plans in various geographic areas. The sample of Blue Cross-Blue Shield members was derived from an I.A.M. population in New Jersey. The second sample was derived from I.A.M. members employed by the General Electric Company in three mid-western states; they belonged to a self-insured company plan that provided "major medical expense" protection, with indemnification and cost-sharing features similar to those marketed by most commercial insurance carriers. The third sample was designed to represent members of a group practice plan. In the end I.A.M. members using the group plan could not be studied, but a set of blue-collar workers, believed to be socially equivalent, was chosen from among the members of the Kaiser-Permanente Health Plan in northern California. About 700 families in each sample were studied through household interviews, records of the insurance carriers, and hospital records.

The findings on medical care use were different in this study from those in the two previous studies. After making various adjustments for age and sex composition, hospitalization experience was found to be quite similar across the three plans. Excluding maternity cases, hospital admissions were 76 per 1000 persons per year in the Blue Plan, 71 in the General Electric Plan, and 79 in the Kaiser Plan. Aggregate hospital days were 580 per 1000 persons per year in the Blue Plan, 610 in the General Electric Plan, and 610 in the Kaiser Plan. Since differences in resources of the three geographic areas might account for these relatively small differences, the investigators regarded these three sets of hospitalization rates as essentially similar. For ambulatory services, on the other hand, the Blue Plan experience was 4.1 patient-doctor contacts per year, the General Electric Plan rate was 4.6 contacts, and the Kaiser Plan rate was 5.9 contacts.

This study also reported on "out-of-plan use," which is use of physicians or hospitals not belonging to the Kaiser plan, hence paid for privately. The out-of-plan use accounted for 8% of the hospital admissions and 14% of the above ambulatory doctor services.

A fourth major comparative study of health insurance plan experience was on federal government workers insured under the Federal Employees Health Benefits Program (Perrott, 1966 and 1971). This system allows federal employees in all parts of the nation a choice of membership in one of several local health insurance plans; hence aggregate data are available on numerous examples of the several principal types of plan operating in the United States. The reports on this experience focus largely on hospitalization rates in a very large population—more than 8,000,000—of plan members (the universe, rather than a sample, has been studied). Analyses were made by age and sex.

Over the years 1961 to 1968 the findings for hospital use in this study have been consistently lowest for the group practice plans, whereas the rates for the Blue Plans and the commercial "indemnity" plans have been consistently highest (while varying from year to year). These general variations hold for each age level examined separately. They are especially striking with respect to hospital admissions for elective surgical procedures (such as tonsillectomy, appendectomy, and gynecological surgery). The differentials have applied to both hospital admissions and hospital days, although they tend to be greater for hospital days; for example, in 1968 the Blue Plan members had 924 (nonmaternity) hospital days per 1000 persons per year, the commercial plan members had 987 such days, and the group practice plan members had 422.

Other comparisons in the federal employee studies simply reflect the differing benefit packages under the several types of plan. Thus insured payments for out-of-hospital ambulatory services in 1968 were received by only 23% of Blue Plan members and 17% of commercial plan members (these plans are known to offer very limited benefits for such care). On the other hand, the group practice plans, in which ambulatory services are a basic benefit, showed 73% of their members having such services paid for in 1968. The picture drawn, therefore, is one in which the insurance premium for membership in the Blue and commercial plans supports a high rate of hospitalization and a low rate of ambulatory service; in the group practice plans the converse is true.

A fifth comparative study concerns health insurance experience in

1962-1963 of California state government employees (Medical Advisory Council to the California Public Employees Retirement System, 1971). This study solicited information through mailed questionnaires sent to 2000 to 3000 members of each of four types of health insurance plan operating in the state. In addition to the three basic types on which the previous studies have focused, this one examines the medical foundation type of plan—that is, county-based plans sponsored by medical societies and offering comprehensive doctor's care (office, home, and hospital) through free choice of private practitioner and fee-for-service payments.

The hospital use findings confirm those of most of the above studies: lowest for both admissions and day rates in the group practice plans. Hospital days per 1000 persons per year were 945 in the Blue plans, 1005 in the commercial plans, 1281 in the "medical foundation" plans, and 770 in the group practice plans. Doctor ambulatory visits per person per year, on the other hand, were Blues, 3.7, commercials, 3.7, foundations, 4.7, and group practice plans, 4.5.

The findings of a sixth comparative analysis were recently summarized in an excellent review paper on the concept of "health maintenance organizations" (Klarman, 1971). These data apply to hospitalization of Medicare beneficiaries (persons 65 years of age and older) and, as it happens, come from southern California (the same locale as our own research). The units of measurement are dollars spent by the government on hospital care, which may be taken to correspond roughly to hospital days used. In a comparison of the expenditures on behalf of aged beneficiaries belonging to the Kaiser-Permanente Health Plan with those for the general Medicare population they were found to be 11 percent lower in the former series.

Donabedian (1969) published a valuable review article on the available evidence of the effects of "prepaid group practice" compared with other patterns of health insurance organization and delivery. This paper summarized the principal findings of the studies reviewed above and also some smaller studies done in Detroit (involving the Community Health Association and Blue Cross-Blue Shield Plans) and St. Louis (involving the Labor Health Institute of that city). The essential findings on one thorny question, the use of services outside the direct service (prepaid group practice) health plans, were summarized by Donabedian:

"Outside physicians are used for 37% of surgical operations in the

Health Insurance Plan of Greater New York, 14% of all paid physicians' services and 33% of house calls in Kaiser-Permanente, and 23% of physicians' and dentists' services in the Labor Health Institute of St. Louis."

These previous studies provide a point of reference for presentation of our findings on use of medical services. Generally, we might expect lower rates of hospital use and higher rates of ambulatory use in the group plans compared with the others. Most of the previous studies, however, are limited in design to particular nonrepresentative samples and to only one example of each plan; also they generally do not take up the problem of statistical significance of differences in use rates and the influence of intervening and confounding variables.

PHYSICIAN SERVICES

Doctor Visits

All data on use of ambulatory services must to some degree depend on the ability of the user to recall his visits to the doctor. The objective of research methodology is to cut down the recall error. In this study we used two sources of information to estimate the rate of doctor visits. First, all respondents were asked to recall doctor visits (office, home, and clinic) for members of their families over the previous three months, one month at a time. Analysis is conducted on doctor visits made by members of the family insured under the study plan only; that is, when uninsured family members were involved in the reported visits, or when insured family members were also covered under some other insurance plan, the family was omitted from the analysis. This does not entirely remove recall error, since even a three-month period involves some guessing, especially for respondents with large families for whom there have been a number of visits. There is evidence from other sources (National Center for Health Statistics, 1965) that respondent recall error on even a two-week basis results in about a 43% underestimation of doctor visits. Given this source of error, however, the important consideration was whether this would produce selective bias against any one or more of the health plans under study. There is a possibility that people visiting physicians in group practice may underestimate the number of visits to a greater extent, since one trip to the clinic may in fact involve more than one physician contact. This would introduce a systematic bias against the group plans by which rate of doctor visits recalled by the respondent would be lower than in other plans.[1]

Medical records were the second source of information on ambulatory care. These were gathered on a 12-month basis, and do not involve the recall factor. Of course, in the commercial and provider plans we relied on recall to some extent to obtain the names of providers used in the past year. This was also true for out-of-plan visits made by members of the group plans. We used a rigorous checking procedure (outlined in Appendix A) to ensure completeness of records and have considerable faith in the accuracy of statistics from this source. Physician visits, in the office, home, or outpatient clinic are defined as provider-patient[2] contacts ("medical care bits").

In order to provide as complete a picture as possible, statistics from both sources are presented by plan.

Variations by plan

The previous research has indicated that studies have found annual doctor visit rates for insured populations ranging from 3.7 per person to 6.0 per person. The figure for the general population of the western United States was about 4.8 in 1966-67 (National Center for Health Statistics, 1966-1967). Our statistics are presented in Tables 3-1A and 3-1B. Questionnaire data indicate a rate of 0.7 visits per person for the three-month period, which translates into about 2.8 visits per person for a 12-month period. Data from the medical records yield a rate of 4.06 visits per person per year, which is 28% higher than the estimate gained from the consumer questionnaire figures. Apparently there is considerable recall error in the questionnaire data.

If we are willing to accept 4.06 as a reasonable estimate of the true doctor visit rate for the total sample, several qualifications should be

---

[1] The three-month period with staggered questionnaire mailings introduces the possibility of seasonal influences on the reported statistics. We discounted this bias by examining doctor contacts for the subsample on which medical records had been gathered. A monthly rate was calculated for the 12-month period and examined for seasonal fluctuations. Significant seasonal variations were not found; visitation rates were roughly equivalent for all 12 months. This would probably not be true in other parts of the country where seasons are severe and influence health to a greater extent.

[2] Office and clinic visits during which the patient did not see an M.D. are counted in these statistics; for instance, somebody coming in for an immunization given by a nurse would be assigned a visit.

recognized. First, it is not a true estimate of visitation rates for the total populations insured by the six plans because it treats all plans equally, thus giving disproportionate weight to the small plans (such as the small group plan). This qualification should be kept in mind for all tables presented in this book. Second, we expect figures for our sample to be lower than those for the population at large, since we are limited to employed people under age 65. Third, there is wide variation around the average, even though very extreme cases were deleted from the computation of means in both the questionnaire and medical records data.

Our primary interest in the figures in Tables 3-1A and 3-1B is in the differences among the plans. The first analytic objective was to determine whether significant differences were demonstrated among the six plans. Statistically the answer is "yes" in this case, since analysis of variance of the means and chi-square tests on the distributions are significant at the 0.05 level or better for both the questionnaire and medical records data.[3] Data from the records confirm findings of previous research that consumers in group health plans see doctors more frequently than consumers in other plans. The large group plan rate of 4.70 visits per person per year is the highest of all six plans, and the small group plan is not far behind at 4.61. At the other end of the spectrum consumers in the large commercial plan have a very low rate relative to other consumers in this study and to all rates reported by previous research. Another statistic of interest in Table 3-1A is the percent of families for whom *no doctor visits* were found for the 12-month period. Overall, some 28% of the families fell into this category. There are very large differences among some of the plans, however. Nearly half the families in the large commercial plan had no doctor visits for the previous year in contrast to less than 10% of the families in the small group plan. The reverse is true for percent of families who are heavy users of doctor services; nearly half the families in the small group plan make four or more visits per person in contrast to fewer than one-fourth of those in the large commercial plan.

---

[3] Differences will generally be regarded as significant throughout the book at the .05 level. This means that one would expect the obtained distribution only five times out of 100 by chance. Generally, statistical significance at a given level is easy to obtain in large samples (such as the questionnaire sample) even though the actual differences are rather small. It should be remembered that the Ns quoted in the tables refer to *families,* but the data reported frequently refer to *persons,* so that the actual N is about three times as large.

TABLE 3-1A

Doctor visits per insured person in three months (questionnaires)

Visits per person in three months	Plan						
	All plans	Large comm	Small comm	Hosp-spon	Phys-spon	Large group	Small group
None (%)	50.2	61.4	52.1	49.2	69.4	34.1	50.2
Fewer than one	19.5	12.3	18.6	15.9	12.1	30.4	18.3
One or more	30.3	26.3	29.3	34.8	18.4	35.5	31.5
Mean	0.71	0.51	0.73	0.96	0.46	0.79	0.81
SD	1.32	1.08	1.38	1.62	1.35	1.13	1.54
N	2223	467	558	234	159	566	240

$F=5.75$, $df=5/2217$, $p<0.001$
$\chi^2=123.7$, $df=10$, $p<0.001$

TABLE 3-1B

Doctor visits per insured person in 12 months (medical records)

Visits per person in 12 months	Plan						
	All plans	Large comm	Small comm	Hosp-spon	Phys-spon	Large group	Small group
None (%)	28.4	47.4	39.1	33.2	19.3	18.8	9.8
Fewer than four	32.5	28.4	22.6	32.1	34.5	36.6	41.9
Four or more	39.1	24.3	38.2	34.7	46.1	44.6	48.3
Mean	4.06	2.77	4.26	3.94	4.09	4.70	4.61
SD	5.29	4.36	5.76	5.10	6.69	5.01	4.59
N	809	137	146	147	109	142	128

$F=2.39$, $df=5/803$, $p<0.05$
$\chi^2=71.5$, $df=10$, $p<0.001$

We conclude from these data that there are significant, although small, differences among plans (except for the large commercial plan) in use of physician services and that generally the consumers in the group plans are the heaviest users and those in the large commercial plan use physician services the least. If we rank the six plans on an average number of doctor visits per person per year, this ordering is achieved:

1. Large group (most visits)
2. Small group
3. Small commercial
4. Physician-sponored
5. Hospital-sponsored
6. Large commercial (least visits)

Unfortunately, these data and the information from the questionnaires do not correspond, as recall from one plan to another seems to differ. Questionnaire data do confirm, however, that the large commercial plan consumers have few physician visits and a large percent of nonusers (61% in a three-month period).

Analysis of ambulatory use was also done by plan type, whereby three types of plan were assumed (commercial, provider-sponsored, and group), each with two representatives. Each plan was assigned a weight so that it would contribute in proportion to its size to the rate for its plan type. The resulting figures can then be interpreted as representing types of health plan in the Los Angeles area. Estimates from questionnaire data are given in parentheses and averages converted to a 12-month period for convenience.

Plan type	Average visits	Percent with no visits
Commercial	3.2 (2.4)	45 (59)
Provider-sponsored	4.0 (3.2)	29 (59)
Group	4.7 (3.2)	17 (35)

By these figures the group plans have the highest average per person rate of doctor visits and the lowest percent of families with no visits during the year (or three-month period in the case of questionnaire data). All statistical tests on these data were highly significant.

Finally, we wish to consider a question discussed earlier in the literature review—that of "out-of-plan" use of physicians by consumers in the two group plans. Out-of-plan use is frequently a criticism of "closed-panel" group practices such as those in our study. This appears to be a legitimate criticism because the consumer who chooses to obtain medical care outside his group plan has to pay for such care himself. This probably indicates dissatisfaction with some aspect of the group plan situation or breakdown of access to group plan physicians in time of need. Of all physician visits made by consumers in the two group plans, 8.6%[4] were to doctors outside the plans. Data for this figure came from the medical records. The large group plan had a higher percent of out-of-plan use—10.5% of physician visits compared with 6.9% in the small group plan. These figures are low in comparison with the 14% of ambulatory visits reported in the Columbia University study discussed earlier. If our figures are accurate, out-of-plan use of doctors in the two study plans is negligible. Comparative figures from the other plans would involve insured services consumed but not claimed, and we have no estimate of this.

Organizational determinants

The second analytic objective was to relate differences in the output measures to structural differences in the plan organizations. We have concluded that there are statistically significant differences in use of physician services among the six plans in the study. Our model indicates that variations in performance must be interpreted in terms of organizational characteristics as well as the characteristics of consumers and physicians, but because of the small number (six) of organizations in the study there is no possibility of meaningful statistical tests to determine organizational influence. Rather we have chosen the path of logical argument to develop the possible relationships involved.

In Chapter 2 we discussed the flow of influence in a health plan organization from the *goals* of the organization to its *structure* and to the characteristics of the *product.* Measures employed by this study lead to the general conclusion that the group plans espoused service goals over profit goals to a greater extent than did the other four plans and that this emphasis resulted in an administrative structure that placed more controls over providers than over consumers. The products of the six organizations were evaluated in terms of the extent to which restrictions were placed on consumer use of insured services. The conclusion was that the provider-sponsored plans were the most restrictive (least comprehensive) and the group plans the least restrictive.

It is obvious that one central organizational determinant of consumer use of medical services is the nature of the product (benefit

---

[4] This figure is a measurement of percent of ambulatory *visits* not of medical bits, which is 12%.

package). Other things being equal, there should be greater use of medical services under a system with fewer built-in restraints. This is particularly true of ambulatory services, where it is by the patient's own initiative that medical care is sought, as opposed to the attending physician controlling hospital services.

The consumer considering a visit to a physician under a plan that makes him liable for the first $200, or for all expenses unless he is hospitalized, is likely to think twice if there is any doubt in his mind about the necessity of the visit. The need to seek out medical care is usually even less evident if the person has no immediate benefits from preventive services.

Of course "all other things" are never equal, and it is recognized in our model that organizational characteristics interact with consumer and physician characteristics to determine output. For instance, comprehensiveness of insurance benefits may be of little importance to upper income families, who could for all but the most catastrophic costs insure themselves.

What is the degree of correspondence between comprehensiveness of benefit packages and use of ambulatory services in the six study plans? In Chapter 2 an index of comprehensiveness devised from three indicators (items in the package, proportion of family bills paid by the plan, and consumer-physician evaluations) allowed us to compare the plans. When these rankings are contrasted with use of ambulatory services, this result is obtained:

Comprehensiveness of benefit package	Doctor visits per insured person in 12 months
1. Large group (most)	1. Large group (most)
2. Small group	2. Small group
3. Large commercial	3. Small commercial
4. Small commercial	4. Physician-sponsored
5. Physician-sponsored	5. Hospital-sponsored
6. Hospital-sponsored (least)	6. Large commercial (least)

The correspondence between the two sets of rankings is perfect for five of the six plans, the large commercial plan being the exception. This plan ranks third in comprehensiveness because of its affiliated clinic plan (admittedly atypical in this type of plan), but ranks last, or sixth, on use of ambulatory services. It is evident that we cannot seek an explanation for the low doctor-visit rates in the large commercial plan in the characteristics of the benefit packages, since comprehensiveness of the packages suggests a visitation rate very similar to that of the small commercial plan.

In view of the above rankings, does the correspondence between comprehensiveness of benefits and doctor visits in five plans suggest that consumers in the group plans tend to make unnecessary visits (overuse) or does it mean that consumers in the other plans tend not to make necessary visits? Answers to this question can be provided only by consideration of characteristics of the consumers.

Consumer characteristics

In our earlier discussion of consumer characteristics the six health plans were ranked in order of *need* and *demand.* The concept of need encompassed such indicators as age, acute and chronic illnesses, and females of child-bearing age. An overall assessment of the relative levels of need of the six samples led to the conclusion that the group plans exhibited the highest level of consumer need. The large commercial and physician-sponsored plans had the lowest levels. On this basis alone we expect that the doctor-visit rate in the group plans should be the highest—and it is. But the question is not really answered because we still might ask, do consumers from families with high need actually make more doctor visits in the group plans than they do in the other plans? If they do, then it would appear, needs are more adequately met in the group plans. If they do not, then low-need consumers must have a higher visit rate in the group plans and we must look elsewhere for an explanation of differences in doctor visits.

We examined the rate of doctor visits per person per year in each of the plans, first for high-need families, then for low-need families. The former is defined in terms of four indicators: average family age of 40 or more, reported chronic or acute illnesses in the family, and presence of females in the child-bearing years. Average doctor visits for high-need families were found to be 5.2 visits per person per year, and for low-need families they were 3.4, across all plans. This suggests that the four items chosen to reflect need are valid indicators. Average visits calculated by plan show the following:

Plan	High-need families	Low-need families
Large commercial	3.8	2.6
Small commercial	5.8	3.4
Hospital-sponsored	4.8	3.2
Physician-sponsored	6.3	3.3
Large group	5.3	4.3
Small group	5.6	3.7

From these figures, high-need families have higher per person rate of doctor visits in each plan than low-need families. Within families of apparently similar need, however, there is no support for the contention that consumers with the comprehensive benefit packages of the group plans visit doctors more frequently than consumers with less comprehensive benefits. In two plans—the small commercial and the physician-sponsored—the rate is higher than in either group plan. The greatest difference in rates among the high-need consumers is between the large commercial plan and the others, with a very low rate in the former.

On the other hand, there is evidence (although the differences are small) that consumers in the group plans who are defined as "low-need" visit physicians more frequently than consumers of similar need in other plans. The rate is highest in the large group plan (4.3) and lowest in the large commercial plan (2.6). The differential between doctor-visit rates between high-need and low-need families is the smallest in the large group plan.

The evidence leads to the conclusion that the higher rates of doctor visits in the group plans compared with other plans is due to greater use by consumers with lower medical need. In the analysis by plan types annual doctor visit rates for low-need families in the group plans are 4.2, compared with 3.6 in the provider-sponsored plans and 2.8 in the commercials. Thus it appears that under comprehensive benefit packages (where annual examinations are more likely to be a part of the contract) the threshold at which the consumer becomes sensitive to illness is lowered so that he visits his doctor more readily. The argument could be made that this lowering of the threshold may be in part responsible for keeping the rate of doctor visits down among high-need consumers in the group plans or that fewer "return visits" are ordered by the doctor. Consumers in the low-need category, for instance, who make regular visits to physicians for preventive checkups or at the earliest signs of illness, would raise the rate of visits in this category. The same behavior among high-need consumers may have the effect of reducing the necessity for a great many visits because illnesses are caught in early stages and prevented from becoming critical and requiring extended care.

On the basis of the above distributions of mean rates an argument might be made that under the comprehensive benefit packages of the group plans the threshold of physician use is lowered too far and doctors are bothered by people who are essentially hypochondriacs at worst or overcautious at best. Physicians in the large group plan (see Chapter 2) did complain of consumers making unnecessary visits to a much greater extent than physicians in other plans.[5] Together with

[5] Percent of physicians making this complaint in the various plans was large group—71%, small group—55%, commercials—46%, and provider-sponsored—42%.

the data on doctor visits by low-need consumers, there is some support for the idea that the more comprehensive benefit packages lead to high use of physician services.

The low rate of doctor visits in the large commercial plan appears to be partly due to the relatively few high-need consumers in the sample (this plan ranks second-last on the need index) in combination with low-use rate by those who are high-need (the rate of 3.8 visits per person per year is the lowest of all plans).

Further investigation brings us to a consideration of *demand* or propensity to consume. In the plan typology, demand encompassed such indicators as income, education, occupation, ethnicity, attitudes toward doctors, insurance, and symptoms. These demand factors are related to the threshold concept discussed earlier, since the higher the demand, the more likely the consumer is to seek out medical care at any given level of need. Demand factors are particularly relevant to physician visits because they involve consumer initiative to a greater extent than hospital admissions. The index of demand across all indicators (see Chapter 2) ranked the small group plan with the highest demand, followed by the small commercial and large group plans. The lowest demand was found in the large commercial plan. This ranking may provide some clue to why high-need persons in the large commercial plan have the lowest rate of doctor visits of all high-need consumers.

The examination of the influence of demand factors on doctor visits begins with *income.* Doctor visits by low-income people should be higher in the plans with the most comprehensive benefits because these people are least able to overcome financial barriers. Table 3-2 reveals that for the entire sample high-income families have significantly more doctor visits than low-income families: 4.97 and 3.54, respectively ($t=3.67$, $df=771$, $p<0.001$). This is true for families in each of the six plans. In addition, 32% of the low-income families, compared with 21% of the high-income families, made no doctor visits in 12 months. Family financial resources apparently play an important role in determining how often family members see the doctor. How are these differences between high-income and low-income families distributed across the plans? It appears that among the low-income consumers those in the large group plan have the highest per person rate of doctor visits. Also the families in the large group plan not visiting a doctor for 12 months are fewer among the low-income families than among the high-income families—the only plan for which this is true. Low-income families visit the doctor least frequently in the large commercial plan and more than half the families in this category have no doctor visits during the year.

TABLE 3-2
Doctor visits per person per year by plan and family income (annual)

Doctor visits per person per year	Plan						
	All plans	Large comm	Small comm	Hosp-spon	Phys-spon	Large group	Small group
Less than $11,000							
None (%)	31.9	52.0	35.8	38.8	18.6	18.2	15.8
Fewer than four	36.0	25.4	28.6	31.9	41.6	46.1	48.7
Four or more	32.1	22.6	35.5	29.4	39.8	35.6	35.4
Mean	3.54	2.66	3.25	3.58	4.18	4.29	3.65
SD	5.43	4.57	4.19	5.46	7.93	5.69	3.89
N	468	104	61	100	69	69	65
	$\chi^2=43.82$, df=10, $p<0.001$						
$11,000 *or more*							
None (%)	20.8	31.5	31.6	23.5	15.0	20.9	4.1
Fewer than four	29.6	38.7	21.0	36.9	22.9	29.8	34.0
four or more	49.5	29.8	47.4	39.7	62.1	49.2	61.9
Mean	4.97	3.16	5.94	4.26	4.24	5.00	5.74
SD	5.08	3.70	6.85	3.98	3.73	4.38	5.21
N	306	32	70	42	37	67	58
	$\chi^2=25.20$, df=10, $p<0.01$						

Table 3-2 illustrates that income is indeed relevant to demand: the more high-income people in a plan, the more doctor visits these people will make. But what is the influence of income on the relations among the plans? We expect the differences in doctor visits among plans to increase for the low-income families, so that the plans with more comprehensive benefit packages will display relatively higher rates. Among the high-income families differences in rates might be reduced. The difference in rate of doctor visits between the plan with the most comprehensive benefits (large group) and the least comprehensive benefits (hospital-sponsored) was shown to be 0.76 in Table 3-1A. For the low-income families this difference is 0.71 and for high-income it is 0.74. The difference between these two plans on percent of families with no doctor visits was found to be 14.4% before income level was introduced. With the introduction of income the difference for low-income families is increased to 20.6% (i.e., 20.6% more families had no doctor visits in the hospital-sponsored plan than in the large group plan) and for high-income families, to 2.6%. A tentative conclusion from these data is that comprehensive benefits for low-income families do not necessarily increase the frequency of seeing the doctor but increase the probability that somebody in the family will see a doctor at least once during a 12-month period.

The latter part of this conclusion might be examined for all plans by combining them into plan types. In terms of comprehensiveness of benefits, the group type is the most comprehensive, followed by the commercials and the provider-sponsored plans in that order. Differences between the group plans and the other two types in terms of percent of families with no medical care for 12 months are the following:

	Group-commercial	Group-provider-sponsored
All families	27.6%	11.3%
Low-income families	31.1%	14.6%
High-income families	13.3%	2.2%

These figures reveal that the gap widens for low-income families and is reduced for high-income families in both cases. The impact of comprehensive plans on the low-income families is relatively small. This is not surprising, since health insurance is only one of myriad influences on doctor-visiting behavior.

The second factor to be considered within the *demand* concept is education. In this case our measure is of educational attainment of the head of household. It is difficult to predict from theory the effect of this variable on rate of doctor visits. On one hand, highly educated people should be heavier users of medical services where consumer initiative requirements are high—for instance, for preventive services. On the other hand, delay in consultation of a physician which might be associated with lower educational levels will more likely result in critical illnesses requiring extended physician visits. Table 3-3 indicates that for all people in the sample there is essentially no difference in rate of doctor visits between high- and low-education levels. The rate for families whose heads of household have a high school education or less is 4.21 and the rate for others is 3.94, a difference that is not statistically or practically significant ($t=0.68$, $df=732$).

Interaction of organizational characteristics and educational level of the consumer should produce a marked advantage for the highly educated people in the group practice plans. We have ranked the group plans at the top in terms of comprehensiveness of benefits. We indicated in Chapter 2 a direct relation between educational level and knowledge of benefits. Therefore the greatest advantage of complete benefits should be taken by the highly educated in the group plans. There should also be an effect of interaction between bureaucratic characteristics of the group plans and consumer education so that the highly educated consumer is better able to cope with the complexities of the system. On the other hand, the consumer with a lower education is at considerable disadvantage in such a system and might be expected to have fewer doctor visits because of these factors than lower educated consumers in the nongroup plans.

There is considerable evidence in Table 3-3 that lower educational level does work against consumers in the group plans. Lower educated families in the large group plan have almost the lowest average rate of visitation, second only to that of the large commercial plan. This is a remarkable change in ranking from its top position in the overall figures (see Table 3-1A). As for lower educated consumers in the small group plan, their average rate of visits is not

TABLE 3-3
Doctor visits per person per year
by plan and education of head of household

Doctor visits per person per year	Plan						
	All plans	Large comm	Small comm	Hosp-spon	Phys-spon	Large group	Small group
High school or less							
None (%)	25.2	45.3	34.4	23.6	24.4	16.6	9.0
Fewer than four	36.8	35.7	27.6	35.2	28.3	44.2	47.9
four or more	38.0	19.0	38.0	41.2	47.3	39.3	43.1
Mean	4.21	2.22	4.61	5.05	4.87	3.81	4.59
SD	5.63	4.26	5.57	5.66	9.54	3.63	4.59
N	402	63	65	88	47	79	60
$\chi^2=34.66$, df=10, $p<0.001$							
Some college or more							
None (%)	31.1	53.1	36.2	44.0	20.6	23.7	9.5
Fewer than four	29.3	27.6	20.9	33.9	38.9	20.4	39.0
four or more	39.6	19.3	42.9	22.1	40.5	55.9	51.5
Mean	3.94	2.51	4.45	1.96	2.96	6.15	4.67
SD	5.14	4.10	6.11	2.90	3.55	6.35	4.73
N	332	57	72	47	36	57	63
$\chi^2=46.72$, df=10, $p<0.01$							

different from consumers in the small commercial and provider-sponsored plans. Consumers from highly educated family backgrounds, however, are very heavy users of physician services in the large group plan and second highest in the small group plan.

To test the relative impact of education level on doctor visits across plans the large group plan (most comprehensive benefits, most bureaucratic organization) is compared with the hospital-sponsored plan (least comprehensive benefits, physicians predominantly in solo practice). For all families in these two plans the difference in average annual doctor visits is 0.76. For the lower educated families the difference is -1.24, an increase of 2.00, meaning that in the hospital-sponsored plan 1.24 visits are made per person per year *more* than by consumers from the same educational background in the large group plan. For highly educated families the difference is 4.19, meaning that 4.19 visits are made per person per year *less* than those in the large group plan. Finally, if one considers only percent of families receiving no medical care during 12 months, a difference of 14.4% was found between these two plans before the introduction of the education factor. For highly educated families this is increased to 20.3% and for lower educated families it is reduced to 7.0%.

Thus, if we consider average visits per year we conclude that lower educated consumers in the large group plan make much less use of physicians than consumers in the hospital-sponsored plan. Considering percent of families with no medical care, the difference between the two plans is increased for the highly educated consumers and cut in half for lower educated consumers.

By examining these percent differences for all plans we obtained the following result, using the plan-type classification for percent of families with no care during the year.

	Group and commercial	Group and Provider-sponsored
All families	26.6%	11.3%
Lower educated families	26.6%	8.2%
Highly educated families	26.5%	15.2%

The differences discussed above in percent of families with no care are maintained in the comparison between the group and provider-sponsored plans. Regardless of educational level, however, about 26% more families in the commercial than in the group plans receive no medical care.

The patient's attitude toward physicians, health insurance, and symptoms are used to measure demand. The symptom attitudes, defined in Chapter 2, can be scaled according to "symptom sensitivity." On this scale people can be identified as symptom insensitive, symptom sensitive, or symptom hypersensitive. This scale is of particular interest, since respondents classified as symptom hypersensitive are thought to be consumers most likely to see physicians unnecessarily; that is, hypersensitive people feel that a physician visit is appropriate for symptoms that a panel of physicians judged to be relatively minor.[6] In our earlier discussion of need we concluded that the higher rate of physician visits in the large group plan was not because medically needy persons (defined by our indicators) made more visits to the doctor but because persons of lower need did.

TABLE 3-4

Doctor visits per person per year by plan and symptom sensitivity of respondent

Doctor visits per person per year	Plan						
	All plans	Large comm	Small comm	Hosp-spon	Phys-spon	Large group	Small group
Symptom-sensitive or -insensitive							
None (%)	31.3	52.5	49.5	31.6	29.9	26.1	3.6
Fewer than four	36.1	28.4	20.8	42.4	41.2	45.7	41.2
Four or more	32.6	19.2	29.7	26.0	28.8	28.2	55.2
Mean	3.53	2.31	3.12	4.21	4.55	2.80	4.87
SD	5.67	4.38	4.34	7.46	13.13	3.02	3.83
N	227 †	42	43	27	18	48	49
$\chi^2=39.92$, df=10, $p<0.001$							
Symptom hypersensitive							
None (%)	23.7	44.0	38.6	29.7	25.4	12.9	13.9
Fewer than four	32.6	29.1	15.6	34.1	32.5	35.1	41.9
Four or more	43.7	26.9	45.8	36.2	42.1	52.1	44.3
Mean	4.76	3.25	4.77	3.25	3.80	5.04	4.46
SD	5.02	5.00	6.28	3.90	5.29	4.38	5.04
N	298 †	38	50	26	20	86	78
$\chi^2=30.23$, df=10, $p<0.001$							

†N is lower in this table because the shortened version of the consumer questionnaire used in the study of nonrespondents did not include the question on symptom sensitivity.

[6] The panel of physicians was asked to judge a list of symptoms on the basis of their experience with those symptoms in practice. That is, if a patient presented a certain symptom, what was the likelihood that there was need for medical attention? Among symptoms judged to be relatively minor, serious illness *could* occur, but it was *less likely* than among other symptoms.

Table 3-4 does not provide a direct test of the influence of symptom sensitivity, because the rate of doctor visits for each plan is for all family members, whereas the classification on the sensitivity scale is for the respondent only. It is not illogical, however, to suppose that the attitude of the respondent would influence the behavior of other family members.

For the entire sample the rate of doctor visits for the symptom-hypersensitive category is 4.76, compared with 3.53 in the other categories. The difference in means is not statistically significant ($t=1.81$, $df=523$) at $p<0.05$ because the sample is small but in the predicted direction.

Symptom hypersensitivity has the greatest influence in the large group plan. The rate of doctor visits for those classified as hypersensitive is 5.04, compared with a rate of 2.80 for other people in the plan. This lends support to the large group's physicians' claims that many consumers in the plan seek unnecessary care.[7]

The influence of symptom sensitivity on the relations among the plans may be illustrated again by comparing the large group and the hospital-sponsored plans. People in the large group plan make an average of 0.76 more visits per person than consumers in the hospital-sponsored plan. For families represented by a symptom-hypersensitive respondent this difference is increased to 1.79—a very substantial change. Among other families represented by a symptom- sensitive or symptom-insensitive respondent there is again a substantial change but in the opposite direction. In these families the rate in the hospital-sponsored plan is 1.41 visits per person *greater*—a change of 2.17 over the base figures. The augmented difference between these two plans for symptom-hypersensitive families may be interpreted as a response to differences in the comprehensiveness of the benefit packages. Comprehensive benefits allow the symptom-hypersensitive consumer to visit his doctor as often as he wants to at no extra financial cost to himself. Interpretation of the difference between the two plans for symptom-sensitive and -insensitive persons is more difficult. Why should these people have higher visitation rates under the hospital-sponsored plan than under the group plan? The answer may again lie in

---

[7] The visits that large group plan physicians characterize as unnecessary may or may not be the same as those rated relatively minor in the symptom-sensitivity scale. The physician questionnaire did not ask physicians to specifiy which visits were unnecessary.

the ease of access to physicians under the plan offering free choice of community physicians. Perhaps those who have a higher threshold to symptoms simply "cannot be bothered" to confront the bureaucracy of the large group plan unless their illness is severe.

Consumer complaints about physicians were expected to be inversely related to doctor visits: the more negative people feel about physicians, the less likely they are to visit them. The data reveal a *direct* rather than an inverse relationship. Doctor-visit rates per year for people with few complaints about physicians is 3.8, whereas the annual rate for the more negative consumers is 4.6. The difference is not statistically significant (t=1.30, df=526) but the direction is interesting.

The most significant differences on this factor are found in the large group plan. Consumers reporting few complaints in this plan have an average visitation rate of 3.8, but those with many complaints have a rate of 6.1. The small group practice plan reveals almost no difference in the two groups, and in some of the plans offering free choice of physician the trend is reversed so that people with few complaints have more visits (this is true in the small commercial and physician-sponsored plans). These data for the large group plan may be a reflection of physician attitudes toward their patients. As mentioned in Chapter 2, physicians in this plan recorded the most displeasure about their patients.

The last attitude indicator of demand is the impact of health insurance on use of physician services. Data indicate a tendency in the expected direction: that is, those who feel health insurance increases their use of physician services have a higher rate of doctor visits than those who do not—the rates are 4.6 and 3.8, respectively (t=1.61, df=522, not significant). This attitude has the greatest impact in the commercial plans. For those families in which health insurance is thought to increase use of services 38% report no doctor visits for 12 months in the large commercial plan and 34% in the small commercial. For families in which this attitude is not present the rate rises to 50%.

If we select two social status items (income and education) and two attitudinal items (hypersensitivity and insurance influence) as indicators of demand, the average annual rate of doctor visits for high-demand families is 4.47 and for low-demand families, 3.76. The difference in rates is not so pronounced as that reported for high-need and low-need families because of differences in impact of the items in each plan. Average annual per capita visits by plan for high-demand and low-demand families are the following:

Plan	High-demand families	Low-demand families
Large commercial	4.27	2.40
Small commercial	5.00	3.62
Hospital-sponsored	3.35	4.12
Physician-sponsored	3.24	4.55
Large group	5.17	3.78
Small group	4.88	4.43

High-demand families have a higher per person rate of doctor visits in all plans except the two provider-sponsored plans. Within families of similar demand levels the highest rate of doctor visits is found in the large group plan, followed by the small commercial and small group plans. Thus, although we concluded earlier that there was no evidence that high-need families made the most physician visits under comprehensive health insurance, there is evidence here that high-demand families do visit the doctor most frequently under comprehensive benefits, whereas our earlier finding showed that high-need families do not.

The general conclusion of the influence of consumer characteristics on the use of physician services by plan-type is the following:

Doctor visits per person per year

Plan type	Low-demand families	High-demand families
Commercial	2.8	4.4
Provider-sponsored	3.6	3.2
Group	4.2	5.1

The higher doctor visit rates for plans with the most comprehensive benefit packages (the group plans) are heavily influenced by use by families needing less medical care (younger families without chronic conditions, without reported acute conditions, and with fewer women of child-bearing age) with high demand (high income, high education, hypersensitivity and influenced by the comprehensiveness of their health insurance).

In summary, the data on doctor visits have documented that the annual rate of visits per person in all plans was 4.06. The highest visitation rate was in the large group plan and the lowest in the large commercial plan. The higher use of doctors' services in the group plans, however, was due in part to greater use by low-need families. In the small group plan out-of-plan use was 6.9%, and in the large group plan it was 10.5%. The comprehensive benefit packages of the group plans appear to increase the probability that persons from low-income families will visit the doctor at least once a year, but the effect is slight. Persons from lower educated families visit doctors significantly less often in the large group plan than highly educated families. This is not true in other plans and may be a result of the "bureaucratic effect." Generally, higher use of doctors in the group plans appears to be, in part, heavy use by low-need, high-demand people.

Total Volume of Care

Use of physician services is usually reported as number of visits. Measurement of use in these terms tells very little about volume of services actually received by consumers because the meaning of "office visit" can vary according to what was actually done during that visit. The same is true of a physician visit in the hospital. We hope to remedy this deficiency by analyzing each unit of medical care, both in and out of the hospital, as measured by the *doctor care index.* All care received by consumers in the medical record subsample was translated into units of the *California Relative Value Study.* These units were in turn converted into "dummy dollars" by multiplying by the "average" conversion factor reported by physicians for each section of the CRVS manual: Medicine, (the term here includes physical medicine and consultations), Surgery, Anesthesia, Laboratory, and Radiology.[8] The mean values obtained from the physicians were as follows:

Type of service	Average charge per unit
Medicine	$7.10
Surgery	7.43
Anesthesia	7.10
Laboratory	5.42
Radiology	5.42

[8] The reason it was necessary to multiply by a conversion factor for each section is that units from section to section are not equivalent and therefore not additive. The *doctor care index* avoids the impossible alternative of dealing with units from each section separately.

The resulting *doctor care index* does not represent actual price of care received because medical expenses not codeable by CRVS manual methods were not included in the calculations (e.g., hospital days, room and board, or private nurse charges), and the doctor care index for the family was then adjusted for family size. The figure now represents the average dollar value of care received per person per year in the given plan. Although these averages were not true dollar values, they were strictly comparable across plans. This enabled us to compare the volume of total medical services use across the six study plans.

Variations by plan

Table 3-5 suggests that the lowest per person volume of medical care received is in the large group plan and the two commercial plans. Large group consumers on the average received 74.8 units of medical care in and out of the hospital in one year, which is the lowest average. The highest is under the small group plan at 115.8.

We note from the table that the major differences among plans are in the percent of consumers with "none" and with "less than 75." Previous discussion has revealed that the group plans have relatively few people who receive no medical care at all during 12 months (less than 10% in the small group plan and 19% in the large group plan). This is in contrast to almost 50% in the large commercial plan. Consequently the mean units of care received by *all*

TABLE 3-5

Units of medical care per insured member for 12 months by plan

Units of medical care per person	Plan						
	All plans	Large comm	Small comm	Hosp-spon	Phys-spon	Large group	Small group
None (%)	27.8	47.8	35.5	33.4	19.3	18.8	9.8
Fewer than 75	37.1	20.2	25.9	27.1	54.9	47.3	51.2
75 or more	35.0	32.0	38.5	39.6	25.7	33.9	39.0
Mean	95.7	81.9	93.4	104.8	107.5	74.8	115.8
SD	181.5	149.7	137.4	146.7	315.7	102.0	196.8
N	793	136	134	145	112	142	125

$F=1.012$, $df=5/787$, $p=$not significant

$\chi^2=39.92$, $df=10$, $p<0.001$

people (averages computed for the entire sample, including consumers receiving no medical care) is influenced in the group plans by relatively few families with no care but by many families in the commercials and the hospital-sponsored plan with no care.

A comparison between the large commercial plan and the small group plan illustrates this well. In the former plan 48% of the families received no medical care during the study year, 20% received relatively little, and 32% were heavy users. In the small group plan 10% received no medical care, 51% received relatively little, and 39% were heavy users. The percent of families in both "heavy users" categories are nearly equivalent; but in the large commercial plan twice the percent of families who were light users received no care and in the small group plan, the figures are reversed—five times as many families who received no care were light users.

If the means were computed only for people who received some care during the the study year, the differences indicated in Table 3-5 would be magnified considerably. Thus for a random sample of families under the six plans those in the large group plan receive the least amount of medical services per person and those in the small group plan receive the most, but the difference is not statistically significant. If one were to consider only consumers receiving some medical care during the year, there is a significantly higher proportion under the group plans and the physician-sponsored plan. Among these people, each person would receive on the average much less care in these three plans, the lowest being the large group plan.

When units of the doctor care index are analyzed by plan type, the following results are obtained:

Plan type	Average units per person	Percent with no medical care
Commercial	85.1	44.4
Provider-sponsored	105.6	28.8
Group	81.1	17.4

This illustrates our conclusion that less care per person is delivered under the group plans, and significantly less is delivered per person when the population under consideration includes only those who make at least one visit to a physician during a 12-month period. The lower rate of hospitalization, of course, in the group plans would also substantially influence these differentials.

Organizational determinants

Although the previous section on doctor visits concentrated on consumer controls built into the benefit package, volume of services is more directly affected by controls over the physician. The consumer determines to a large extent whether he will visit a physician, but the physician is responsible for the type and amount of care delivered. In Chapter 2 the health plan organization has two types of control over physicians: direct control built into the system, as in the group plans in which physicians provide care within a peer-review system and indirect control enforced through the benefit package.

Proponents of the prepaid group practice health plans argue that peer review encourages appropriate medical care. For volume of service this means the correct volume of service for the patient's condition. This is encouraged in the group plans in this study by comprehensive benefit packages that largely remove financial barriers to complete medical care and by the salaried mode of remuneration of physicians. Under the salary system, it is argued, physicians are free to respond to the patient's condition without consideration of the patient's income. Under the fee-for-service system a greater volume of services provided to the patient results in higher incomes for the physician (provided insurance benefits cover the services or the patient is personally able to bear the extra costs).

But a danger of the group-plan system with respect to volume of certain services is that it also might tend to err on the side of overservicing. Physicians may more readily order tests "just to be sure" in a system in which he does not bear the direct financial responsibility for the costs. The reverse, however, appears to be true because consumers in the group plans, on the average, receive fewer services per person than consumers in the fee-for-service plans. For laboratory and radiology testing only the next chapter will analyze the data more fully. It is sufficient to note here that CRVS units of laboratory work for all care (ambulatory and hospital) is 3.2 per person in the small group plan, 2.7 in the large group, and 2.4 per person in the other plans. Percent distributions reveal that 45% of the families in the small group plan received more than two units per person of laboratory testing, compared with 38% in the large group and 28% in the other plans. This leads to the conclusion that consumers in the group plans receive more lab testing on the average than consumers in the other plans. Data on CRVS units of radiology per person do not reveal clear differences: small group, 2.0; large group, 1.2; other plans, 1.5. Percent distributions for radiology in the small group are 27% of families with more than 1.5 units per person, in the large group, 26%, and other plans, 24%.

Physicians were asked to give their opinions about the influence of insurance on treatment patterns—that is, whether health insurance led to "overtreatment" or "limitations on treatment." When physicians were classified according to one of the six study plans which they felt insured most of their patients, the following results were obtained:

Plan insuring most patients	Insurance causes overtreatment	Insurance limits adequate diagnosis and treatment
Commercial[9]	17.7%	36.0%
Hospital-sponsored	18.7%	32.5%
Physician-sponsored	17.6%	37.8%
Large group	22.3%%	16.1%
Small group	22.3%	15.5%
	$\chi^2=3.1$,df=4,NS	$\chi^2=50.5$,df=4,$p<0.001$

Thus about 20% of physicians in all plans feel that health insurance leads to overtreatment, and the differences among plans are not significant. Physicians whose patients are largely from the commercial and provider-sponsored plans, however, are significantly more aware of limitations on diagnosis and treatment procedures related to insurance than are physicians in the group plans. When specifically asked about the influence of insurance on laboratory work outside the hospital, the complaint is registered by about 50% of the physicians whose patients are insured under the commercial and provider-sponsored plans.

From these data it appears that the greater volume of laboratory testing in the group plans is not overtreatment, but rather that the lower rates in the other plans may be due to limitations on the benefit packages.

Consumer characteristics

The analysis of data on doctor visits revealed that consumers in the group plans classified as low-need and high-demand visited physicians more frequently than the same type of consumer in the

[9] N for the large and small commercial are combined because of the small number of physicians choosing each commercial plan. Combined N for these plans in this table is 164.

physicians more frequently than the same type of consumer in the other plans. In this section on volume of services we have concluded that consumers in the large group plan tend to receive fewer services per person than consumers in the other plans, although the differences among plans are not significant. Considering only user families, however, the group plans and the physician-sponsored plan deliver fewer services per person than other plans. Although the data are not directly comparable to doctor visits because volume of services includes in-hospital physician services, one suspects that the lower average volume per person in the group plans may be due to routine work for many low-need consumers.

We again selected four indicators for need: average family age, presence of chronic illness, presence of acute illness, and presence of women of child-bearing age. Using doctor care index units, an average volume of care per person was calculated for high-need and low-need consumers in each plan. An average was computed for families with average age of 41 years or older and an average for families with average age of 40 years or younger. The former are defined as high-need families, the latter as low-need. The procedure was repeated for each of the four indicators. When all indicators were averaged for all six plans, the high-need families received an average of 120.1 units of medical care for 12 months, compared with 80.3 for the low-need families.

Plan	High-need families	Low-need families
Large commercial	87.3	71.3
Small commercial	107.5	80.4
Hospital-sponsored	132.1	84.4
Physician-sponsored	180.8	80.5
Large group	84.3	68.9
Small group	129.2	83.6

In each plan the volume of care for the low-need families is considerably less than that for the high-need families. The greatest differential in volume of care for the two groups is in the physician-sponsored plan, in which high-need families receive 100.3 units per person more than low-need families. The smallest differential is in the large group plan at only 14.4 and the large commercial at 16.0.

Whether we speak of low-need or high-need families, consumers in the large group plan receive the lowest volume of services per person.

Combined with a higher frequency of visits by people in the low-need category, this would help explain the lower volume in this plan. The greatest differences, however, are not among the low-need families but among the high-need families, where the large group and large commercial plans provide significantly less service per person than the other plans. For instance, the large group plan delivers only 84.3. units to consumers from high-need families, compared with 180.8 units in the physician-sponsored plan: less than half as much care.

A more detailed examination of the data on one or more family members with chronic illnesses is provided in Table 3-6.

TABLE 3-6

Units of medical care per insured member by plan and reported presence of chronic illness in the family

Units of care per insured member	Plan						
	All plans	Large comm	Small comm	Hosp-spon	Phys-spon	Large group	Small group
No reported chronic illness							
None (%)	41.6	51.6	60.8	41.9	25.9	32.4	23.7
Fewer than 75	36.3	15.9	14.7	35.1	57.2	53.5	64.0
75 or more	22.1	32.5	24.4	23.1	16.9	14.1	12.3
Mean	67.2	82.8	66.2	50.5	94.0	49.8	35.2
SD	129.8	160.2	136.7	76.7	65.7	88.8	51.9
N	402	88	75	76	76	48	38
$\chi^2=66.7$, df=10, $p<0.001$							
One or more reported chronic illnesses							
None (%)	15.6	41.6	5.7	24.1	7.6	11.8	5.2
Fewer than 75	37.3	28.0	42.2	18.3	54.7	43.9	41.1
75 or more	47.1	30.4	52.1	57.6	37.7	44.3	53.7
Mean	118.2	79.5	127.9	165.3	136.6	87.9	121.6
SD	206.2	130.6	131.7	179.7	508.8	106.5	130.3
N	358	47	58	68	35	93	55
$\chi^2=52.9$, df=10, $p<0.001$							

Assuming that a chronically ill person should see a physician at least once a year, it is not surprising to find that only 16% of the families reporting chronic illnesses received no care at all during the 12 months under study, compared with 42% of the families not reporting chronic illnesses. In the large commercial plan 42% of the families reporting chronic illness received no medical care. This is the lowest plan performance in this study. The comparable figure in the small group plan is 5.2% and in the small commercial plan, 5.7%.

These plans have the "best" performance in this respect.

What has the introduction of "reported chronic illnesses in the family" done to the relationships among the plans? In order to examine the change, we select the two plans discussed earlier which delivered the highest and the lowest volume of medical services to high-need families: the physician-sponsored and the large group plan. Coincidentally, these two plans also exhibit large differences in the comprehensiveness of the benefit packages they sell: the large group plan was rated the most comprehensive, the physician-sponsored as the next-to-last in comprehensiveness. It would not be unreasonable (if one ignores incentives to low hospital use) to expect that the health plan with the most comprehensive benefits would deliver the largest volume of care per person. In fact, the data indicate the reverse. On the average, consumers in the physician-sponsored plan receive 32.7 more units of doctor care and have about the same percent of families with no care—19%. Consumers from families without reported chronic illnesses receive 44.2 units more and have 6% fewer families without doctor care. For families with reported chronic illnesses the differences are 48.7 and 4%. The introduction of chronic illness as a factor does not appreciably change the relationship between these two plans, but there is a tendency for the volume of doctor care to increase in the physician-sponsored plan for families with chronic illnesses.

This tendency of the doctor care index is illustrated clearly when the plans are collapsed into plan types and all indicators of need are averaged.

Plan type	All families	High-need	Low-need
Commercial	85.1	93.1	74.2
Provider-sponsored	105.6	147.2	83.7
Group	81.1	90.8	71.2

The volume of care for the low-need families is fairly consistent across the three plan types, but the rise in volume per person is precipitous in the provider-sponsored plans for high-need families.

The relatively low volume of services across the board for the group plans (especially the large group plan) is probably attributable to the emphasis of these plans on ambulatory care. Lower rates of hospitalization have been found in other studies. Volume of services in an ambulatory situation is likely to be lower than in the hospital situation. Analysis of hospital rates is reported later in this chapter.

Our major emphasis in considering the determinants of volume of services has been on physician response to consumer *need.* Consequently, consumer *demand* is not seen to have a major influence on volume of services. There is often, however, the necessity for the physician to consider financial resources of the patient in his treatment program. Limitations of insurance policies are less a factor in the group plans than in other plans because of the comprehensive nature of their benefit packages. With this in mind, then, we expect that income levels of consumers will influence the volume of medical services to some extent in the provider-sponsored and commercial plans but have little or no influence in the group plans.

TABLE 3-7

Units of medical care per insured member by plan and family annual income

Units of medical care per insured person	Plan						
	All plans	Large comm	Small comm	Hosp-spon	Phys-spon	Large group	Small group
Less than $11,000							
None (%)	32.0	52.0	35.8	39.0	18.6	18.2	16.0
Fewer than 75	36.7	18.3	33.4	24.8	55.9	53.5	47.5
75 or more	31.3	29.7	30.8	36.2	25.5	28.5	36.5
Mean	91.6	89.1	70.8	86.8	104.9	73.7	127.7
SD	206.4	165.8	106.9	122.1	380.5	110.8	248.9
N	465	104	61	98	70	69	64
	$\chi^2=58.9$, df=10, $p<0.001$						
$11,000 *or more*							
None (%)	20.0	33.3	27.4	23.5	15.0	20.9	4.1
Fewer than 75	38.7	27.1	21.4	35.9	57.6	37.2	55.8
75 or more	41.3	39.6	51.2	40.6	27.4	41.8	40.2
Mean	105.1	59.8	129.9	138.4	114.5	75.8	107.2
SD	138.9	76.6	162.8	187.4	152.5	94.7	122.8
N	300	32	61	98	70	69	64
	$\chi^2=30.6$, df=10, $p<0.001$						

The influence of income on volume of services is not significant for all the plans. Table 3-7 shows, however, that the higher income consumers tend to receive a higher volume of doctor's care: 105 units per person compared with 92 units per person in the lower income levels (below $11,000 per year). Even if we conclude that there is no difference in the volume of services by income level, it is still of interest because studies have generally found a greater incidence of illness among people in lower income levels. On the basis of need one would expect more services for these people, for we have already found that volume of services varies in all plans according to *need.*

The direct relation between need and volume of services may be limited to those with the financial resources to afford services beyond insurance policy benefits. Let us examine this one step further by controlling for income level in each plan.

Considering the average units of doctor care per person in each plan, there appears to be a greater influence of family income in the provider-sponsored and commercial plans than in the group plans. In the two provider-sponsored plans and the small commercial plan the means are considerably higher in the "$11,000 or more" categories than in lower income families. The large group plan consumers in both categories have almost identical averages, whereas in the small group and large commercial plans the lower income people have higher average units per person. If the two group plans are combined as a type of health plan, it is clear that consumer income has little impact on volume of doctor services in these plans.

Plan type	All families	Below $11,000	$11,000 and more
Commercials	87.1	85.7	90.1
Provider-sponsored	104.1	92.3	129.8
Group	81.5	82.4	80.6

The distributions in Table 3-7 indicate that families receiving a large volume of doctor services (75 units or more per person) are predominantly in the upper income class in all plans.

Our discussion of the influence of income on use shows that higher income people make more doctor visits and tend to receive more medical services than lower income people. The influence on doctor-visit rates was observed across all plans, but volume of services is increased with high income predominantly in plans with less comprehensive benefits.

Education does not appear to have an overall effect on volume of doctor services. In the large group plan, however, the highly educated families do receive a greater volume than those with lower educations. This is probably the same effect described under doctor-visit rates and may be due to the fact that these people visit their doctors more often. It may be caused, also, by their receiving more services at each visit. In any case, it appears to be a consequence of "knowing how to work the system."

Hypersensitivity to symptoms was analyzed for its effect on volume of doctor services. It was the only attitudinal dimension of demand thought relevant to this dependent variable. Theoretically the symptom-sensitive person might not only make more visits (as he was found to do under comprehensive benefits) but also demand more "attention" at each visit. Again it should be recognized that our test is very indirect, since symptom sensitivity was measured only on the respondent, whereas volume of services applies to all insured people in the family.

In four of the six plans the hypersensitive people were found to receive a greater volume of medical services: large group, large commercial, and the two provider-sponsored plans. In addition, all plans, except the small group plan, had a predominance of heavy users in the hypersensitive category.

An overall index of volume of doctor services was computed for high-demand and low-demand families, as defined by income, education, health insurance influence on use, and symptom sensitivity. Averages computed for all four indicators show demand having almost no influence. For the high-demand families the average number of units per person is 89.2, and for the low-demand families it is 87.4.

Plan	High-demand	Low-demand
Large commercial	70.1	59.4
Small commercial	111.0	80.1
Hospital-sponsored	77.9	86.1
Physician-sponsored	105.9	103.2
Large group	84.4	63.1
Small group	91.7	130.5

The effect of demand is not consistent from plan to plan. In the hospital-sponsored and the small group plans the volume per person is actually higher in the low-demand category.

One indication of how sensitive the plans are to need and demand on volume of doctor services is the variance in their average units per person for high and low categories of need and demand. On such an index the provider-sponsored plans would be most sensitive to need, since the differential between high-need and low-need families in those plans is the highest (100.3 for the physician-sponsored, 47.7

for the hospital-sponsored). The least sensitive is the large group plan (difference of 15.4). The greatest sensitivity to *demand,* on the other hand, is demonstrated by the small commercial and the large group plan (30.9 and 21.3, respectively) whereas the small group plan and the hospital-sponsored plan demonstrate negative influence of demand.

One must be cautious in interpreting these data, especially those concerning responsiveness to need in the different plans. A possible conclusion might be that the provider-sponsored plans, despite their low comprehensiveness rating, provide the most *appropriate* distribution of doctor services between the high-need and low-need families. There are at least two other interpretations, however, that are equally plausible. One is that the high-need persons in these plans have greater needs due to the lack of preventive programs that can forestall the serious or critical illnesses. The other is that of overtreatment—the provision of unnecessary services to people in the high-need category because of fee incentives.

All of these are hypotheses for further investigation. We shall have more to say concerning the characteristics of the medical services provided in each plan in the next chapter.

In summary, greater need leads to greater volume of services in every plan, but the group plans and the physician-sponsored plan deliver the lowest volume of services to those who receive care, with the large group plan having the lowest volume. Physicians in the provider and commercial plans complain more frequently about the laboratory and radiology limitations than do physicians in the group plans. More laboratory testing is provided in the group plans. Persons having higher incomes use more services in plans having less comprehensive benefits.

HOSPITAL CARE

Admissions

Major national interest has focused, with good reason, on hospitalization experience and factors associated with high or low admission rates. The reason is mainly financial. Hospital care is the most expensive and most rapidly increasing component of medical care expense for the patient. Figures reported for 1969, the last year in which we collected data for this study, showed an average per capita expenditure in America of $256 annually for personal health care. Of this total, $109.75 was spent on hospital care, compared with $58.04 for physician services. Over the three years of our study hospital expenditures increased by 54.1% (California Medical Association, 1970). The Social Security Administration estimates that by 1975 Americans will be spending $500 per capita on health care, and a large portion of that will be for hospital care.

Our review of the literature suggested that different patterns of health insurance organization had different effects on rate of hospital admissions, with comprehensive prepaid group practice plans best able to contain hospital costs. Much of the argument for "health maintenance organizations" is based on this belief. Our data will provide more fuel for the controversy.

Our data on hospital admissions is derived from medical records and the consumer questionnaire. The questionnaire asked the respondent to recall the number of hospital admissions for anybody in the family during the preceding 12 months. Analysis of the resulting data was conducted only on families without multiple insurance coverage and whose members were all insured under the study plan or when the number of members having hospital care was equal the number of insured family members. Thus the base for the rates is the insured family only; hospitalization for uninsured members or for families with multiple coverage is excluded.

We again have a problem of accurate recall, although it is less of a problem with infrequent and dramatic occurrences such as hospitalization. Figures from a nationwide survey in the late 1950s demonstrated a good correspondence between medical records data and respondent recall information on number of hospitalizations (National Center for Health Statistics, 1965). Eighty-seven percent of the hospitalizations recorded in medical records were also reported by the respondent on a 12-month basis. This size of recall error could be tolerated, especially since our primary interest is in the relative hospital admission rates across the plans rather than in absolute rates. There is no reason to believe that there would be a different rate of recall in one type of plan over another.

Data on hospital admissions from the medical records is accurate, but suffers from the problem of small sample sizes. The accuracy of the records for hospital experience is relatively certain, since we were not likely to have missed clues to a hospital admission in our many checks. They are also accurate in terms of the time period covered. For the records this is exactly 12 months from the time of signing the authorization. For the questionnaire estimates the respondent might have difficulty remembering whether a hospitalization was within the last 12 months.

In order to report data by averages, extreme values were deleted from the upper end of the distribution to prevent undue influence on the mean. For medical record data on hospitalization three such families with a rate of six hospital admissions per person were deleted and for the consumer questionnaire data six families with a rate of four or more per person were deleted. All families are included in the percent distributions.

Variations by plan

Three estimates of hospital admission rates were computed for the six plans in the study. The first rate is computed from the total sample of consumer questionnaires; the second is from the consumer questionnares of those respondents who were included in the subsample for the study of medical records; the third is from the medical records. The large sample, in which the respondent was asked to recall his family's hospitalization experience for 12 months, yielded a rate of 82 per 1000 insured persons; the subsample questionnaire data showed a rate of 150, and the medical records a rate of 132.

Obviously the estimates from the subsample are significantly different from those of the overall consumer sample ($p \leq 0.001$ in both cases), but the difference between the estimates within the subsample are not significant ($t=1.07$). We thus conclude that respondents in the overall consumer sample did not recall hospitalization experience very well, leading to an underestimate of about 40%. We feel that the bulk of the difference between the hospitalization rates for the overall sample and the subsample is attributable to recall rather than differences in actual rates, because the mean obtained from the medical records (132/1000) is nearly identical to that reported for the population of California as a whole for 1966 (134/1000) (California Medical Association, 1969). We might suspect the rate for our study people to be somewhat lower than the state figure because of the exclusion of people over 65 years of age in our sample, but the rate of hospitalization might also be higher because of the influence of insurance. In any case, the figure obtained from the questionnaire (82/1000) seems out of line.

An interesting note is that of the two recall estimates reported in Table 3-8 one is lower and one is higher than the actual rate computed from the medical records. The underestimate for the total sample is not difficult to explain, although the extent of it is perhaps surprising for an event such as hospitalization: people in the subsample had their memories jogged by the request to fill out the authorization form giving our research staff access to medical records. This procedure apparently made them think carefully about hospital experience for the family. It is indicative of the thoroughness with which these forms were filled out that these respondents actually estimated *more* hospitalizations than they had during the previous year (150/1000 compared with 132/1000). The reason, of course, is the difficulty of pinpointing events exactly within the 12-month period.

The question facing the analysts was which sample should be in the subsequent analysis? Underestimation is not really a problem because we are interested primarily in the relation among rates for the six plans. Underestimations, however, are acceptable only if they are relatively uniform from plan to plan so as not to bias the relationships among the plans. Table 3-8 indicates conclusively that such biases *would be* involved in using the overall sample, since the recall for people in the group plans is very accurate compared with the recall of those in the other plans.

TABLE 3-8
Estimates of hospital admissions per 1000 persons annually from three sources

	Plan						
	All plans	Large comm	Small comm	Hosp-spon	Phys-spon	Large group	Small group
Consumer questionnaire: total sample							
Mean	82	59	85	98	46	84	102
SD	250	213	232	232	211	207	339
N	2820	500	621	283	236	580	599
	$F=2.84$, $df=5/2814$, $p<0.05$						
Consumer questionnaire: subsample							
Mean	150	136	133	250	136	85	163
SD	355	298	286	474	350	220	416
N	805	136	138	146	114	142	129
	$F=3.84$, $df=5/799$, $p<0.01$						
Medical records							
Mean	132	126	194	152	150	71	104
SD	318	280	416	309	385	200	271
N	805	137	138	146	114	142	129
	$F=2.54$, $df=5/799$, $p<0.05$						

In the large group plan the estimate from the total sample (consumer questionnaires) was 84/1000; the figure obtained from the medical records was 71/1000, which is not a significant difference ($t=.69$). In the small group plan the difference is almost nonexistent. In all other plans the differences are very large. Therefore, if we were to use the large consumer sample to estimate hospital experience, we would be introducing a systematic bias *against* the group plans which would show them to have a much higher rate of hospitalization in relation to the other plans than they actually have. Consequently, we decided to use the medical records figures for subsequent analysis. This obviously puts limits on the reliability of estimates using control variables because the samples are small.

It is not easy to explain why respondents in the group plans provide much more accurate information on hospital experience than those in other plans. In Table 3-8 the major interest is the difference in rates among plans. There seems little doubt that our study provides confirmation of earlier studies (see review of literature) that the group practice plans have lower rates of hospitalization. Are these differences statistically significant? In reporting the significance of infrequently occurring events, using a small sample, we are cognizant of the fact that differences must be relatively large to satisfy the same significance level we have used in other tests for more frequently occurring events (doctor visits) or for larger samples. As an illustration, the difference between 71 (large group plan) and 126 (large commercial plan) appears substantial from a practical perspective, but its level of statistical significance is not quite 0.05, which is the level we have been using.

The rate of admissions in the large group plan is significantly lower than rates in all other plans but the small group plan in which the difference does not reach statistical significance. Rates in the small group plan are significantly lower than those in the small commercial plan. Differences among other plan pairs are not significant.

Testing for overall differences among the plans, we find significance at the 5% level. It is evident that this is largely due to the differences between the large group plan and all others (except the small group plan).

If the plans are collapsed into plan types according to the relative sizes of their insured populations, the group plans have an admission rate of 76 per 1000 per year,[10] the commercial, 145 and the provider-sponsored plans, 151. These differential figures are, however, mainly due to the influence of the low rate in the large group plan.

Organizational determinants

Two organizational deteminants of hospital services use are emphasis on in-hospital care and limitation of ambulatory services in the benefit packages and the relation of the physician to the hospitals.

On the first point much contention has been made that a majority of health plans help to increase the cost of medical care by concentrating on in-hospital benefits. Pressure is placed on the physician to hospitalize a patient so that benefits are received from the insuring agency. We asked our sample of physicians used by consumers in these six plans to comment on this contention relative to health plans in the Los Angeles area. These physicians were classified according to the one of the six plans which they thought insured most of their patients. These results were obtained:

Plan insuring most patients	Percent who feel plans are geared to hospitalization
Commercial	47%
Hospital-sponsored	48%
Physician-sponsored	43%
Large group	28%
Small group	33%

For further evidence of the providers' perceptions on this point they were asked to rate one of the six study plans about which they knew most on "effectiveness of the plan in controlling costs." Since hospital expenses contribute heavily to costs, responses may in part reflect physician opinions of plan ability to control these costs.

[10] In "Health Insurance Effects," published in 1972, calculations were based on hospital admission data from questionnaires. The calculations presented here, however, are based on admission rates from the medical records.

Plan best known to physician	Percent who feel cost control is excellent
Commercial	13%
Hospital-sponsored	3%
Physician-sponsored	5%
Large group	52%
Small group	33%

Finally we may recall an earlier discussion of physician opinions concerning benefit adequacy under each plan for laboratory and radiology work *outside* the hospital. Physicians in the group plans were much less likely to indicate that they are differentially aware of this complaint. We conclude that physicians' perceptions on this issue are vital, since they are the key decision makers on whether and for how long to hospitalize.

The second point mentioned was the relation of physicians to hospitals. In Chapter 2 we pointed out that physicians in the large group plan had a vested interest in controlling costs incurred by the health insuring agency because they participate in the excess earnings resulting from effective cost controls. Controlling rates of hospital admission is to their financial advantage and yet not financially detrimental to the patient, since the benefits include both ambulatory and hospital care. For instance, if the patient requires laboratory and radiology testing for a diagnosis, it is unlikely that the large group physician will admit him to a hospital if such testing can be done on an ambulatory basis. In other plans, however, there is some pressure to hospitalize, since such testing is more likely to be paid for by the insuring agency. The two group plans differ on this vital point of physician-hospital relations. The small group plan is more like the commercial and provider-sponsored plans in this study, as it does not have group-owned hospitals.

Availability of hospital beds is another influence. In the large group plan there are about two beds per 1000 persons insured, a rate much lower than the community ratio. As reported earlier, these beds are efficiently used in the large group plan: 84% occupancy as compared with 77% in the other hospitals.

The variations of plan organization and their influences are not difficult to understand. It still remains to be seen how these variations are influenced by need and demand characteristics of the consumers.

Consumer characteristics

The influence of consumer need on rate of hospitalization was based on the same indicators: average family age, presence of acute illness, presence of chronic illness, and women of child-bearing age. When average hospital admissions per 1000 insured persons were calculated for each group, the mean for the high-need families was 161 and for the low-need families, 112. Overall differences on each of the four indicators were significant except for *age:* the rate for those families averaging 41 or more years and for those averaging 40 or less was equal—128. Since people over 65 are not included in our study, the very high risks were eliminated.

Averaging all need characteristics together for each plan, the following distribution of mean hospital admissions per 1000 persons per year was obtained:

Plan	High-need families	Low-need families
Large commercial	142	106
Small commercial	148	154
Hospital-sponsored	212	116
Physician-sponsored	146	125
Large group	77	67
Small group	135	52

For each plan except the small commercial plan the average is greater for high-need families. Both types of family in the group plans have the lowest rate of hospital admissions, but the major difference between the small group plan and the commerical and provider-sponsored plans is in the rate of admission for low-need families, which is less than half the rate of all four plans. This is even lower than the large group practice rate.

According to these data, high-need families in the large group practice have a remarkably low rate of hospital admission compared with the other five plans. Hospitalization is significantly higher in low-need families in the commercial and provider-sponsored plans having a significantly higher hospitalization rate than either group plan. The difference in hospitalization rate between low-need and high-need families is least in the large group and small commercial plans and greatest in physician-sponsored plans.

The response of the large group plan to high-need families is illustrated in Table 3-9, where distributions and means for families with and without chronic illnesses are shown. Again the lowest illnesses are in the large group plan, although the mean is not significantly different from that of the small group plan or the large commercial plan. There are interesting shifts in rate of admission for some plans between families with and without chronically ill members. If we compare the amount of shift in the two group plans, it is evident that the large group plan tends to hospitalize at a nearly constant rate across the two family types, but the small group plan hospitalizes families with chronically-ill members more than five times as frequently as it does others. The percent distributions of the two plans show the same pattern: 23% of the families reporting chronic illnesses in the small group plan have at least one hospital admission per person compared with 2% of other families. The corresponding figures for the large group plan are 14 and 16%—a highly significant reversal.

The ranking of plans according to medical need in Chapter 2 placed the large group plan first and the small group plan second. In terms of hospital admissions these plans are on the bottom—the large group plan being the lowest. Although need predicts a higher rate of hospital admissions, there are very differential responses to need in various health plan social systems. The tendency revealed by our data seems to be, for instance, that the large group plan does not hospitalize for chronic illness to the same extent as other plans—especially the small commercial and hospital-sponsored plans.

TABLE 3-9

Hospital admission per 1000 insured persons by plan and presence of chronic illness in the family

Hospital admissions per 1000 persons	Plan						
	All plans	Large comm	Small comm	Hosp-spon	Phy-spon	Large group	Small group
No reported chronic illness							
None (%)	81.8	74.2	78.3	84.6	83.5	83.6	95.3
Fewer than 500	9.3	14.2	13.6	12.0	.6	8.2	3.1
500 or more	8.9	11.6	8.1	3.5	15.9	8.2	1.6
Mean	98	141	97	49	159	62	20
SD	264	292	224	133	414	167	98
N	402	88	75	76	76	48	38
	$\chi^2=23.7$, df=10, $p<0.01$						
One or more reported chronic illness							
None (%)	74.8	82.3	62.7	59.1	82.9	85.9	76.8
Fewer than 500	9.8	3.3	18.8	10.9	4.4	4.5	16.8
500 or more	15.4	14.4	18.5	30.0	12.7	9.6	6.4
Mean	145	99	201	264	132	76	106
SD	307	259	339	396	323	216	
N	365	48	58	70	37	93	58
	$\chi^2=34.7$, df=10, $p<0.001$						

Demand is not generally found to influence doctor visits or volume of services, although there have been interesting effects from plan to plan. On hospital admissions demand has very little minimal overall effect: families classified as high-demand (one or more of high income, high education, perceived influence of health insurance on use, and symptom hypersensitive) have a hospitalization rate of 110, whereas low-demand families have a rate of 118—not a significant difference. Taking each of the four indicators separately, there is no significant difference in hospitalization rates for three. There is, however, for *education* but in the opposite direction from that predicted. Consumers from families whose heads of household have a high school education or less have a higher hospitalization rate (148) than other consumers (85). Yet there is a tendency for higher income families to have a higher rate than lower income families.

If we examine the impact of education and income further, we again find it is not the same across all plans. In five of the six plans lower educated consumers are hospitalized more frequently than those with better educations, whereas in the large group plan the reverse is true. This may be interpreted as education probably being linked to need, so that the lower educated families have higher need. In this instance the education variable merely reflects the same result we obtained with the need indicators: that is, the large group plan is relatively unaffected by need in its hospitalization patterns. Otherwise the "bureaucracy effect" discussed in relation to doctor visits may also apply: that is, those with better educations are better able to obtain medical services in a large bureaucracy like the large group plan. The latter effect is true demand impact.

Better family financial resources mean higher hospitalization rates in three plans and lower rates in the remaining three. The direct effect of family income is apparent in the small commercial and the provider-sponsored plans. Lower income families have higher hospitalization rates in the other plans. The relationship according to plan types is the following:

	Average admissions/1000		Percent of families 500/1000 or more	
Plan type	High income	Low income	High income	Low income
Commercials	196	127	15.0	12.9
Provider-sponsored	175	145	23.9	13.6
Group	60	96	7.1	11.5

Although data presented by plan type conceal the different rates of the two commercial plans, they illustrate the reversal in the effect of income from the group plans to the others.

The different effect of income is probably due to the greater comprehensiveness of the benefit packages under the group plans which greatly softens the blow of costs due to hospitalization for families with limited incomes and typically higher rates of sickness. The blow probably is softened also for those in the small commercial plan by generally higher incomes; thus those below $11,000 may actually have higher incomes in this plan than the same category of people in other plans.

One of the indicators commonly associated with the concept of "social class" is occupation. Our data reveal that occupational level apparently has a direct relation to hospitalization rates for the overall sample and for each of the six plans. Workers in upper class occupations (white-collar and up) have an admission rate of 87 per 1000 per year, whereas workers in blue-collar and the lower class occupations have a rate of 206 ($t=3.43$, $df=750$, $p<0.001$). The relationship appears constant in all plans. According to plan types, the results are as follows:

Average admissions/1000

Plan type	High-occupational status	Low-occupational status
Commercial	104	134
Provider-sponsored	70	168
Group	60	93

Our discussion of *demand* has centered on social class indicators because the relationships in the data indicated a greater impact for these than the attitudinal variables.

In summary, the annual hospitalization rate for all plans is 132 per 1000 insured persons. The rate was significantly lower in the large group plan and next lowest in the small group plan. Aspects that might explain these differences in rates are the group plans' comprehensive benefits for ambulatory care and the large group plan's physician-hospital relationship. In all plans high-need families had a higher rate than low-need families, but the large group plan was very low for the high-need group compared with other plans. High income leads to higher hospital rates in the provider-sponsored plans and the small commercial plan, but the reverse is true in the other plans. Lower education leads to lower hospitalization rates only in the large group plan. Lower occupational status leads to higher rate of hospitalization regardless of health plan.

Hospital Days

Days in the hospital were measured from the medical record data. No attempt was made to have the respondent recall days in the hospital for hospitalized members of his family. Thus, although the dependent variable is measured very accurately, the sample size for each of the six plans is again rather small. It should be noted, however, that the figures in the tables apply to *families.*

For presentation of means a few families with a very large number of hospital days had to be removed from the sample. With small numbers a few extreme values on a variable of this sort can result in a misleading average. Five such families were removed from the sample, three of which had 59 hospital days per person, one had 86 days, and another had 163 days. The reported means are thus based on 99.6% of the sample. In tables involving *percent* distributions there is, of course, no distortion caused by extreme values and all families are included.

The reported means refer to the total sample rather than only to persons or families with hospital care. Our purpose is to provide some estimate of the total number of hospital days generated by populations insured under different health plans.

Hospital days are significant, particularly in California, where the cost of hospitalization is higher than in other states. A survey conducted in May 1969 revealed that the average price per day of a private room in California was $55.88 and a semiprivate, $49.73. Comparable figures for metropolitan United States as a whole, as of December 1968, were $45.70 and $40.70 (California Medical Association, 1970). Rates for special accommodations are much higher, and rates are increasing rapidly. Longer hospital stays, therefore, can result in large expenses for the patient or the health insurance agency. Considerable attention is currently directed toward reviewing length of hospital stay to prevent overuse of these expensive facilities. This study makes no pretense of judging appropriateness of length of stay reported but it does point out the possibility of abuse at both ends of the spectrum: that is, overuse is financially expensive but underuse could be fatal or lead eventually to longer stays.

Variation by plan

The importance of the variability in length of stay from one type of plan to another deserves the emphasis we place on determining whether significant differences among the study plans can be demonstrated.

Base figures with which we begin our comparisons are those for the United States and for California. For the country the average hospital days per person per year in 1966 was 1.22, for California it was 0.96 (California Medical Association, 1969). The comparable figure for our sample is 0.96—in exact agreement with the state figures. Even with five extreme cases removed, however, the variation around the mean is quite large—more than three times the mean.

When length of stay per person across the six plans is examined in Table 3-10, the figures for the commercial and provider-sponsored plans and the small group plan hover very close to the overall mean; the rate is close to one hospital day per insured person in the sample. The rate for the large group plan, however, is only about one-third the rate for the other plans—a rather remarkable drop.

Using the F-test, the difference among all plans is not significant. There is apparently as much variation in hospital stay *within* plans as there is *among* the plans. The lack of significance appears to be caused by large variances and the similarity in means among five of the six plans. Tests of differences between *pairs* of means reveal that the average length of stay in the large group plan is significantly different

TABLE 3-10

Hospital days per insured person per year by plan

Hospital days per insured person	Plan						
	All plans	Large comm	Small comm	Hosp-spon	Phys-spon	Large group	Small group
None (%)	77.8	77.2	69.5	72.4	81.1	85.4	82.1
Less than two	9.7	13.1	15.4	8.4	2.7	11.2	6.0
two or more	12.5	9.8	15.1	19.2	16.2	3.4	11.9
Mean	0.96	1.15	1.20	1.15	1.09	0.34	0.87
SD	3.23	4.74	3.49	2.55	3.40	1.84	2.65
N	805	137	138	146	113	142	129

F2=1.46, df=5/799, not significant

$\chi^2=35.4$, df=10, $p<0.001$

(at 0.05 level) from each of the other five plans but that differences in length of stay between each of the remaining pairs are not significant. This finding is similar to that reported for hospital admissions, except that for length of stay the difference between the two group plans is statistically significant.

We conclude that consumers in the large group plan spend significantly less time in the hospital than consumers insured under the other plans. The examination of the distributions confirms this conclusion. As we have seen previously, a greater percent of families in the large group plan have no hospitalization (85.4%) and a smaller percent hospitalized (3.4%) than any other plan. If we compare the large group plan against each of the other plans in terms of "long stay" vs. "short stay" rates, the large group plan has significantly fewer families (at the 0.01 level) with the long-stay rate.

Length of hospital stay in the six plans *per admission* rather than *per person* should now be considered. The latter figure is useful in terms of policy planning, since it provides guidelines for expectations of extent of hospital use for a population as a whole. Considering only people who *are* hospitalized, however, results are somewhat different. In the total sample of 817 families we found 175 families with one or more hospital admissions, with an average of 6.8 days for each admission. Length of stay per admission for each plan is:

Plan	Days per admission
Large commercial	4.8
Small commercial	5.3
Hospital-sponsored	9.1
Physician-sponsored	9.0
Large group	4.8
Small group	8.2

From these data the very low rate of admission per person reported earlier for the large group plan may be caused by a *combination* of more people with no hospitalization and a relatively low average hospital stay for those who are admitted. The small group rate, however, on the latter measure is not different from that of the commercial plans.

Thus our "hospital days" data should be regarded as a combination of both rate of admission and length of stay for those who are admitted. These are the important data from the perspective of the policy maker, who is interested in the amount of hospital care consumed by a given population under various forms of health care financing and delivery.

Organizational determinants

Many of the same organizational characteristics discussed under hospital admissions apply in the same manner to length of stay. It is of further importance that in the large group plan, where there is the dual influence of comprehensive benefits for ambulatory services and motivation on the part of the physician to avoid costly hospital stays, length of stay may be decreased by doing diagnostic and preliminary testing in the clinic before admission.

Consumer characteristics

The postulate that a population insured under a type of health plan similar in vital respects to the large group plan will consume less hospital care than a population under any other major type of health plan is examined. We have already demonstrated that the large group plan has significantly lower admissions than any other plan, and other plans do not differ significantly among themselves, nor do they appear to have any important influence on the rate reported for the state as a whole.

The response of the large group plan to medical need may not be the same as that of other types of health insurance in terms of hospital use. This is demonstrated by the following figures:

Plan	Days of stay per person (high-need families)
Large commercial	1.28
Small commercial	0.85
Hospital-sponsored	1.58
Physician-sponsored	1.77
Large group	0.42
Small group	0.95

Translated into dollar amounts this means the large group plan can count on budgeting about $21 per insured person per year to cover the cost of hospital rooms for its high-need subscribers. At the other extreme the high-need families in the physician-sponsored plan will cost that plan about $88 for hospital accommodations (1969 figures). This is perhaps one of the reasons why the physician-sponsored plan charges the highest premiums in the study, pays only 37% of its insured families' total medical expenses (see Table 2-5, Chapter 2), and still, according to our figures, loses money (see Table 2-3, Chapter 2).

The critic of this evidence would first of all want to know something about the medical needs of the populations insured under the health plans. Perhaps the lower hospital use under the large group plan is not due to organizational features but rather to the fact that consumers under this plan have significantly fewer needs than those under the other plans. In Chapter 2 we showed that the large and small group plans ranked 1 and 2 in terms of need as measured by several indicators. In the preceding section of this chapter we also demonstrated that our need indicators indeed appear to be related to consumption of hospital services measured by hospital admissions: the high-need families had an admission rate of 161, whereas the low-need families had a rate of 112 for the total sample. This lends some credibility to the four indicators used in terms of hospital admissions.[11]

Thus we cannot explain the lower rate of hospital admissions or the shorter stay in the large group plan by demonstrating lower need in the insured population. In fact, the reverse appears to be the case. The high-need consumers in the large group plan receive more hospital care than the low-need consumers in this plan, but in both instances the hospital care is less than that received in any other plan (except the small group plan, where admissions for the low-need category are not significantly different from those in the large group

---

[11] At this level of analysis we cannot satisfactorily deal with the argument at a more sophisticated level: namely, that high-need consumers in the nongroup plans really have a higher level of need than the same category of consumers in the group plans. The reverse makes more sense, since it is logical to predict a drift of people with greater medical needs to the health plans with the more comprehensive benefits. This, of course, assumes that the consumer has a choice of plan, which is always the policy when the large group plan is offered but not necessarily the case in other situations.

plan). If the population insured under the large group plan resembled the populations insured under the other plans in terms of need, the hospitalization rates would be even lower than they are reported here for that plan.

Is it possible that consumers in the large group plan have lower use of hospitals because their needs are not adequately met? According to one item of information from our data, this argument can be discounted; that is, consumers in the large group plan do not miss more days of work because of illness than do respondents in any other plan (nor do they miss fewer).[12]

Before leaving the influence of need on hospital days we emphasize that the large group practice plan finding cannot be generalized to all "prepaid group practice plans." To illustrate, data on hospital days per person per year for each of the four indicators of need may be compared for the two group plans in our study.

Need Indicator	Large Group	Small Group
Average age 41+	0.34	0.87
Chronic illnesses reported	0.46	0.77
Acute illnesses reported	0.59	0.55
Females in child-bearing years	0.28	0.62
Average	0.42	0.95

Turning to the influence of *demand,* if this criterion does increase the amount of services, then one would expect consumers from families in which the head of household is college-educated to take up more medical services than consumers from other families.

First, evidence shows the higher educated are less likely to be hospitalized; 82% have none, compared with 75% of the lower educated. The average number of hospital days per person for the

[12] This enticing bit of data is derived from an item in the consumer questionnaire which reads "How many days have you been away from work in the *last year* (12 months) because you were sick?." Response categories were provided. Although this is the only measure we have which taps health status outcome, detailed analysis was not pursued because of obvious recall problems.

lower educated is 1.30, compared with only .36 for the higher educated.[13] This tendency is consistent for all plans except the large group plan, in which almost no differences exist between the two education categories. Interpretation of the data in five of the plans is that education acts as an indicator of need rather than demand in that there is probably higher medical need in the lower classes (education is one traditional index of social class). For the large group plan the effect of education as a *demand* indicator may be quite important.

The "bureaucracy" effect, as previously discussed, may operate so that people from the lower socioeconomic classes (but especially those with lower educations) are less capable of dealing with a relatively complex bureaucracy than people with college educations. The possible consequence is that use might be lower in the lower classes. Some people with medical needs may never even see a doctor. This would be a vital demand effect and might offer some explanation for the data in Table 3-11.

Lower hospital rates in the large group plan in terms of demand may be the result of consumers from lower educated families having significantly *fewer* physician visits than those from highly educated families (see Table 3-3). We might attribute this to the bureaucracy effect, for if previous research is reviewed there is generally found to be more illness in the lower classes. Under five health plans this is demonstrated by greater use of medical services by people from lower educational levels. In the large group plan this is not the case, and one is led to conclude that *possibly there are those in this plan from lower educated families who have medical needs but are never seen by a physician.*

---

[13] The figures for families with college-educated heads of household may look a little low (.36 days per person as opposed to 1.30 in families whose heads have less education). Other traditional social class indicators consistently show the upper classes to have fewer hospital days: high-income families .90 compared with low-income families 1.06; high-occupation families .43 compared with low-occupation families 1.37. Data in the preliminary report from this study (Roemer et al., 1972) were given by social class (Hollingshead: 1957), and the rates for the upper classes were also quite low (average about .30 per person). By plan type the main difference between data in the preliminary report and these is the flip-flop between provider and group plans: in the preliminary report the group plans had a very low rate among upper class families; in these data the provider plans have the lowest rate among these families. We feel that the medical records data are more reliable, although the reader should be aware of the relatively small samples in each plan and large variances in some plans.

TABLE 3-11

Hospital days per insured person per year by plan and by education of head of household

Hospital days per person per year	Plan						
	All plans	Large comm	Small comm	Hosp-spon	Phys-spon	Large group	Small group
High school or less							
None (%)	75.4	83.5	65.2	64.3	75.4	86.0	79.9
Fewer than two	9.9	8.5	19.4	10.3	1.2	10.7	7.0
two or more	14.7	8.0	15.4	25.3	23.4	3.3	13.1
Mean	1.30	1.88	1.59	1.60	1.60	0.34	0.96
SD	3.25	6.80	3.95	3.02	4.42	1.61	2.52
N	405	63	65	88	49	79	61
	$\chi^2=33.17$, df=10, p<0.01						
Some college or more							
None (%)	81.9	75.7	73.2	90.0	85.2	83.2	88.0
Fewer than two	11.2	22.0	11.8	7.5	6.5	13.1	5.4
two or more	6.8	2.3	14.9	2.9	8.3	3.7	6.6
Mean	0.36	0.19	0.86	0.12	0.22	0.37	0.21
SD	1.74	0.51	3.02	0.48	0.60	2.21	2.67
N	334	57	72	47	38	57	64
	$\chi^2=21.75$, df=10, p<0.001						

This "demand" interpretaton is confirmed again in the hospital use data, where it is shown that consumers from low educational backgrounds spend a great deal less time in the hospital than similar consumers in other plans, but the relationship does not hold up for college-educated consumers. The overall constraining effect of a very limited hospital bed supply in the large group plan must also be considered.

Although it is beyond the scope of this study to investigate the suspected differences in need and demand between the large group plan and other plans, it is possible to provide some information. In order to cross-classify three variables simultaneously (plan, education, and need), a larger sample is required. We feel justified in analyzing data from the total sample (consumer questionnaires) on hospital admission rates for the two group plans only, since we demonstrated a very high correlation between recall and medical records data for those samples. Therefore we tested for the interaction effect on these two plans, recognizing that the so-called bureaucratic effect is not best demonstrated by comparing them because they both exhibit the problem. Because of smaller size and less complexity in the small group plan, however, we expect education to have less of an effect in this plan than in the large group plan. If we could test interaction differences between the large group plan and one of the plans in which solo practice is predominant, we feel the effect would be greater.

Introduction of education into the relation between plan and need on hospital admissions per 1000 insured persons produces the following:

	High school or less		Some college or more	
	High-need	Low-need	High-need	Low-need
Large group	82	81	90	82
Small group	115	77	72	42
(N)	(298)	(232)	(243)	(209)

We recall that the differences in admission rates for high-need people between these two plans without considering educational level was 58, with the small group having the higher admission rate. For people who are both high-need and highly educated, however, the data show the large group to have 22 admissions per 1000 *more*, a shift of 80 from the overall figures. On the other hand, for high-need, lower educated people the small group has 33 admissions per 1000 more than the large group, a shift of only 25 from the original data. Thus these data provide further confirmation that the lower rate of hospital use in the large plan is at least partially due to the relatively low rate among those in the plan who have *high needs* but *low educations.* Comparable information on doctor visits is even more striking, but our confidence in the accuracy of recall data for doctor visits is low and is therefore not reported here.

In summary, the aggregate use of hospitals for the sample was .96 days per year per insured person. This figure is in agreement with rates reported in California as a whole. The large group plan had a much lower rate of hospital days per person than the other plans. Even so, this plan's length of hospital stay per admission is nearly equivalent to the commercial plans' rates. The average stays of the small group and provider plans are much higher. The large group plan's performance on annual hospital days per person is largely a result of the low overall admission rate, which is affected by a significantly lower rate of admissions for people with high needs but low education. This appears to be due to the "bureaucratic effect" that operates only in the large group plan.

CONCLUSION

The use of services analysis has emphasized four aspects: number of doctor visits, volume of care, hospital admissions, and hospital days.

The data used for studying doctor visits were those taken from the medical records rather than the questionnaires, as patient recall was not accurate. An overall rate of doctor visits per person was 4.06 annually, with the highest rate of visits in the large group plan and the lowest rate in the large commercial plan. Generally there was more use of doctor services in the group plans compared with other plans. Contrary to some arguments, the comprehensive benefit packages of the group plans have only a slight effect on low-income family visits to doctors. Only the probability that these persons may make at least one visit during the year is increased. Also, the large group plan's "bureaucratic effect" may cause lower educated families to visit doctors less than highly educated families, since the difference between these two groups of patients occurs only in this plan. The greater use of doctors in the group plans seems partly the result of more visits by people who have lower needs and higher demands.

Every plan demonstrated that greater need leads to more medical services. In the group plans and the physician-sponsored plans, however, the lowest volume of services is delivered to those who receive care. The group plans provided more laboratory testing, whereas physicians in the provider and commercial plans frequently complained about limitations on laboratory and radiology testing outside the hospital. In the plans offering less comprehensive benefit packages people with higher incomes used more services.

Analysis of hospital admissions and hospital days was conducted on the medical records data, as patient recall again proved faulty. The overall annual rate of hospitalization was 132 per 1000 persons. In the large group plan the hospitalization rate was significantly lower, with the small group plan having the next lowest rate. These rates might be explained as the result of the comprehensive benefits for ambulatory care in the group plans, and in the large group plan, the relationship of member physicians to hospitals. A look at consumer characteristics showed that high-need families had a higher rate in all plans than low-need families. In the provider-sponsored plans and the small commercial plan there was a relation between income and higher hospital rates. The reverse tended to be true in the other plans. In the large group plan lower education led to lower hospitalization rates. Regardless of plan, lower occupational status results in more hospitalizations.

The overall days of hospital stay for the sample was 0.96 day per year per insured person. Taken individually, the large group plan had the lowest rates per person but not per admission. The performance of this plan on days of stay per person is largely the result of the low admission rate, especially for people with high needs but low education. The hypothesis is that the "bureaucratic effect" operating in this plan serves as a deterrent to these people.

REFERENCES

Anderson, Odin W. and Sheatsley, Paul B. "Comprehensive medical insurance: a study of costs, use and attitudes under two plans." Research series #9, Health Information Foundation, New York (1961).

California Medical Association."Trends in U.S. health care expenditures, 1966-1969." *Socioeconomic Report,* 10, no. 12 (December 1970); "Recent data on hospital rates in California." *Socioeconomic Report,* 10, no. 2 (February 1970). "Per capita health care expenditures—measurements in the U.S. and in California." *Socioeconomic Report,* 9, no. 10 (October 1969).

Columbia University School of Public Health and Administrative Medicine. "Family medical care under three types of health insurance." Foundation on Employee Health, Medical Care and Welfare, New York (1962).

Committee on Fees of the Commission on Medical Services, California Medical Association. "Relative value studies." Six Ninety Three Sutter Publications, San Francisco (1964).

Densen, Paul M., Balamuth, Eva, and Shapiro, Sam. "Prepaid Medical Care and Hospital Utilization." Chicago: American Hospital Association, 1958. (Monograph #3)

Donabedian, Avedis. "An evaluation of prepaid group practice." *Inquiry,* 6, no. 3 (September 1969), 3-27.

Greenberg, Ira G. and Rodburg, Michael L. "The role of prepaid group practice in relieving the medical care crisis." *Harvard Law Review,* 84, no. 4 (February 1971), 889-1001.

Hollingshead, A. B. "Two-factor index of social position." New Haven, Connecticut, 1957. (Monograph)

Klarman, Herbert E. "Analysis of the HMO proposal—its assumptions, implications, and prospects," in proceedings of the thirteenth annual symposium on hospital affairs. *Health maintenance organizations: a reconfiguration of the health services system.* Center for health administration studies, Graduate school of business, University of Chicago, 1971.

Medical advisory council to the board of administration of the Public Employees' Retirement System. "Final report on the survey of consumer experience under the State of California employees' hospital and medical care act." Sacramento, 1971. (Monograph)

National Center for Health Statistics. "Health interview responses compared with medical records." *Vital and health statistics,* 2, no. 7 (July 1965), 64-65. "Volume of physician visits, United States." *Vital and health statistics,* 10, no. 49 (July 1966—June 1967), 49.

Perrott, George S. *Federal employees health benefit program: enrollment and utilization of health services 1961-1968.* Washington, D.C.: Public Health Service, Health Services and Mental Health Administration, 1971. See also: Perrott, George S. "Federal employees health benefits program: utilization of hospital services." *American Journal of Public Health,* 56, no. 1 (January 1966), 57-64.

Roemer, Milton I., Hetherington, Robert W., Hopkins, Carl E., Gerst, Arthur E., Parsons, Eleanor; Long, Donald M. "Health insurance effects: services, expenditures, and attitudes under three types of plan." Bureau of public health economics, School of public health, University of Michigan, 1972. (Research series 16)

IV

Quality of Care and Range of Services

PERSONAL SERVICES OF ANY KIND, whether a haircut or a thoracotomy, are subject to a wide range of variation between and within provider organizations. Some characteristics of service are associated with different utilities to the consumer. The set of characteristics associated with utility, if they can be delineated, constitute a *quality of service* scale ranging from very bad to very good.

There are both quantitative and qualitative differences in the medical care provided for remedy of a given condition. Normal maternity is managed with 2 to 3 hospital days in California, 3 to 7 days on the East coast, 10 to 12 days in England. Some medical centers treat a liver cirrhosis with medicines, others use surgery. As any burlesque buff knows, some surgeons will leave a nearly invisible scar, others an ugly keloid. To the extent that these differences have significance for the outcome, or the *value* of the service, they are called *quality of medical care.* If this attribute of service is important to us, we should have a way to measure, rate, or at least rank it. A measure of quality is needed for the following:

- Research into causal relations between service and outcome.
- Management control of operations—monitoring.
- Service, program, or system design or selection (Bickner, 1970).

Many approaches to measurement of quality have been tried (Roemer, 1971; Goldsmith, 1972). The ultimate measure is, of course, the *outcome* or end result. For half a century there have been innumerable *therapeutic trials* in which one drug has been tested against another, one surgical operation against another, etc., in double blind randomized experiments. In these experiments an outcome or criterion for quality is relatively easy to identify: an illness can be cured as in the case of tuberculosis or other infections, immunity provided as in the case of the polio vaccine, or survival lengthened as in the case of surgery or radiation for breast cancer. In such cases it is relatively straightforward to measure the relative value of alternative elements of technique or treatment.

Measurement of the overall quality of a physician's activities, or that of a clinic, a hospital, or a large system such as the British National Health Service, or of a large group practice health plan is not so straightforward. Here we wish to assess a large bundle of services or service elements, and the controlled experiment is usually thought of as unfeasible (Cochrane, 1972). We must instead resort to pseudo-experiments: after-the-fact observation and analysis of operating systems.

Criteria for evaluating the quality of services provided by such complex systems are difficult to determine. Only a handful of system studies using an outcome or end-result criterion have been done. The best known are the studies of perinatal mortality in the Health Insurance Plan of Greater New York (Shapiro, 1967) Perinatal mortality experience within the plan, which features the group mode of physician practice, was compared with that of a similar population served under the usual individual practice mode. Recently in California perinatal outcomes have been compared under six different modes of delivery of medical care being used by the state plan for medical care for the poor—Medi-Cal. Another California study has compared service outputs of different configurations of health insurance plans: for example, commercial insurance, provider-sponsored group practice, and the "Blues." Observational analyses such as these can never be entirely satisfying because of self-selection of the consumers and other confounding exogenous variables intervening between plan and the outcome. No matter how many variables we control there may be others that are causing (or concealing) differences in outcomes. The RAND Corporation is planning a direct randomized experiment to compare the performances of several different modes of medical care delivery, but it will be several years before the outcome of this real-time experiment will emerge (Roemer and Shonick, 1973).

Moreover, outcome, in terms of health status of the target population, can seldom be measured directly. This difficulty has pushed most studies back to proximal or proxy criteria. Process variables are commonly measured as proxies for outcome. For example, the quality of a physical examination is rated on whether or not a rectal examination is done; quality of a gynecologist is rated on whether he routinely does Papanicolaou tests on apparently healthy women. Further, quality is not a homogenous attribute: a physician may be good at diagnosis, poor on treatment, or vice versa. A health plan may deliver high quality services for adults but mediocre for children.

Process variables may be good or poor indicators of quality, depending on the articulation between process and outcome. If for example, a Pap smear has a beneficial outcome in every case, then the procedure may be used as a proxy for the outcome. But relatively few of the many procedures and elements of the process of medical care are that certain.

Hence it is common practice to retreat still further to structural variables to ensure quality of care. Quality control of drugs in manufacture, sample tests of potency of vaccines, standards for certification and licensure of medical schools, hospitals, physicians and other structural elements of the system provide necessary though never sufficient guarantees of quality of care.

Most definitions of quality of medical care are based on process and structure variables—the inputs. Most agree that quality has multiple dimensions. Much effort has gone into development of composite indexes (Goldsmith,1972) for expressing the overall health status of a population as a single easily understood number comparable from place to place and from time to time. While such an index has value, like the GNP, for public information and broad policy, it would tell us nothing about what should be done to improve health status, and so we certainly need many more specific indicators of specific health problems. The single-number index has the further weakness that it integrates many influences on health status other than medical care, which determines only a small part of health status (Bickner,1970).

Most professionals (physicians, dentists, etc.) are wary of defining quality explicitly but are sure that they know it when they see it. They commonly believe only a professional can judge quality of medical care: hence the popularity of peer review. Objective or mechanical audits are generally distrusted. Case review, either through the medical record (Lembcke, 1967), or by direct observation of the physician at work (Peterson, et al., 1965), is the only method trusted by the professionals, and this with reservations. This usually means an expert judging without use of explicit criteria, since physicians will rarely agree on particular criteria.

Implicit in their judgment of quality of care is a set of attributes which Lee and Jones, in their study for the Committee on the Costs of Medical Care (1933), labeled "articles of faith." Lee and Jones identified eight characteristics of the professional behavior of "recognized leaders in medicine." In this way they defined "good medical care".

1. The practice of *rational* medicine based on the medical sciences.
2. Emphasis on *prevention.*
3. Intelligent *cooperation* between the lay public and the practitioners of scientific medicine.
4. Treatment of the *patient as a whole.*
5. Maintenance of a *close and continuing personal relation* between physician and patient.
6. *Coordination* with social welfare work.
7. *Coordination* of all types of medical services.
8. The application of *all the necessary* services of modern, scientific medicine to the needs of all the people.

These basic themes are still found throughout the rhetoric of quality of care (Brook, DeGreyndt, and Williamson, 1973). They make it clear, however, that "quality" of care is not a unitary dimension.

The Lee and Jones eight-point statement of the "articles of faith" provide us with a relatively solid foundation on which to build our examination of the *content* of medical services received by consumers under the six study plans. In Chapter 2 the amount of services received was discussed. Now information is needed on the composition of those services. If we could systematically describe the medical care in terms of the articles of faith, the resulting information would be relevant to the concept of "quality" thereby defined and would constitute an advance toward measuring this difficult concept.

Quality of medical care is a multidimensional concept implying judgment and results in the judges using different sets of indicators and giving different sets of weights to them. Thus we decided to abandon the unitary concept of "quality" and focus on the elements of delivered services. In order to avoid the appearance of arrogating the mystique of the physician, we call our study Range of Services. If the composite of services delivered to patients had indeed some underlying structure, we would let the data tell us the dimensions and the weights.

EMPIRICAL MEASUREMENT

The first approach to conceptualization is by enumeration, as in the Lee and Jones statement. The more difficult the concept, the greater the tendency to leave it at that. There has been no shortage of volunteers offering their opinions on what good medical care really is. Zetterberg points out the difficulties with such definitions:

> Definitions by enumeration give the scientist easy directions for concrete empirical references to a concept. There seem to be, however, at least two problems involved in the usage of definitions by enumeration. For one, we have the risk that the factors enumerated are empirically unrelated. As a matter of fact and research, the various dimensions. . . (may) show rather low intercorrelations, occasionally negative ones . . . Secondly, the factors enumerated may have no conceptual attribute in common . . . Enumerations, thus, easily become conceptual patchworks, more confusing than illuminating.

Applying Zetterberg's critique to the Lee-Jones statment, our conclusion is that Lee and Jones have made a first step toward the definition of "quality of medical care." Beyond this first step, however, we wish to examine the empirical basis for the definition so that it will be reasonably valid as well as easily put into operation. In order to avoid the "conceptual patchwork" referred to by Zetterberg, empirical data can be used to order the enumerated factors in such a way that any subconcepts can be clearly measured, defined, and applied systematically to empirical examples of medical services. If we are successful, this will provide a response to Donabedian's call for measures of the quality of medical care which are "easily, sometimes routinely, measurable and reasonably valid."

Indicators

From the literature (Donabedian, 1969), plus very extended discussions with physicians, we hypothesized five major qualitative aspects of medical care. The five dimensions and associated indicators obtainable from medical records are exhibited in Table 4-1. The major dimensions were represented by associated procedures and activities that could be determined reliably from the medical chart. The indicators were designed to provide the operational lines between the defintions of Lee and Jones and the empirical definition toward which we were working. Some procedures, for example, 1.9, pelvic examination, may seem arbitrary and debatable, but the empirical analysis to follow will test these hypothesized relations. Some items, such as 1.7, well-baby checkup, are age or sex-limited, and suitable statistical adjustment was necessary to correct for this element of the problem. That is, a physician should not be down-graded because of absence of a Pap smear if the patient is male.

All data for analysis were derived from medical records. The

TABLE 4-1

Descriptive categories (tentative)
and indicators of range of services

Prevention	*Continuity*
Checkup examination	Followup visit
Chest X-ray	Followup visit requested
Pap smear	Continuity of medical personnel
Prenatal checkup	Continuity of medical record
Immunization	Progress notes
Advice on preventive procedures	Rehabilitation services
Well-baby checkup	
Rectal examination	
Pelvic examination	
Serology	
Comprehensiveness	*Coordination*
Social factors	Referral to specialist
Secondary conditons found	Referral to paramedical personnel
	Consultation services
Rationality	
Chief complaint	Treatment: other physician seen
History	Complete blood count
Physical examination	Urinalysis
Diagnosis	Other laboratory work done
Laboratory work ordered	Other radiology done
Laboratory results recorded	
Treatment: injection	
Treatment: prescription	Surgery (amount)
Control Variables	
Location of care	Type of illness
Pregnancy	New or continuing
	Level of seriousness

medical records were cut up (literally) into discrete "bits" of service, a medical care bit (MCB) being a single patient-server contact and its associated laboratory, radiology, and other ancillary services (see Appendix A). The MCB was the smallest discrete unit of medical care with substantive meaning. Bits may be combined or added to form new units of study, such as a patient, a family, a physician, a hospital, or a health plan. On 1215 records some 11,379 bits were coded on each of 60 items of information. Most of the events coded were dummy variables (simply occurring or not), but some such as "physical examination" were scaled. Subjective judgments of *appropriateness* of procedures were not attempted. Thus the records could be analyzed according to content by properly trained non-medical coders.[1] This measurement system had the additional feature of being unobtrusive with respect to the events being observed.

Content analysis may be defined as "a method of studying and analyzing communications in a systematic, objective, and quantitative manner for the purpose of measuring variables" (Kerlinger, 1966). In this case the "communications" were medical records and the purpose was to obtain quantitative data to serve as measures of the dimensions identified for study. Since the coding procedure necessarily required the use of coders as interpreters of the record to scale or code relevant items, the reliability of the coding process was critical. It was necessary to measure the agreement between coders and if the results were not reliable to examine the causes. There are at least two main components of low reliability (North et al., 1963). These are differences between one coder and another and lack of consistency in one coder's orientation to the items being scaled. The first might occur when the two coders have differing concepts of a variable and the second when one coder does not have a clear concept of the variable and changes his definition from one instance to another. Pretests were undertaken both to develop clear working concepts of the variables and to identify the reliability problems that might occur. Practicing physicians and three non-medical coders familiar with medical terminology and procedures were asked to code 12 randomly selected records on six variables. These were variables that, it was felt, required most judgment in content analysis and for which medical experience was most necessary.

The results of this pretest were subjected to thorough statistical

---

[1] The coding form and coding manual may be obtained by request to the authors.

analysis and careful discussion. We tested for exact agreement of coding between each pair of coders and overall agreement among all coders, correlation between pairs of coders, and significance of agreement of the overall ranking of the variables by all coders.

Exact agreements were found to vary from 44 to 63%. Goodman and Kruskal's gamma measuring correlations between pairs of coders varied from 0.62 to 0.95. Significance tests using Kendall's coefficient of concordance (W) were postive at the 0.01 level. We found that the agreement between physicians was no better than that between other coders or between the physicians and the non-medical coders.

The experience of the first pretest allowed us to define the variables more clearly for the second pretest, and the amount of coder decision required was reduced by collapsing nearly all variables to dichotomies. Five non-medical coders participated in the second pretest. Results were encouraging, but there was still enough variability in the coding of certain variables to cause concern.

Consequently, a permanent *group* of coders was established chosen from the most experienced staff members and physician consultants. In the final process, when an individual coder felt competent to code independently, his work was tested for reliability against a set of records that had been coded by the group without his presence.

When a coder's reliability had been established on a variable, he was considered trained on that variable only and continued the pretesting process for variables he had not coded reliably. The coder then began coding the records on his own.

Approximately 72,000 pieces of information resulted from this process, providing us with an empirical base to test for the existence of dimensions in the data.

Factor Analysis

Empirical verification of the existence of underlying dimensions in the data was accomplished by application of factor analysis (Varimax rotation). Factor analysis (Harman, 1967; Rummel, 1967) is a statistical technique designed to identify "clusters" of variables that correlate more with one another than with the others. Such a cluster is called a "factor," or a "dimension." As Harman explains it:

> "The principal concern of factor analysis is the resolution of a set of variables linearly in terms of (usually) a small number of categories or "factors"...The preferred types of factor solutions

statistical simplicity, (2) meaningfulness.

Both general principles enunciated by Harman are important to our study. First, statistical simplicity is essential because the raw data provide us with information far too complex to be readily understood and analyzed in their raw form. Second, the clusters (factors) that are identified must be meaningful in terms of the real world, for in studying *range of services*—a concept closely allied to quality of care but nearly devoid of subjective judgment—certain subconcepts were suggested which had logical meaning for range of services and quality of care: prevention, comprehensiveness, etc.

Factor analysis finds the first, most distinct factor. The remaining variance is then analyzed and a second factor found that is orthogonal to, or independent of, the first. This continues until all the variance is explained or no more significant clusters are found. The factor analyst then examines the clusters of variables that load heavily on each factor to see if any substantive meaning is apparent in the way the variables cluster. With luck a few, usually not more than four or five distinct factors will emerge. If the investigator can associate any reasonable substantive meaning to these factors, he has gained some insight into the structure of the data and reduced his problem from a relatively fuzzy one of 60 dimensions to a relatively clear one of a few dimensions.

For this study two reiterations to clear out redundant or meaningless variables were completed. The final factor analysis was conducted on 20 "best" variables: 15 that had highly significant loadings on at least one of the first four factors, plus five that, although low on correlation with the factors, we felt had conceptual significance (16 20).

Results of the factor analysis are shown in Table 4-2. The 5 hypothesized dimensions (Table 4-1) did not turn out to be entirely distinct. Instead the data gave us four major factors or dimensions, that appeared to us to represent "prevention," "rationality," "verification," and "continuity." Although no single factor explained a great deal of the variance, the four factors combined explained 42%. Variables 1 to 5—Pap smear, pelvic examination, check-up, rectal examination, and physical examination—all had significantly high correlations (0.49 to 0.82) with the first factor and, with the exception of physical examination, had no correlation with any other factor. This factor seemed clearly to be prevention.

TABLE 4-2

Factor analysis of 11,379 medical care bits first numbers are factor loadings; numbers in brackets are average score coefficients.

Variable	Factor I	II	III	IV	h2
Pap smear	.82(.386)†	-.04(-.101)	.00(-.108)	-.07(.008)	.68
Pelvic examination	.81(.367)†	.14(.004)	.02(-.117)	.02(.059)	.68
Annual examination (checkup)	.71(.308)†	-.10(-.142)	.18(.011)	-.17(-.060)	.58
Rectal examination	.49(.173)†	.14(.006)	0.31(.081)	-.00(.010)	.36
Physical examination	.49(.159)†	.50(.221)†	.18(-.023)	.03(.041)	.53
Chief complaint	-.01(-.088)	.68(.381)†	.04(-.038)	-.16(-.091)	.49
History	.23(.023)	.64(.315)†	.26(.039)	.19(.117)	.57
Diagnosis	.11(.014)	.51(.274)†	.02(-.061)	.18.(.107)	.30
Progress notes	-.07(.052)	.43(.262)†	-.12(-.097)	.15(.084)	.23
CBC	.16(-.037)	.07(-.050)	.77(.374)†	.01(-.003)	.63
Urinalysis	.14(-.039)	.06(-.049)	.71(.347)†	-.01(-.012)	.53
Serology	-.04(-.115)	.04(-.034)	.66(.343)†	.03(.001)	.43
Chest X-ray	.10(-.042)	.04(-.040)	.57(.181)†	-.06(-.043)	.34
Followup visit	-.10(.005)	-.06(-.021)	.01(-.021)	.86(.473)†	.76
Followup visit requested	-.02(.035)	-.05(.032)	.06(.022)	.85(.473)†	.74
Continuity	-.10(.010)	-.30(-.146)	-.12(-.023)	.25(.137)	.18
Social factors	.11(-.012)	.32(.150)	.22(.068)	-.08(-.040)	.17
Lab-radiology results noted	-.08(.047)	.24(.160)	-.16(-.094)	-.16(-.088)	.12
Referral to specialist	-.07(-.078)	.22(-.078)	.08(.037)	-.16(-.097)	.10
Immunizations	.02(.001)	-.07(-.043)	.02(.017)	-.26(-.143)	.07
Percent of Total Variance Explained	17.5	9.5	7.9	7.5	42.3

†Variables used to define the underlying concept. Selection is on the basis of loadings equal to or greater than 0.40.

Table 4-3 presents the items used to define each of the factors.[2] Each factor score is contributed to by those indicators that are specified here. They also, however, take into account all 20 variables to some extent.

Table 4-3 indicates that we have employed both of Harman's "principles" in the statistical solution. As for simplicity, the original range of variables has been reduced to four different dimensions which we have termed *prevention, rationality, verification,* and *continuity.* The important indicators of each of these concepts have been identified and their statistical "weights" (factor loadings) determined. Regarding meaningfulness, all four factors are readily interpretable as relevant dimensions of the range of services concept.[3]

TABLE 4-3

Factors and their most important indicators

Factor	Indicators
I. Prevention	Pap smear Pelvic examination Annual checkup Rectal examination Physical examination
II. Rationality	Physical examination Chief complaint History Diagnosis Progress notes
III. Verification	Complete blood count Urinalysis Serology Chest X-ray
IV. Continuity	Followup visit Followup visit requested

[2] The variables in Table 4-2 are not defined in detail because of their complexity. The information is available and can be obtained by writing to the authors.

[3] Immunization, although an obvious preventive procedure, does not weight heavily on the prevention factor. It will be treated separately. Immunization is clearly of different quality than the examination procedures that dominate the prevention factor.

As we observed earlier, a "factor score" on each dimension ranges from zero to one for each MCB (medical care bit).[4] In terms of the medical procedures involved, a *prevention* score of "one" would be assigned to any MCB of a woman who came in for an annual checkup, was given a physical examination that included a pelvic and rectal, a Pap smear, and the other 20 procedures that have positive factor score coefficients. Any other procedure contributes relatively little to the assigned score for the MCB. This is how all factors are measured.

A nearly maximum score can be attained by performance of the procedures identified in Table 4-3 for each factor. The theoretical minimum score on the other hand, "0", is assigned when all procedures *negatively* related to the factor are performed and none of those positively related is performed.

In keeping with the objective nature of the range of services concept, we offer no judgment on the adequacy of medical services. The scales are meant only to reflect range of services. Certain logical exigencies, however, arose during the medical record coding which forced us to make judgments of "does not apply."For instance, the variable "diagnosis" was coded only for the first visit that appeared in

---

[4] The factor score coefficients presented in Table 4-2 are average regression weights of each standardized variable. The actual factor score for any given medical care bit, say for factor 1, would be calculated as FI=.386 (MCB value on "Pap smear" —mean value for all MCBs on "Pap smear"/standard deviation for "Pap smear") + .367 (MCB value on "pelvic examination") +...+ .001 (MCB value on "immunizations" - mean value for all MCBs on "immunizations"/standard deviation for "immunizations"). Actual ranges computed in this manner for each of the four dimensions were as follows: prevention—2.79 to 6.27; rationality—3.40 to 3.51; verification—1.79 to 8.29; continutiy—4.28 to 2.28. Because these ranges are not equivalent, the scores were converted to range from zero to one, where zero represented the theoretical lowest possible score and one, the highest possible score attainable on each factor. For instance, in factor 1, in order to attain the highest possible score, an MCB would have to exhibit 12 of the 20 procedures that have positive factor score coefficients but not the 8 with negative coefficients.

the record. Subsequently, MCBs with no diagnosis were coded "does not apply," since it was apparent that the physician had already made his judgment of the nature of the illness. If following MCBs either repeated or altered the diagnosis, they were coded. Beyond this no judgments were attempted.

The units of this scale are similar to those used in Chapter 3 to reflect total volume of medical services (CRVS units), except that the range of services units reflect extent of care in categories conceptually and statistically related to quality. Generally, it might be agreed that higher scores in each of the four categories are more desirable than the lower scores: for instance, the more preventive services delivered, the better but even this conclusion must be qualified because officers of the most preventive-oriented health plan in our study (the large group practice plan) have recently decided that preventive care in low-risk populations should be applied at a lower rate than in high-risk populations.[5] Similar qualifications could be advanced for all four factors.

An examination of the correspondence between factor scores and professional subjective judgments of quality of care would be interesting and would provide valuable information concerning both the "peer review" method and the factor scores. This is beyond the scope of the present research.

FINDINGS

The average factor scores by plan did not differ greatly, as shown in the ranges given in Table 4-4. The plans, accordingly, were ranked on each factor.

---

[5] Given the resources available, the plan would rather concentrate on the high-need families. The ideal, however, would be, to provide equal care for each patient no matter what his individual needs.

TABLE 4-4
Rank of plans on factor score (1=highest)

Factor and range of plan score averages	Plan					
	Large comm	Small comm	Hosp-spon	Phys-spon	Large group	Small group
Prevention (0.375-0.455)	6	3	5	4	1	2
Rationality (0.501-0.531)	4.5	6	2	4.5	1	3
Verification (0.118-0.153)	4	5	6	3	2	1
Continuity (0.556-0.625)	6	2	1	4	3	5
Sum of Ranks	20.5	16	14	15.5	7	11

Prevention

Variations by plan

On all of the indicators presented in Table 4-5[6] one or both of the group practice plans demonstrates a higher score, whether we examine average occurrence of the procedure per person in the sample or percent of families in which nobody received the type of service under study. Between the group plans, the small group has a higher rate for adult annual checkups, pap smears, and rectal exams; the large group is higher on well-child checkups, pelvic examinations, and immunizations. There appears little doubt that the group plans deliver more of these preventive services overall than any other plan in the study.

Some of the differences are significant from a practical standpoint; for instance, 82% of the families in the study had no adult annual checkup, and this representation rises to 90% and higher in the commercial plans. In contrast, 61% of the families in the small group practice plan had at least one annual checkup, and the overall mean

[6] This table shows distributions for each indicator used in the definition of the prevention factor except "physical examination" which is dealt with under the next factor.

rate indicates that almost one in three adults received an annual checkup. For children the record of the large group practice plan is the most impressive, where only 58% of the families with children 18 years and under went without annual checkups and about three out of five of these children had such an examination during the study year. In contrast, fewer than three among 20 children 18 years and younger received annual checkups under the large commercial plan.

TABLE 4-5

Preventive procedures by plan (average per person)
(N represents total families used to calculate the per person rate. "Percent with none" refers to % of families.)

	Plan							
	All plans	Large comm	Small comm	Hosp-spon	Phys-spon	Large group	Small group	
Annual checkup (19+ *years*)								
None (%)	82.4	96.1	90.6	87.5	83.7	73.6	61.2	
Mean	0.13	0.03	0.05	0.09	0.11	0.21	0.30	
SD	0.31	0.17	0.18	0.25	0.26	0.39	0.44	
N	817	137	146	147	117	142	129	
Annual checkup (18 *years and under*)								
None (%)	77.5	90.6	79.5	86.9	76.0	57.8	74.6	
Mean	0.32	0.14	0.18	0.38	0.38	0.59	0.30	
SD	0.95	0.67	0.45	1.20	1.13	1.37	1.74	
N	390	83	86	48	41	76	56	
Pap smears (adult females)								
None (%)	64.2	80.7	63.9	66.9	60.9	55.7	54.1	
Mean	0.38	0.20	0.39	0.36	0.40	0.45	0.53	
SD	0.55	0.41	0.54	0.55	0.51	0.52	0.68	
N	705	130	126	117	99	116	116	
Pelvic exams (adult females)								
None (%)	65.2	76.2	66.7	69.1	59.6	58.6	57.8	
Mean	0.69	0.45	0.74	0.69	0.72	0.82	0.73	
SD	0.58	0.33	0.77	0.66	0.50	0.64	0.49	
N	705	130	126	117	99	116	116	
Rectal exams								
None (%)	76.7	94.6	85.5	75.6	81.7	63.8	58.8	
Mean	0.13	0.03	0.06	0.14	0.13	0.18	0.24	
SD	0.30	0.15	0.20	0.28	0.38	0.36	0.36	
N	812	137	141	146	117	142	129	
Immunizations								
None (%)	79.2	87.8	84.5	82.9	85.0	58.8	77.6	
Mean	0.12	0.04	0.09	0.12	0.10	0.22	0.18	
SD	0.39	0.22	0.26	0.36	0.50	0.37	0.54	
N	812	137	141	146	117	142	129	

If annual checkup rates for adults and children are combined, differences among the plans are statistically significant. The group practice plans have higher rates than the other plans but are not different from each other.

Considering the "high risk" category of women in childbearing years, the differences among the plans on this variable are not so striking. About 50% of the women in the group practice plans received Pap smear tests compared with the overall rate of 35%. The large group practice plan has a higher rate than all other plans, and the large commercial plan has the lowest.

The aggregate scores on the prevention factor are provided in Table 4-6. These scores reflect characteristics of medical services *received* and are thus calculated only for persons who did make at least one doctor visit during the study year. This is a different base from that used in Table 4-5, in which we reported services received for the entire sample, including people who received no care at all. Prevention factor scores reported are "per person per visit" for ambulatory care. The figures thus represent the extent to which ambulatory visits in the six plans were for preventive services.[7]

Much the same conclusions may be drawn from the factor scores as from the separate indicators. The large group practice plan emerges as having the highest overall score, as well as the smallest percent of people with "low" scores.[8]

Tests for statistical significance on both the means and percent distribution indicate the probability of obtaining these results by chance to be less than one in 1000. Although the differences among the means do not appear large, the means are very stable (variances low) and even small fluctuations in their size reflect changes in the distribution.

t-tests were run on each pair of means. It was found that the group practice plans had higher average scores than each of the

---

[7] Certain of the procedures loading heavily on this factor could, of course, be performed during a visit for an illness rather than a preventive checkup (e.g., rectal and pelvic examinations). But the factor analysis tells us that usually they will go together with the annual examination which also has a high loading on this factor. The existence of the factor is based on the covariation of the high-loading items with some underlying characteristic—which in this case we have identified as "prevention."

[8] Distributions are based on dividing the overall distribution into three groups so that the upper and lower 20% are separated out.

TABLE 4-6

Prevention factor scores (averages per person per visit) by plan, ambulatory care

Average factor score per person per visit	Plan						
	All plans	Large comm	Small comm	Hosp-spon	Phys-spon	Large group	Small group
Low (%)	19.2	32.1	18.8	19.9	23.4	12.4	16.6
Medium	60.9	54.6	67.1	68.9	56.1	55.9	62.8
High	19.9	13.4	14.1	11.2	20.5	31.8	20.6
Mean	0.421	0.375	0.412	0.401	0.410	0.455	0.435
SD	0.119	0.099	0.109	0.085	0.120	0.137	0.124
N (persons)	1215	144	199	171	161	181	259

$F=11.6$, df=51209, $p=.001$

$\chi^2=60.2$, df=10, $p<.001$

other plans but did not differ significantly from each other. Thus we may conclude that, whether we consider separate indicators over the entire sample or factor scores over the sample of medical services received, the group practice plans provide a greater amount of preventive services.

Organizational determinants

The group practice plans produce the most comprehensive benefit package overall, but they are the only plans (with the exception of the small prepaid clinic portion of the large commercial plan) with benefits for no-illness examinations. The large group plan sends out a monthly "newsletter" of health education, and this might have the effect of heightening awareness on the part of their consumers. Benefits for routine examinations are complete in the large group practice plan, but a small coinsurance fee is charged in the small group practice plan.

Access to medical services, however, may play a part in use of preventive services in the large group plan. Many people who responded to our questionnaire complained about the difficulty of making an appointment for a routine physicial examination (implying that they expected such services to be available). The small group plan's subscribers did not share this complaint. This may in part account for the lower rate of annual checkup for adults found in the large group practice plan compared with the small group practice plan.

When physicians were asked whether they thought health insurance "helped promote preventive medicine,"their response was as follows:

Plan insuring most patients	Percent responding "yes"
Commercial plans	18.3
Hospital-sponsored	16.4
Physician-sponsored	16.1
Large group	52.9
Small group	53.4

Few physicians with patients subscribing to other plans felt that insurance had an impact on the use of preventive services.

Plan officials and physicians in the large group practice plan encourage the use of preventive services by categories of people most likely to benefit from those services. The effect of this policy, if any, can be examined only by the consideration of consumer characteristics.

Consumer characteristics

The group practice plans have the most members of high medical need according to measures of age, sex, and illness experience (Chapter 2). If the people in higher need categories (older people, women in child-bearing years, people experiencing chronic or acute illnesses) have greater need for all types of medical service, perhaps especially preventive, then preventive services are highest in the group practice plans because they are required. But this line of logic was disproved in the preceding chapter on use: the people needing less care use more services in the group practice plans than in other plans. Is this also true of preventive services?

To categorize persons in terms of need two person characteristics and two family characteristics were used. High need persons were thus those who had one or more of these characteristics: age over 40, women of child-bearing age, and a family reporting at least one chronic or one acute illness. The results illustrated here are the average prevention factor scores per person per visit.

Plan	High-need persons	Low-need persons
Large commercial	0.382	0.376
Small commercial	0.431	0.408
Hospital-sponsored	0.404	0.396
Physician-sponsored	0.408	0.409
Large group	0.438	0.469
Small group	0.434	0.442

For the entire sample we find almost no difference in the averages between the two categories of persons, but there is an interesting contrast in the scores between the group practice plans and all other plans; the relationship is reversed. In the two group practice plans the low-need persons receive *more* preventive services (+0.019); in the other plans they receive *less* (-0.013) than the high-need persons.

The conclusion from these data and data presented in the preceding chapter is that people in the low-need category visit doctors more frequently in the group practice plans and the visits are more likely to be for preventive procedures than visits made by similar people in the other plans. Again the effect is most pronounced in the large group practice plan.

This is an interesting phenomenon because, according to the officials of the large group practice plan, the relation between amount of preventive services delivered and need should be positive—as it tends to be in the commercial and provider-sponsored plans. The complete benefits for routine examinations and the comprehensive benefits for most procedures has lowered the "threshold" for low-need people to visit the doctor. Why the effect of the lowered threshold should be greater for the low-need people than the high-need might be explained in terms of *demand,* since low-need people are frequently found in the higher socioeconomic classes.

The effect of demand on consumption of preventive services is measured by indicators of social class (income, occupation, and education) and personal attitudes (toward symptoms and health insurance). These socioeconomic characteristics are more those of the family and head of household than those of the person for whom the rate is calculated. Attitudes of the *respondent,* who may not necessarily be the head of household, may have a much more indirect effect or none at all. Thus there is slippage in two attitude indicators used to explain variations in preventive services rates.

Elements of the demand concept have been tested elsewhere for effect on use of preventive services (Moody and Gray) and found to be rather good indicators. Two reasons cited are education and economic resources. The lower classes are generally thought of as less knowledgable about potential advantages of preventive services and also less able to afford medical services except in time of illness. Defining demand in terms of the five indicators listed above, we find that the high-demand category averages 0.435 on preventive services and the low category, 0.416. This difference is upheld for each of the five indicators except symptom sensitivity, for which there is no difference in the total sample between the symptom-hypersensitive and the symptom-sensitive and -insensitive.

Plan	High-demand	Low-demand
Large commercial	0.396	0.365
Small commercial	0.435	0.398
Hospital-sponsored	0.405	0.392
Physician-sponsored	0.444	0.401
Large group	0.477	0.461
Small group	0.439	0.434

For the high-demand persons roughly equivalent (statistically) amounts of preventive services are provided under the group, small commercial, and physician-sponsored plans. For low-demand persons the group practice plans provide more preventive services than any of the other four plans but do not differ much from each other. Thus a similar effect to that found for need is displayed: differences among the plans are reduced for the high-demand persons as they were for the high-need persons.

High-demand persons receive more preventive services per visit than low-demand persons in five of the six plans; in the large group practice plan the relationship is reversed. Thus the overall effect of demand is diminished in the large group practice plan. People from high-income families ($11,000 per year and more) do not consume more preventive services in this plan but in fact consume less than the low-income people. This inverse effect of income is also found in the small group practice plan, but in all other plans the effect is direct. The inference is that the comprehensive benefit packages of the two group practice plans effectively remove consideration of finances, allowing low-income people more access to preventive medical services.

It is surprising to find that people from lower educated families receive more preventive services than people from highly educated families in the large group plan. This was not found in Chapter 3: the large group practice plan is the only one having this relation to education. All other plans, including the small group practice plan, show higher preventive scores for persons from highly educated families. Table 4-7 demonstrates our general conclusion of how

TABLE 4-7

Prevention factor scores (average per person per visit) by plan and education of head of household (ambulatory care)

Average factor score per person per visit	Plan						
	All plans	Large comm	Small comm	Hosp-spon	Phys-spon	Large group	Small group
High school or less							
Low (%)	22.7	35.1	31.1	20.6	22.0	14.2	22.5
Medium	61.5	55.6	64.0	75.0	62.2	53.2	61.3
High	15.8	8.7	4.9	4.4	15.8	32.6	16.2
Mean	0.414	0.369	0.382	0.394	0.389	0.468	0.424
SD	0.119	0.099	0.089	0.074	0.081	0.154	0.120
N (persons)	638	80	93	128	56	180	102
	$\chi^2=73.3$, df=10, $p<0.001$						
Some college or more							
Low (%)	12.4	26.8	8.0	18.5	12.0	9.7	11.0
Medium	60.7	49.0	69.9	46.0	57.3	58.2	65.0
High	26.9	24.2	22.1	35.5	30.7	32.1	24.0
Mean	0.437	0.396	0.438	0.429	0.459	0.432	0.446
SD	0.118	0.102	0.119	0.114	0.135	0.099	0.125
N (persons)	512	51	106	38	67	95	154
	$\chi^2=20.7$, df=10, $p<0.05$						

demand influences use of preventive service. If we examine the means within plans (columns), every plan except the large group practice plan demonstrates the same relation between education and average prevention score: a family with a college-educated head of household receives more preventive care. The means among plans for the same educational category consistently show higher average scores for persons in the group plans only in the lower educated category. In the highly educated category differences among the plans are not large.

The effect of more comprehensive benefits in the group practice plans have proved to affect, to a greater extent, people with limited financial resources where preventive care is concerned. But a more detailed examination of the effect of education within plans leads to an unexpected finding: that lower educated persons receive higher average scores than highly educated persons in the large group plan. Taken together with the conclusion from Chapter 3 that persons from lower educated families make fewer doctor visits of all types in this plan, it is surprising that those who do make doctor visits go for preventive services.[9] The "bureaucratic effect" discussed previously apparently does not apply to this service.

Explanation of this finding must be speculative, as it requires further research. Since the relation between education and preventive scores is found only in the large group practice plan, it is possible that the health education program of this plan has a greater effect on people with less education than it does on college-educated families. Pamphlets sent out regularly by the health plan discuss various types of symptoms and in so doing may raise the awareness of those readers who have not considered them previously. During the period of our study this health plan literature was stressing the benefits of preventive examinations. Preliminary investigation of the impact of health-plan literature indicates that it has some effect on lower educated families. Fifty-five percent of the lower educated respondents in the large group practice plan affirmed that the literature was a "valuable source of health information." In contrast, 20-44% of the lower educated families in the other plans checked this questionnaire item, but highly educated families were even more aware of this source of information than lower educated families in the large group practice plan; 79% checked it in the questionnaire.

Further investigation indicates that health-plan literature does not have a greater effect on people with lesser education in the large group plan. As a proxy for the prevention factor score we used the response from a question in the consumer questionnaire regarding frequency of annual checkups. When this was controlled for education and awareness of health plan literature, we found that college-educated respondent who also checked the health plan literature as a "valuable source of health information" was as likely to have a regular annual examination as the same type of respondent with less education. The reader should be aware, of course, that this test is imprecise, and that it involves respondent recall error and a

---

[9] The reader may suspect this unusual effect is in some way connected to the nature of the factor scores themselves. Since they are a new method of assessing preventive services, they have not been tested previously. But statistical tabulations of one of the high loading indicators of this factor, annual checkups, leads to much the same conclusion. For this variable alone we found essentially no difference in rates between lower educated and highly educated persons for the large group practice plan, but all other plans demonstrated higher rates for the highly educated category.

proxy variable which is only one indicator of 20 associated with the factor score on prevention.

A further explanation is offered but not studied. Possibly the college-educated person in the large group practice plan obtains annual checkups by presenting an illness designed for the occasion. Comments in the questionnaire make it obvious that it is difficult to obtain an appointment in the large group practice plan for an annual checkup. An illness visit on the other hand is less difficult to arrange. Since the prevention factor score reflects medical services usually received in the absence of a complaint, such visits would not be scored as preventive. If this is the case, it is reasonable that the college-educated person would be more aware of this method of "working the system"; hence his preventive score would be correspondingly lower. This also provides a possible explanation of the high rate of doctor visits reported for the college-educated people in Chapter 3—that is, many of the visits by low-need persons apparently for trivial complaints may actually be visits for preventive checkups.

The last of the socioeconomic indicators of demand (occupation) has a consistent effect across all plans. White-collar workers score higher in the total sample than blue-collar workers, and in each plan they have higher scores (although the differences are not signficant in some plans). The effect is probably due to at least two factors. White-collar occupations are more likely to provide the opportunity for time from work for preventive examinations and are more likely to require annual checkups.

Physician determinants

The physician typology presented in Chapter 2 described the study plans in terms of the characteristics of physicians seen by consumers. The dimensions of the typology were *limiting, qualifying, facilitating,* and *motivating.* If physician characteristics relate to these concepts, they might be important determinants of the kind of medical services delivered.

The same unit of analysis, the person who receives some medical care during the study year, is retained. In this section, however, characteristics of the *physicians* visited by the patient are considered. The dependent variable is still the average prevention factor score per person per visit and analysis is limited to ambulatory care.

From the analysis of physician characteristics it is concluded that they do influence level of preventive care. The effect is more noticeable in the commercial and provider-sponsored plans than in the group practice plans. Persons visiting the more qualified (e.g., board-certified) physicians in terms of our typology have an average prevention factor score per visit of 0.423, compared with 0.413 for others, but for persons visiting physicians in the group practice plans average scores are identical. This is not unexpected, since the influence of supervision in a group of physicians tends to equalize performance. We found that regardless of the physician characteristic we tested, persons in the group practice plans have higher average factor scores on prevention.

Taking each dimension separately, "limiting" was measured by age, father's socioeconomic status, country of medical training, and status of medical school attended as measured by rate of applications per student position. Optimal performance was expected from physicians with one or more of the characteristics-age 40 or under, upper class (Hollingshead classes I through III), trained in the United States, Canada, Great Britain, or Scandinavia, and having attended a medical school with a relatively high rate of applications. Persons seeing physicians with none of these characteristics had an average prevention score of 0.420, whereas others averaged 0.423—not a substantial difference. Significance for the total sample was reached for one of the four indicators: persons seeing physicians who had attended much sought-after medical schools received higher preventive scores ($t=3.13$, $df=916$, $p<0.01$). There was a strong tendency for persons visiting physicians trained in the western countries to receive *less* preventive care than others (0.419 to 0.431), but the difference is slight.

The ranking of plans in terms of average preventive score was not altered for the two groups of physicians. For both the "limited" and "not limited," the group practice plans had higher scores.

Two indicators were selected for the *qualifying* dimension: certification status and formal courses in continuing medical education. Persons receiving care from physicians with one or both of these qualifications had higher scores on prevention than others, with both indicators reaching significance (certification, $p<0.05$; continuing medical education, $p<0.01$). Within the plan the care provided by the more highly qualified practitioners (by our measures) and the less qualified did not differ much for the group practice plans but did for the other plans.

The *facilitating* dimension was measured by two behavioral indicators (the structural indicators were omitted because there was no variaton in the two group practice plans). The indicators were number of professional journals read and number of patients seen per hour. Persons visiting physicians who read much professional literature or had a relatively low rate of patients per hour (four or fewer) attained higher preventive scores per visit than others (0.428 to 0.398). Both indicators were significant: journal reading at 0.05 and patients per hour at 0.001. Average scores per plan are the following:

Plan	High facilitating	Low facilitating
Large commercial	0.395	0.342
Small commercial	0.428	0.404
Hospital-sponsored	0.406	0.408
Physician-sponsored	0.406	0.390
Large group	0.450	0.446
Small group	0.435	0.420

These data reveal that within every plan except the hospital-sponsored the difference between the two categories described for the total sample is maintained. Looking at the two indicators separately, the effect of journal-reading on preventive care is mainly observed for physicians in private practice and has little effect on the group-practice physicians. The self-education value of keeping up with information in the journals may be of less importance to the practitioner in group practice because of regular interaction with colleagues (consultations and regularly scheduled medical meetings). Average prevention scores are higher for both group plans regardless of journal-reading behavior of the physicians, but the gap between either group practice plan and the other plans is increased considerably for physicians who are not heavy journal readers.

The impact of patient load is consistent in all plans. When the patient load is high, physicians tend to reduce the amount of preventive care delivered regardless of plan. The efficiencies of the large group practice type of organization could give member physicians the opportunity to see patients at a higher rate without reducing level of service. The data in Table 4-8 do not support this. The average reduction in preventive score for the group practice plans is 37 points, whereas it is 27 for the other plans. In terms of percent of people receiving high prevention scores, the reduction is 4.3 percentage points for the groups and 10.7 for the other plans. The conclusion is that no clear advantage can be demonstrated from these data for the group plans in handling a higher volume of patients per hour without reducing level of preventive services. Such advantages may be more logically demonstrated for other factor scores in which some medical procedures involved may be taken over more readily by paramedical personnel.

The final dimension is of *motivating,* under which physician attitudes toward patients and toward medical care are measured. The implicit hypothesis is that physicians with a positive orientation are likely to behave differently in their service to patients than those with negative orientations.

TABLE 4-8

Prevention factor scores per person per visit (ambulatory care) by plan and average patient load of physicians seen

	Plan						
Average factor score per person per visit	All plans	Large comm	Small comm	Hosp-spon	Phys-spon	Large group	Small group
Physician patient load: 4 or less per hour							
Low (%)	16.2	20.9	20.9	15.8	24.4	9.7	15.8
Medium	60.7	62.0	60.5	69.3	50.7	59.4	62.6
High	23.1	17.1	18.6	14.9	24.9	30.9	21.6
Mean	0.431	0.391	0.424	0.409	0.416	0.454	0.437
SD	0.124	0.103	0.130	0.008	0.130	0.130	0.124
N (persons)	784	74	101	75	85	222	117
	$\chi^2=24.7$, df=10, $p<0.01$						
Physician patient load: 5 or more per hour							
Low (%)	26.9	52.8	13.3	18.7	26.6	23.3	35.8
Medium	62.6	41.6	72.7	76.1	65.7	51.0	46.0
High	10.5	5.6	14.0	5.2	7.7	25.7	18.2
Mean	0.389	0.345	0.411	0.399	0.376	0.423	0.394
SD	0.094	0.095	0.083	0.078	0.090	0.117	0.118
N (persons)	286	56	63	68	56	32	12
	$\chi^2=40.5$, df=10, $p<0.001$						

Motivating attitudes are degree of agreement with the necessity of annual checkups, "negativity" toward patients reflected in number of complaints made about patients (see Chapter 2 for details of this Guttman scale), and agreement or disagreement with the complaint that patients tend to make unnecessary visits.

As with the other dimensions, consumers were divided into two groups; depending on the characteristics of the physicians they visited during the 12-month study period. In the first group consumers visited highly motivated physicians (by our measures) who were characterized by one or more positive attitudes toward annual checkups, low negativity toward patients, and disagreement with the complaint about unnecessary visitation.

For the total sample there was little difference between the "high" and the "low" categories. In both categories the group practice plans retained their prevention rankings. Of the three indicators used one was statistically significant for the total sample, but the direction of the relationship is reversed: patients visiting physicians who frequently complain that unnecessary visits are made receive higher prevention scores than others ($p=0.05$). This may be a reversal of influences which were also encountered in studying the relationship between consumer complaints about physicians and rate of doctor visits. The physicians who provide the most preventive services are apparently more critical of unnecessary visits. The attitude itself becomes the variable that is influenced (dependent variable) rather than the one that influences. This negative attitude is significant only in the group practice plans and especially in the large group practice plan. In this plan the difference in average score between the two categories is 80 points, compared with 28 in the small group practice plan and -10 in the other plans. Physician attitudes toward the annual checkup, which are mostly negative in the large group practice plan, are the probable cause. Only in the group practice plans do physicians who agree with the necessity of the checkup provide more preventive services than those who do not agree. The relationship does not hold in the other plans.

The attitude toward the annual checkup seems to deteriorate when high levels of preventive services are covered under comprehensive benefits. In the group practice plans there is a positive relationship between agreement with the necessity of the annual checkup and level of preventive services. But there is also a positive relationship between high level of preventive services and complaints about patients making unnecessary visits. Since these relationships do not appear in the other plans, which have less comprehensive benefit packages, physicians in the group practice plans may be reacting with some annoyance to the relatively high rate of preventive services actually delivered to low-need consumers.

In summary, the group practice plans place first and second on "prevention." The highest performance on this dimension is found in the small group practice, with the best scores on three of the six indicators (well-child checkup, pelvic examination, and immunization). The large group practice had the highest scores on the remaining three (adult checkup, Pap smear and rectal examination and immunization). The hospital-sponsored and the small commercial plan were lowest on the prevention factor. In the group practice plans, however, low-need persons received more preventive services than high-need persons. In the other plans the reverse is true. High-demand patients receive more preventive care in all plans except the large group practice plan. In this plan low-demand patients receive the most service.

The indicators by which demand was measured illustrated that white-collar families receive more preventive care regardless of plan, and people with higher incomes have more preventive care in the commercial and provider-sponsored plans. In all plans except the large group practice plan higher education is associated with more preventive care. Lower educated families have more preventive care in the large group practice plan.

In the group plans the physician is the manager of the patient's health care and has incentives to maintain health. In the other plans consumers are the managers, that is, making decisions on when and where to get care, with no visible incentive to seek preventive services. Consequently, the physicians in the large group practice plan had higher prevention scores.

Physicians classified as *limited* in terms of backgound did not differ from others on the prevention score, but patients seeing physicians who had attended high prestige medical schools received more preventive care. The better qualified physicians, measured according to certification and continuing medical education, provided their patients with more preventive services, except for those in the group practice plans in which physician qualification had no influence on these services. Physicians rated as high on *facilitation* (readers of professional journals and low patient load) rated higher prevention scores. Patient load had a consistent effect on all plans. Highly motivated physicians in the group plans regarded annual examinations more favorably, provided more preventive services, and complained less about unnecessary visits.

Rationality

Variations by plan

Items included in this concept are largely procedural, indicating the various steps followed by the practitioner to evaluate, diagnose, and treat a given illness.

Table 4-9 presents the distributions of seven items relevant to the

TABLE 4-9
Rationality procedures per visit by plan
(ambulatory care)

	Plan						
Rationality procedures per visit	All plans	Large comm	Small comm	Hosp-spon	Phys-spon	Large group	Small group
Physical examinations							
None (%)	34.8	42.1	41.8	38.0	42.5	19.7	24.9
mean (rge 0-3)	0.95	0.78	0.86	0.83	0.74	1.33	1.12
SD	0.87	0.79	0.89	0.79	0.78	0.91	0.85
Histories							
None (%)	47.7	51.0	53.2	56.0	51.2	30.8	44.3
Mean (rge 0-3)	.68	0.62	0.63	0.56	0.61	0.87	0.69
SD	0.77	0.75	0.81	0.76	0.76	0.74	0.74
Diagnosis							
None (%)	39.6	48.7	45.3	41.2	33.4	32.8	36.7
Social factors							
None (%)	91.4	93.3	92.4	92.7	94.0	87.4	87.4
Consultations							
None (%)	99.4	99.7	99.3	99.7	99.6	98.6	99.5
Mean (CRVS units/1000 persons	20	8	30 7		12	42	16
SD	277	158	403	135	193	351	243
Treatment: injections							
None (% visits)	78.7	72.0	74.2	82.1	74.4	96.0	73.1
Mean/person	1.30	1.26	1.82	1.40	2.26	.17	1.39
SD	4.43	358	4.93	2.62	5.76	.67	6.43
Treatment: surgery							
Mean (CRVS units/1000 persons	1.39	1.24	1.74	1.25	1.40	1.21	1.50
SD	4.84	3.02	5.25	3.02	3.82	3.57	7.48
N	1215	144	199	171	161	281	259

concept of rationality, including three of five items used to define the rationality factor.[10]

[10] The other two items (*progress notes* and *chief complaint*) were examined but did not demonstrate large differences between plans and are thus omitted from separate tabulation.

For *physical examinations* our data indicate a better performance in the large group practice plan, whether we are considering incidence or extent of the exams. The simple statistic on percent of ambulatory visits for which no physical examination is recorded reveals 20% for the large group, 25% for the small group, and roughly 40% for the other plans. Average extent of all physical examinations, scored on a four-point scale (zero to three, with three representing complete physical), again is considerably higher in the group practice plans for ambulatory visits.

With the data being presented in the same manner, differences found in physican *histories* have the same variations that occur in physical examination data. Percent of visits for which no history was noted is considerably lower for the large group practice plan (31% compared with about 50% in the commercials and provider-sponsored plans, 44% in the small group practice plan).

The variables *diagnosis* and *social factors* also follow the pattern. Social factors are taken into account almost twice as often in the group plans as in other plans. The highest rate of *consultation* is found in the large group plan, as the questionnaire data indicated earlier. In all plans, however, less than 1% of the ambulatory care visits involved consultation.

The statistics on *treatment* show that injections or "shots" (this does not include immunizations) are roughly *five times* as frequent in the small group, commercial and provider-sponsored plans as in the large group plan. For instance, only 4% of the medical care bits recorded shots in the large group plan, compared with a high of 28% in the large commercial plan and 27% in the small group practice plan. *Surgery* is also less frequent in the large group practice plan.[11]

When rationality factor scores are computed for each person with some medical care, the average per ambulatory visit is significantly higher in the group practice plans. Presented by plan types, these averages are the following:

Plan type	Average index
Commercials	0.503
Provider-sponsored	0.518
Group practice	0.527

The data in Table 4-10 reveal that the higher scores for the group practice category are due to the performance of the large group

[11] This is particularly striking in hospital care, where the average CRVS units per person in the hospital-sponsored plan is more than 11 times that of the large group practice plan, and the latter is significantly lower than all plans except the small group practice plan.

practice plan. The large group practice plan has a higher average factor score than any other plan with the exception of the hospital-sponsored plan. Average factor scores for the small group practice plan, the physician-sponsored plan and the two commercials are almost identical. Statistical tests on each pair of means reach significance for the comparison of the large group practice plan and every other plan except the hospital-sponsored. The only other significant difference is found between the hospital-sponsored plan and small commercial plan ($t=2.01$, $df=370$, $p<0.05$).

TABLE 4-10
Rationality factor scores per person per visit by plan (ambulatory care)

Rationality factor scores per person per visit	Plan						
	All plans	Large comm	Small comm	Hosp-spon	Phys-spon	Large group	Small group
Low (%)	20.4	28.4	20.5	15.7	20.9	15.9	23.4
Medium	57.8	52.5	63.7	58.6	57.0	57.4	56.7
High	21.8	19.1	15.8	25.7	22.1	26.7	19.9
Mean	0.513	0.504	0.501	0.526	0.504	0.531	0.506
SD	0.120	0.137	0.126	0.112	0.107	0.117	0.117
N	1215	144	199	171	161	281	259

$F=2.67$, $df=5/1209$, $p<0.05$

$\chi^2=20.9$, $df=10$, $p<0.05$

The factor scores substantiate the conclusion from examination of separate indicators—that the major difference we find among plans on the concept *rationality* is between the large group practice plan and all others. In contrast to the prevention factor, there appears to be very little similarity in performance on rationality between the two group plans.

Organizational determinants

The *rationality* factor reflects a thoroughness and logic of approach to medical case handling by the attending physician. One of the articles of faith set down by Lee and Jones was "good medical care (may be defined as) the practice of rational medicine based on the medical sciences."It is in the rationality factor, more than any other, that this article of faith finds expression.

The physician and the characteristics of the illness should be the prime determinants of level of rationality. Proponents of the prepaid group practice mode of organization claim that there are other important influences, namely, the method of financing the cost of care and the method of delivering it to the patient. In both instances group practice seems to have an advantage. First, with physicians under salary there is no direct relation between amount of care delivered and amount of remuneration for the physician (with the exception of the indirect influence of hospital care in the large group practice plan, as previously discussed). Under this system, it is argued, the physician is free to concentrate on appropriate treatment for illness at hand. Second, the group mode of organization may raise the average quality of medical care delivered because of better facilities, access to specialists as consultants, peer review and control of work, adequate paramedical support, in-house training programs, and opportunities for continuing education.

Proponents of the fee-for-service solo mode of practice claim that disadvantages can be as easily seen as advantages. The very absence of competition among physicians in a guaranteed-income situation can reduce their motivation to provide the most thorough and competent medical care. The group situation reduces individual responsibility and as such becomes a haven for those who cannot make it on their own. By virtue of their own bureaucratic weight large group practices become laden with requisite forms and procedures, thus making a meaningful doctor-patient relationship difficult. The physician becomes more interested in impressing colleagues than in meeting patient needs because it is those colleagues and the "organization" to which he must answer.

These pros and cons frequently take on the emotional overtones of debates over the relative advantages of "free enterprise" and "socialism" in the field of medicine. As such they are sometimes reduced to statements of values, devoid of objective consideration of evidence.

The evidence offered by our data on the rationality factor is that there are significant differences between these two modes of organizing and financing medical care. If we look at the data for the group plans as opposed to others, our conclusion is that rationality scores are significantly higher in the groups, but if we compare data within the prepaid group category we find that the large group has higher scores than the small group and the latter is no different from the plans based on fee-for-service medicine. Higher scores are apparently not generated by all types of group practice but rather by a group practice organized in the manner of the large group.

Consumer characteristics

A major determinant of rationality, as we have defined it, would be characteristics of the illness presented to the physician. If we divide the consumer sample in each plan into "high-need" and "low-need" categories, we expect average factor scores for persons in the high category to be higher in response to greater need.

In terms of need indicators measured in Chapter 2, the plans with the consumers needing the most care were the small group practice plan, the large group practice plan and the hospital-sponsored plan in that order. Rationality scores are highest in these three plans, although only in the large group practice plan is statistical significance achieved. Are the higher scores in these plans simply due to more high-need people?

Need categories are defined in terms of age, women of child-bearing age, and presence of chronic and short-term illnesses in the family. The high-need category had an average rationality score per person per visit of 0.518, whereas the low-need scored 0.510. Two of the four indicators attained significance for the sample as a whole. Persons from families in which either chronic or short-term illnesses are reported receive higher scores ($p=0.05$) on this factor.

Rationality factor scores for each plan and category of need are the following:

Plan	High-need persons	Low-need persons
Large commercial	0.517	0.495
Small commercial	0.483	0.502
Hospital-sponsored	0.530	0.521
Physician-sponsored	0.504	0.506
Large group	0.542	0.521
Small group	0.514	0.498

For both low-need and high-need persons the large group and hospital-sponsored plans retain their higher averages. For high-need persons the spread between the large group plan and the other plans is greater (59-point difference between highest and lowest) than for low-need persons (26-point difference). This indicates that if each health plan covered a population with need characteristics similar to those of the large group practice plan sample differences in rationality scores would be greater and the large group practice plan would score significantly higher than *all other plans.* This is simply illustrated if the large group practice plan scores are compared with an overall average score for all other plans (not weighted) for the two need categories.

Plan	High-need persons	Low-need persons	Difference
Large group	0.542	0.521	0.021
All others	0.509	0.504	0.005
Difference	0.033	0.017	0.016

In answer to the question posed earlier, the higher overall factor score for the large group practice plan cannot be attributed to a greater proportion of its consumers being high-need. If consumers of higher need were insured under the other plans to a greater extent than they are, this would not affect the rationality score of those plans.

Turning to a consideration of *demand,* we should not expect to find that it has any true effects on rationality. When the samples were divided into two categories of high demand and low demand, using the same five indicators as previously, the difference between them was not significant. The tendency was for the low-demand persons to receive higher factor scores than the high-demand, which probably can be interpreted as a need effect rather than an inverse effect of demand, that is, the more serious illnesses are usually associated with our category of "low demand" (low socioeconomic status), and we have seen in the previous section that high demand leads to a higher rationality score.

For both the high-demand and low-demand categories the large group practice plan consumers receive the highest rationality scores. Within plan it is interesting to note that the commercial and provider-sponsored plans consistently record higher factor scores for the low-demand category, but this is reversed in the group practice plans: the high demand-category tends to have higher scores.

Following this further, consumers in the large group plan from high-income families, or from families with college-educated heads of household, receive more thorough care by our measures than persons in the low-income, low-educated categories. The difference in scores between the two income classes is significant ($t=3.36$, $df=266$, $p<001$), and this is the only plan for which this is true. The explanation for this association of income level with physician behavior is not obvious. The consumer's financial resources are not expected to influence the physicians in the large group practice plan, since there is no direct financial relationship between provider and consumer.

Examination of consumer rate of complaints about physicians relative to the factor score on rationality reveals that consumers who have few complaints have more thorough medical care by our measures ($t=3.05$, $df=881$, $p=0.01$). Again much of the overall significance of this association is caused by the large group practice plan, where consumers who receive less thorough medical care tend to be more critical of physicians than such consumers in other plans.

Physician determinants

Aspects of physicians' backgrounds, training, and attitudes may be prime determinants of level of rationality factor scores. Consideration of the prevention factor indicated that the impact of physician characteristics tended to be less in the group practice situation, and it is again possible to test for the effect on rationality scores.

An important consideration is the contribution of record keeping to scores on this factor. Many of the indicators used here are affected by the tendency of the physician to keep full and systematic records because the records were our only source of information on procedures performed.

For certain variables the accuracy with which the record reflects procedures performed is likely to be greater than for others. For instance, with *social factors,* lack of a written record does not necessarily mean lack of consideration by the doctor of those factors; for a variable such as *physical examination* lack of *any* written record indicating a physical examination probably does indicate that no physical examination of any significance was performed.

We also observed, along with a majority of the physicians in our sample, that record keeping itself is an important aspect of quality of medical care. Procedures which are performed by the physician and not written down are of limited value in ongoing treatment programs—especially if a number of different doctors are involved with the same case.

In Chapter 2 we pointed out that our indicators of record-keeping habits[12] showed no differences between plans. Tendency to keep complete records had two measures: the attitude that good medical records are determinants of good quality medical care and reported tendency to record social and psychological information in the medical records. Both questions were categorized "yes" and "no," and it was shown that about equal percentages of the four resulting types were found in the plans (small group, large group, and others). Do these two questions really reflect behavior in keeping medical records? If they do, then this should be observable in the factor scores derived from the records.

The results of the analysis clearly indicate a direct relationship between responses on both questions concerning medical records and average factor score per physician. Physicians who respond positively on both questions have higher factor scores than physicians who respond negatively on both questions. Responses that are positive on one question and negative on the other generally place scores between the extremes.[13]

We thus conclude that our measures do reflect record-keeping behaviors of physicians and that these behaviors do not vary greatly from plan to plan.

We next analyzed the rationality factor scores of consumers in

---

[12] An attempt was made to estimate the differences among physicians in their tendencies toward complete record keeping. Two indicators were used in the questionnaire to determine the extent of a physician's record keeping. The first asked whether the physician considered social, psychological, and economic factors when treating a patient. Since this type of information is less likely to be recorded, it was thought of as a particulary sensitive indicator of the extent of record keeping. The second indicator asked the physician about his attitude toward systematic and complete record keeping as a determinant of quality of care.

[13] Responses to the two questions produced four categories:

1. Physicians who think complete and systematic record keeping is an

terms of the "limiting" characteristics of physicians visited. The same four variables were used to divide the sample into two groups—the "high" and the "low" on limiting characteristics (age, SES background, application ratio of school attended, and country of medical school). We found that persons who visited physicians characterized as "low" had significantly higher scores than other persons for the sample as a whole (factor score averages of 0.523 and 0.506). The direction of differences between the two groups for all four indicators was as expected, with *age* of physician proving statistically significant ($t=7.80$, $df=1168$, $p<0.001$). Patients whose attending physicians were 40 years of age or younger received much higher scores than other patients or other persons in the total sample. Within plans this difference in physician age was statistically significant for every plan.

Average scores per person per visit for the two groups of

---

important determinant of quality of care and who say they record socioeconomic and psychological information on their patient in the medical record. Average rationality score per physician in this category is 0.508.

2. Physicians who think complete and systematic records are important quality determinants but do not record socioeconomic and psychological data in the records for any reason. Average score in this category is 0.478.

3. Physicians who do not think complete and systematic records are important determinants of quality of care but who do record socioeconomic and psychological data in the medical records. Average score in this category is 0.499.

4. Physicians who do not think complete and systematic records are important determinants of quality of care and do not record socioeconomic and psychological information in the medical records of their patients. Average score in this category is 0.432.

The same results were obtained by using average rationality factor scores per consumer per visit. Persons seeing physicians who were poor record keepers had an average score of 0.502, whereas those seeing good record keepers by our measures had 0.520. If the sample were large enough, it would be desirable to use only information for persons in the latter category, since the quality of information is obviously superior. Analysis indicates, however, that this would not change the conclusions in any way. Among persons visiting only good record keepers in all plans those in the large group practice plan had significantly higher factor scores on rationality.

physicians by plan are the following:

Plan	Limiting: high	Limiting: low
Large commercial	0.507	0.524
Small commercial	0.465	0.508
Hospital-sponsored	0.491	0.552
Physician-sponsored	0.503	0.531
Large group	0.537	0.531
Small group	0.503	0.506

Two observations are that physician characteristics do not have the impact on medical care in the group practice plans that they have in the others and that the large group practice plan records the highest factor scores per person only in the high-limiting category of physicians. With respect to the first observation, differences within these plans from the high-limiting category to the low-limiting category are not significant. Differences in the other plans are significant toward advantage for the low-limiting physicians. Concerning the second point, in the low-limiting category the hospital-sponsored plan has a higher average, the physician-sponsored plan an equivalent average, and the large commercial plan is not much lower. This effect is not gained by the averages in the large group practice plan decreasing but rather by the averages in the other plans increasing under conditions of few limitations in the background characteristics of attending physicians. These observations might be interpreted as a result of an "equalizing" effect of the group practice plans so that the impact of characteristics of the individual physician is effectively reduced.

Qualifying characteristics of physicians were considered next, involving the certification status of physicians and amount of continuing medical education received in the preceding 12 months. Persons visiting physicians categorized as "low" on one or both of these variables were found to have lower rationality scores on the average (0.508 to 0.519). The differences were not significant for the sample as a whole, nor were the differences generated by either indicator taken separately, although the direction was as expected. The gap between average scores in the large group plan and those in the other plans was maintained for both types of practitioner, being slightly greater for those more highly qualified.

The lack of impressive differences on this dimension is probably due to the routine nature of the procedural variables involved in measuring the rationality factor. The type of training necessary for certification or in continuing medical education might have a greater effect on more specialized tasks and esoteric procedures.

Much the same type of result was obtained for the behavioral aspect of the *facilitating* dimension. Persons visiting physicians classified as "low" on this dimension (either low readers of professional journals or with a high patient load) scored 0.510 on the average, whereas those visiting physicians classified as "high" had an average score of .514—not a significant difference. Within plans there are almost no differences in average scores between the two categories for five of the six plans. The large group practice plan shows a higher average for the physicians who are high readers and have a low patient load. Furthermore, the advantage of the large group plan in terms of factor scores is significant only for persons visiting this type of physician. Among persons visiting physicians who read fewer journals and see more patients per hour differences among the plans almost disappear.

It appears once again that the variable measuring patient load is primarily responsible for this finding. Under conditions of heavy patient load (meaning the physician sees five or more patients per hour) the thoroughness of medical care as measured by the rationality factor scores drops sharply in the large group practice plan. This drop is such that the large group practice plan has a lower factor score for these physicians than the other plans—a most unusual occurrence for this plan. As found for prevention, increased patient load appears to have a greater effect on level of medical services in the large group practice plan than in other plans.

On the indicators of the dimension termed *motivating,*[14] there were no significant differences between those visiting physicians classified as highly motivated and those visiting practitioners categorized as "low." Persons visiting physicians who complained about unnecessary patient visits had significantly lower scores on the rationality factor in the large group practice plan, but this was not true in any of the other plans. We also note that the superior performance of the large group practice plan in terms of this factor holds up only for persons visiting

---

[14] The motivating dimension used in relation to rationality does not include attitude toward the preventive annual checkup, since this was not thought to be relevant to this factor. In its place we used attitude toward the right of all people to good medical care. In the questionnaire the question was phrased, "Access to good quality medical care should be a basic right for all people," with the opportunity to check responses ranging from "strongly agree" to "strongly disagree." Physicians classified as "highly motivated" on this indicator were those checking the first alternative. This constitutes 44.7% of the total physician sample.

physicians classified as low on this dimension. People visiting "highly motivated " physicians receive statistically equivalent levels of medical care regardless of health plan.

In summary, rationality scores are based on medical procedures of physical examinations, histories, reported diagnosis, chief complaint, consideration of social factors, consultations, progress notes, and the use of injections and surgery in treatment. The large group practice plan ranked highest on rationality, with the physicians' plan second. The two group practice plans do not perform equally well on this measure.

Organizationally, determinants of physician behavior on the rationality items may be associated with the influence of ongoing peer review and opportunities provided for continuing medical education—whether through formal or informal channels.

Differences between the large group practice plan and others is greatest for the high-need persons, but for the sample as a whole persons in this classification have higher rationality scores. Demand factors have relatively little influence over rationality scores. Income has a significant effect only in the large group practice plan, in which higher income persons have higher factor scores. A significant relationship was found between level of consumer complaints about physicians and average rationality factor scores.

Data from the physician survey indicated that across all plans rationality scores were higher for specialists, younger physicians, and physicians who see fewer than four patients per hour. Physician record-keeping behavior had a direct influence on the rationality factor scores, and good and poor record keepers were evenly distributed over the plans. Persons visiting physicians classified as "high" on the limitation dimension (age, class background, medical school attended) received lower factor scores. *Qualifying* characteristics of physicians (certification, continuing medical education) showed positive but not significant relationships with factor scores. Persons visiting "high motivated" physicians (believe in right to good medical care for all people, low negativity to patients, do not complain about unnecessary visits) receive statistically equivalent levels of care in all health plans.

Verification

Variations by plan

Indicators relevant to the concept of verification are presented in Table 4-11. The first indicator presented is the average laboratory and radiology CRVS units received per visit (medical care bit) by plan for ambulatory care. As the CRVS system does not permit adding units from different sections together, the statistics presented in Table 4-11 have been converted to dollar equivalents (see earlier discussion of method for converting CRVS units to units of the doctor's care index), which can then be added together.

The results from Table 4-11 indicate that the large group plan makes more extensive use of all types of laboratory and radiology testing taken together than any other plan.[15]

The least amount of laboratory and radiology testing per visit for ambulatory care is done in the small group plan and the physician-sponsored plan which perform an average of 0.2 units per visit less than the large group practice plan.

Percent of MCBs in which no laboratory or radiology is ordered provides the same results. It is evident that the large group practice plan makes greater use of laboratory and radiology testing.

Specific verification procedures are presented by plan. The large group plan performs 36% more complete blood counts in ambulatory care than the commercial and provider-sponsored plans. The small group lies between the large group and the other plans on this indicator. It should be noted that the variances for each plan are very large, indicating a great deal of variability from visit to visit within each plan.

Figures on *urinalysis* lead to the same conclusion as those on CBCs. *Serologies* are performed more frequently in the large group practice plan than in other plans. *Chest X-rays* are performed most frequently in the large group practice plan, followed by the small group.

Statistics on percent of ambulatory visits in which laboratory and radiology results are noted (only applicable visits are included here) indicate that physicians seen by subscribers to the commercial and provider-sponsored plans pay more attention to the results of their verifications than physicians in the group practice plans. The

---

[15] This is true for both ambulatory and hospital care.

TABLE 4-11
Verification procedures by plan
(ambulatory care)

Verification procedures	Plan: All plans	Large comm	Small comm	Hosp-spon	Phys-spon	Large group	Small group
Laboratory and radiology (doctor's care index units)							
None (% visits)	75.7	76.3	75.8	75.9	78.1	70.1	78.4
Mean/visit	.695	.668	.738	.724	.614	.810	.615
SD	1.903	1.874	2.320	1.929	2.245	1.798	1.570
Results of laboratory and radiology reported							
None (% visits)	42.0	39.3	40.4	47.8	49.4	41.3	34.0
CBC							
Mean/1000 visits	77	66	80	60	69	94	82
SD	266	249	271	37	53	292	274
Urinalysis							
Mean/1000 visits	108	112	91	108	88	139	102
SD	311	327	288	311	283	346	303
Serology							
Mean/1000 visits	13	8	18	9	18	17	8
SD	114	91	135	93	132	131	88
Chest X-ray							
Mean/1000 visits	34	1	29	17	29	52	38
SD	181	173	169	131	169	221	191
N (visits)	7320	1017	1403	977	1087	1300	1536

difference is most marked between the commercial and provider-sponsored plans and the small group practice plan (44% compared with 34%). Considering that in the group practice plan physicians consistently (except in the instance of serologies)order significantly greater laboratory and radiology testing but note results less frequently, there is some evidence that the testing is somewhat routine in the group practices. If this is the case, results are probably less frequently abnormal and there is less reason to make a note in the record of the findings. The problem with performing a laboratory or radiology test and not noting the results in the medical record is that very frequently it is difficult to find the results of the test, since they tend to get lost in the medical record as a whole. The coders found this to be particularly true of the group plans' medical records. Many cases were encountered in which the laboratory or radiology orders were noted in the medical record, but no indication was given whether the test was actually run and what the results were. The researchers spent a great deal of time ferreting out the results of such orders.[16]

Verification factor scores per person per visit are presented in Table 4-12. The title "verification" is applied to this factor because the variables that contribute most heavily to the scores are laboratory and radiology procedures—CBC, urinalysis, serology, and chest X-ray. It appears to be measuring the extent to which the physician relies on laboratory and radiology procedures to "verify" and substantiate his findings in the physical examination and medical history.

TABLE 4-12
Verification factor scores per person per visit by plan (ambulatory care)

Verification factor scores per person per visit	All plans	Large comm	Small comm	Hosp-spon	Phys-spon	Large group	Small group
Low (%)	41.8	37.1	44.5	47.3	41.8	43.9	36.3
Medium	41.6	51.2	44.5	44.9	39.9	33.2	42.2
High	16.6	11.6	11.0	7.7	18.2	22.9	21.5
Mean	0.138	0.133	0.126	0.118	0.139	0.148	0.153
SD	0.097	0.065	0.092	0.063	0.080	0.127	0.105
N	1215	144	199	171	161	281	259

$F=4.16$, $df=5/1209$, $p<0.001$
$\chi^2=38.3$, $df=10$, $p<0.001$

Data in Table 4-12 substantiate the earlier discussion of separate indicators. Greater use of verification procedures is made in the group practice plans than in other plans. If the plans are collapsed into types, the following results:

Plan type	Average score	Percent "high"
Commercial	0.130	11.4
Provider-sponsored	0.125	11.5
Group practice	0.149	22.7

[16] Large group physicians, in hospital care, tend to note laboratory and radiology test outcomes more frequently than other physicians, but the interesting thing about the statistic is the overall infrequency among all physicians to note results of tests in the hospital: only 13% of the applicable MCBs contain any mention by the physician of test results.

The plan type comparisons indicate a generalizable difference between the group plan type and the other types, since the data are weighted according to the populations in each representative of the types. Either separately or in types, the group practice plans score higher on this factor. Within type of plan there is no significant difference between the large and the small group in their employment of verification procedures. The small group practice plan has the highest average factor score and is significantly higher than all other plans except the physician-sponsored and the large group. The large group practice plan's score is significantly higher only in comparison with the small commercial and the hospital-sponsored plans. The factor score is thus not merely reflecting the procedures identified in its definition and presented in Table 4-12, since on these procedures the large group practice plan had the highest rate.

Organizational determinants

The factor "verification" is highly weighted on laboratory and radiology procedures which are frequently performed routinely by a physician to provide baseline information on his patient. In some instances they might be done as case-finding procedures when the patient's complaints are nonspecific and the physician wishes to run general checks. The factor analysis indicates that the four procedures—CBC, urinalysis, serology, and chest X-rays—generally occur together. Also, the verification factor is not in this instance measuring procedures occurring in non illness visits, since the variable "annual checkup" has insignificant loading on this factor and the procedures themselves do not weight heavily in the prevention factor.

The verification factor measures procedures that may be routine and carried out during illness visits. The higher scores in the group practice plans on this factor are probably influenced to a great extent by the comprehensiveness of the benefit packages that permit routine use of laboratory and radiology procedures without hospitalization.

Consumer characteristics

Persons classified as "high need" received lower scores on the verification factor than persons in the low-need category. Three of the indicators of need were statistically significant ($p=0.01$), whereas the relation with age was in the same direction but not significant. We conclude that the laboratory and radiology procedures reflected in this factor score are negatively associated with level of need.

Within plans there is a consistent rise in average score from the high-need to low-need categories except in the large group practice plan, where the rise is much larger. On all four indicators the large group practice plan patients are more sharply divided between high-need and low-need than in any other plan. The difference in this factor is illustrated by the following

Plan	High-need persons	Low-need persons
Large commercial	0.128	0.137
Small commercial	0.116	0.127
Hospital-sponsored	0.115	0.120
Physician-sponsored	0.128	0.144
Large group	0.126	0.170
Small group	0.147	0.156

Analysis of *demand* reveals very little impact on verification scores. Those classified as low-demand have slightly higher scores on the average than the high-demand persons (0.143 and 0.136 respectively—not significant). Again the gap between the two categories is significant in only the large group practice plan, in which the low-demand category has the higher score. The inverse effect of demand in this one plan is curious. But in the large group practice plan the persons of low demand receive much more routine laboratory and radiology work than others.

This effect is well illustrated by considering education:

Plan	High education	Low education
Commercials and provider-sponsored	0.128	0.127
Large group	0.122	0.161
Small group	0.151	0.157

Across educational categories the level of the verification factor is about the same for the commercial, provider-sponsored and small group practice plan; but the lower educated persons in the large group practice plan have considerably higher average scores than the highly educated persons.

We conclude that low-need persons in the large group plan are more likely to receive routine laboratory and radiology work than these persons in other plans. For persons with characteristics of high need or high demand the difference among plans is reduced.

Physician determinants

For the overall sample persons visiting physicians in the "low-limiting" category (age 40 or less, from upper socioeconomic background, attending school in the United States, Canada, Great

Britain, or Scandinavia) had slightly higher verification scores. In the large group practice plan persons visiting "foreign-trained" physicians had a much higher verification score (0.211) than others (0.136). physicians (in terms of certification status and experience with continuing medical education) achieved higher factor scores than those visiting the more qualified practitioners. This is probably a function of the type of physician seen by persons with minor complaints. The effect is most dramatic in the large group practice plan.

Plan	High-qualified physicians	Low-qualified physicians
Commercials and provider-sponsored	0.126	0.130
Large group	0.130	0.158
Small group	0.156	0.156

This difference in the large group plan may be due to the advancement in the group of experienced physicians to Chiefs of Service and other responsible positions. In such positions they become involved with more difficult and serious cases. Moreover, the less qualified physicians are often assigned to "walk-in clinic" duties, where time pressures lead the doctor to order numerous tests as a substitute for careful clinical examination. As we concluded earlier, higher verification scores are associated with low need, a category that is not likely to include the "difficult and serious" cases. In the other plans this allocation of patients is not a factor.

A *facilitating* variable directly relevant to this factor is one measuring physicians' perception of the accessibility of the laboratory. In the physician questionnaire the respondent was asked to give an average waiting time for an emergency blood-sugar determination. Consumers who visited physicians with access of "one hour or less" had higher verification scores than those who had to wait longer than one hour. The effect of this variable was found mainly in the two group practice plans, as illustrated by the following figures.

Plan	Lab: 1 hour or less	Lab: more than 1 hour
Commercials and provider-sponsored	0.125	0.144
Large group	0.140	0.120
Small group	0.167	0.129

When the laboratory is perceived as relatively inaccessible, verification scores in the group practice plans fall below the average found in the commercial and provider-sponsored plans. When laboratory turn-around is fast, the group practice plans do more of this routine work.

Regarding the *motivating* dimension of physician characteristics, a higher average verification score was found for persons visiting highly motivated physicians (by our measures). The main contributor to the significance of this finding was the Guttman five-item negativity score measuring physician attitudes toward patients. Persons visiting physicians who are "highly negative" by this measure received factor scores averaging .122; those visiting physicians with positive attitudes toward patients had an average of .142. Within the positive category the two group practice plans had the highest scores; for highly negative physicians the large group practice plan dropped to fourth, ranked behind the small group, physician-sponsored, and large commercial plans.

In summary, the two group practice plans score first and second on verification. The small group plan was highest on use of all four of the tests: CBC, urinalysis, serology, and chest X-ray. The *verification* factor score mainly reflects administration of these routine procedures. Absence of direct financial cost to the consumer is cited as a possible determinant of higher verification scores in the group practice plans.

Consumer need is inversely related in the total sample to verification factor scores. This suggests that the factor scores are representing routine laboratory and radiology work for minor complaints. For the low-need persons the group practice plans have the highest average score on this factor.

Demand has an inverse relation to verification in the large group plan but no effect in any other plan.

Persons with high verification scores are more frequently those who visited physicians characterized as 40 years of age or younger, graduated from a medical school in a country other than the United States, Canada, Great Britain, or Scandinavia, not certified, without continuing medical education courses in the preceding 12 months, with short turn-around time from his laboratory, and a positive orientation toward patients.

Continuity

Variations by plan

Two referral patterns, *referral to specialists* and *referral to paramedical workers,* are reflected in *continuity.* For ambulatory care physicians in the large group practice plan have a higher rate of referral to specialists than physicians in all other plans. A referral to a specialist occurs in 7% of the visits. One in three patients receiving care in the large group practice plan is referred to a specialist in a twelve-month period, one in five in the small group practice plan, and one in eight

TABLE 4-13

Continuity items by plan (ambulatory care)

Continuity items	Plan: All plans	Large comm	Small comm	Hosp-spon	Phys-spon	Large group	Small group
Referral to specialists							
None (% visits)	97.3	98.4	98.4	98.6	98.5	93.4	96.5
Mean/1000 persons	189	203	102	75	114	347	200
SD	480	408	335	323	378	653	496
N	1215	144	199	171	161	281	259
Referral to paramedical worker							
None (% visits)	99.1	99.6	98.4	99.7	99.3	98.8	98.8
Mean/1000 persons	56	6	37	9	65	57	126
SD	274	78	200	97	247	242	455
N	1215	144	199	171	161	281	259
Continuity of physicians [17]							
None (% visits)	32.3	23.4	15.7	13.5	13.9	46.8	32.3
Followup requested (or end of illness noted)							
None (% visits)	53.7	58.0	54.1	50.8	59.3	50.9	49.3
Followup visits							
None (% visits)	49.5	53.2	50.0	46.1	58.9	50.8	38.1
N (visits)	7320	1017	1403	977	1087	1300	1536

in the other plans. Physicians in the small group practice plan tend to refer people more frequently to paramedical workers than physicians in other plans.

A person making a doctor visit in either of the group practice plans is less likely to see the same physician he saw on his last visit

[17] Coded (yes) when the same physician was seen within the same specialty or a doctor was seen to whom the patient had been referred.

than a person making a doctor visit under any other health plan.[18]

The difference between the two group practice plans for ambulatory care appears to reflect the difference in size of the practices. Fifty-three percent of the visits to large group physicians were to the same physician within one specialty or to a physician to whom the patient was referred, in contrast to 68% of the visits in the small group practice plan. The average for the other plans is 83%.

Followup visits requested did not vary greatly across the six plans , although the rate was slightly lower for the commercial and provider-sponsored plans. It appears that the rate of followup visits is higher in the small group practice plan (62% of visits) than in all other plans (average of 50%).

TABLE 4-14
Continuity factor scores per person per visit by plan (ambulatory care).

	Plan						
Continuity factor scores per person per visit	All plans	Large comm	Small comm	Hosp-spon	Phys-spon	Large group	Small group
Low (%)	21.4	34.0	18.6	11.8	22.9	17.7	26.0
Medium	62.7	57.5	66.5	53.7	60.3	69.8	62.6
High	15.9	8.5	14.9	34.5	16.8	12.5	11.4
Mean	0.587	0.556	0.603	0.625	0.587	0.589	0.567
SD	0.101	0.090	0.091	0.109	0.112	0.099	0.096
N (persons)	1215	144	199	171	161	281	259

$F=10.9$, $df=5/1209$, $p<0.001$
$\chi^2=76.7$, $df=10$, $p<0.001$

The continuity factor score predominantly reflects the variables *followup requested, followup,* and *continuity* of medical personnel, since these variables have the highest loadings. Table 4-14 reveals somewhat the same pattern observed in the distributions of the separate indicators; the average score in the group practice plans is 0.78 (unweighted), whereas in all other plans it is 0.595. The percent distributions also indicate fewer people in the group practice plans are followed up and have continuity of physicians.

Statistical significance is reached in tests for differences among the

[18] The extent of continuity is less in the group practice plans for both ambulatory and hospital care.

plans. The greatest contributor to this significance is the hospital-sponsored plan which scores higher than any other plan. More than one-third of the persons in this plan have "high " scores in the percent distributions, compared with a little more than 10% in the group practice plans. If the plans are collapsed into plan types, the following results:

Plan type	Average score	Percent "high"
Commercials	0.572	10.7
Provider-sponsored	0.611	28.1
Group practice	0.585	12.4

Differences between the commercial and group practice plan types are not statistically significant, but the provider-sponsored plans are significantly higher than both of them.

Determinants of continuity

The continuity factor reflects a combination of two points made by Lee and Jones. There should be "a close and continuing personal relationship between physician and patient" and there should be "intelligent cooperation between the lay public and the practitioners." It is probable that this close relationship cannot develop if the patient sees a different physician each time he seeks care.[19] This has long been a criticism of the group practice plans. Officials of these plans, however, claim to make it possible for each consumer to choose his own personal physician within the group and make appointments to see that physician each time he seeks medical services. Both the data on the indicator of continuity of medical personnel and the continuity factor suggest that discontinuity remains a greater problem in the group practice plans.

In the physician questionnaire we asked the respondents to evaluate private practice and large group practice on several dimensions, one of which was the "doctor-patient relationship." The data support the expectation that community physicians are in favor of private practice. Classification of physicians according to the insurance plan covering most of their patients results in the following:

[19] Access to *some* doctor at all times and diligent records may, however, compensate for the patient's not seeing the same doctor each time. Continuity may require waiting or other inconveniences: the patient may prefer timeliness and convenience.

Plan of most patients	% Responding doctor-patient relationship is better in private practice
Commercials	70.7
Provider-sponsored	75.3
Group practice	49.5

These data reveal that about one-half the physicians in the group practice plans believe that the doctor-patient relationship suffers in this setting compared with private practice. Of further interest is the apparent correspondence between these percents and the continuity factor scores; there is a tendency for a greater proportion of physicians to endorse their own type of practice when the continuity factor scores are high.

Lee and Jones's second point, "intelligent cooperation" between the doctor and his patient, requires a certain degree of patient compliance with physician requests. The continuity factor score, reflecting a combination of "followup requested" and "followup ," incorporates the physician initiative in requiring the patient to return if needed (or indicating in the record no need for further visits) and patient compliance in returning.

Persons in the consumer sample who were classified as "high-need" had on the average higher continuity scores than those in the low-need category. For both the high-need and low-need consumers the provider-sponsored plans retain their advantage over the other plans. It is probable that the higher average scores among high-need consumers is caused by more serious illnesses, and both physician and consumer tend to have a greater interest in following up. It is in the low-need category that the gap between the group practice and the other plans is greatest.

Demand characteristics of consumers have little overall effect on the level of continuity. The factor averages are 0.586 for the high-demand category and 0.583 for the low-demand category. Comparisons between plans indicate that demand has a greater effect in the large group practice plan than in others. For example, people from lower educated families in the commercial and provider-sponsored plans have higher continuity scores than those from highly educated families. This is probably in reality a need effect rather than a true demand effect. Another demand characteristic which has a signficant effect in the large group plan is *symptom-sensitivity.*The symptom-hypersensitive category has an average continuity score of 0.601 in this plan, compared with 0.550 for those classified as either symptom-sensitive or symptom-insensitive.

classified as either symptom-sensitive or symptom-insensitive.

Physicians classified as "low" on the *limiting* dimension are more likely in most plans to provide continuous medical care (by our measures) for their patients. This effect is most dramatic in the hospital-sponsored plan and least evident in the large group practice plan. In fact, among the persons visiting physicians in the high-limiting category those in the large group practice plan have the highest scores on continuity. In the low-limiting category the hospital-sponsored plan has a higher average than all other plans. Among the remaining physician characteristics tested on this factor physician complaints concerning unnecessary visits by patients was related most strongly to level of continuity. For the total sample consumers visiting physicians who had this attitude had lower continuity scores ($p=0.01$).

There is a correspondence between *consumer* negativity toward physicians and level of the continuity score. This relationship indicates a less critical attitude toward doctors generally for those consumers who have higher continuity factor scores. The effect is consistent across all plans, but among those consumers with a low complaint rate the differences among the plans on the continuity score is greatly reduced from its level among the "high complainers."

In summary, the continuity factor score heavily emphasizes the two followup variables and the continuity of medical personnel. It generally reflects distributions of the separate indicators, with the group plans having an average score of 0.578 and the other plans 0.595. The hospital-sponsored plan has the highest average of all plans. Continuity of medical personnel (measured by the frequency of seeing the same doctor from one visit to the next or seeing a doctor to whom one is referred) is lowest in the group practice plans, with the large group practice plan having the lowest rate. This has long been a criticism of this type of plan. However, in the large group practice plan there is a higher rate of referral to specialists than in all other plans, whereas the small group practice plan makes greater use of paramedical workers.

Greater continuity was found to be associated with higher consumer need. Among the low-need consumers the gap between the group practice plans and others was the greatest. In the large group practice plan the better educated and most symptom-sensitive receive greater continuity of medical care in this plan.

The physicians with more limited backgrounds, and those with negative attitudes toward patient visitation, generated the lowest continuity scores.

CONCLUSION

The two goals in this chapter were to devise a method of assessing the content of medical services from medical records and to apply this method to medical services received by consumers in the six health insurance plans.

Our search for an answer to the first problem began in the literature on quality of medical care. There we found a great many opinions on quality of care and studies that relied on the subjective judgment of medical professionals to identify it. We selected from these opinions a statement made many years ago by Lee and Jones in their landmark work for the Committee on the Costs of Medical Care. This statement, incorporating eight articles of faith, we felt best represented the spirit of what was said by many others.

We pursued the concepts found in the articles of faith, attempting to build from them a method of measuring content of medical services. Measures of *range of services* were devised, analyzed by a technique of factor analysis, and described in terms of four dimensions: prevention, rationality, verification, and continuity. The data to measure each dimension were derived from medical records by non-medical coders. No judgments were used. The dimensions were expressed merely in terms of "more" or "less" of each type of medical service.

The second goal of the chapter led us through a detailed consideration of medical services received under the six health plans. Preventive services, as measured by our prevention factor, were more frequently provided in the group practice plans. But we were also able to show that this higher rate in the group practice plans was due in large measure to use by consumers classified as "low need" —that is, the people who are least likely to benefit from these services.[20] More preventive services were provided by the better qualified practitioners except in the group practice plans, in which the major determinant was physician attitude toward the necessity of preventive services for all people.

Rationality factor scores—measures of the thoroughness of the physician's work—were higher only in the large group practice plan, and the advantage of this plan was greatest among consumers of high need. We found consumers were sensitive to the thoroughness of the medical care they received; they were especially so in the large group practice plan as indicated by higher negativity toward physicians

[20] It may also be argued that "low need" with respect to chronic illness is *due to* a higher level of preventive services.

whose rationality scores were low. Characteristics of physicians were related to rationality. Physicians who were young, from a privileged-class background, and who attended the better medical schools provided more thorough medical services by our measures in private practice, but the effect was greatly reduced in the group practice plans. In the large group practice plan physicians' attitudes toward patients were important determinants of rationality—especially the attitude concerning patients making "unnecessary" visits.

We found more laboratory and radiology testing of all kinds in the large group practice plan. But group practice plan physicians seemed to pay less attention than other physicians to the results of these tests. The verification factor, measuring routine laboratory and radiology procedures, peaked in the group practice plans for low-need consumers. Physicians providing the most of this type of service tended to be young, trained in foreign countries, not specialty certified, without continuing medical education, and with a positive attitude toward patients. In terms of the Lee and Jones statement on the need for coordination of different medical workers, the group practice plans tended to make more referrals to specialists and paramedical workers. But, as a kind of trade-off for the above assets, continuity of medical personnel, an important factor in the doctor-patient relationship, was lowest in the group practice plans. We found that many physicians working within the group practice plans felt this was a disadvantage of large group practice. The better educated consumers are apparently able to "work the system" in the large group practice plan so that they receive higher scores on the continuity factor. Continuity apparently also concerns the patient; higher continuity scores were associated with less complaints about physicians.

The great diversity of information generated by our data on range of services cannot be adequately summed up by a few general conclusions as the above. Much more careful analysis is required to substantiate the suggested findings. But at the most general level we cannot escape the recurring impression that prepaid group practice leads to a higher rate of visits for relatively minor symptoms. When we consider only those consumers characterized by high need for medical services, many of the overall advantages found for the group practice mode cannot be consistently demonstrated.

REFERENCES

Bickner, R. E. "Measurements and indices of health," in Carl E. Hopkins (editor). *Outcomes conference I-II: methodology of identifying, measuring and evaluating outcomes of health services programs, systems and subsystems.* Department of Health, Education and Welfare, Public Health Service, Health Services and Mental Health Administration, National Center for Health Services Research and Development, U.S. Government Printing office, 1970.

Brook, R.H. "Quality of care assessment: choosing a method for peer review." *New England Journal of Medicine,* 288, no. 25 (June 21, 1973), 1323-1329.

Clute, K.F. *The General Practitioner.* Toronto: University of Toronto Press, 1963.

Cochrane, A.L. *Effectiveness and efficiency; random reflections on health services.* London: Nuffield Provincial Hospital Trust, 1972.

DeGreyndt, W. "Five approaches for assessing the quality of care." *Hospital Administration,* 15, no. 1 (Winter 1970), 21-39.

Donabedian, Avedis. *Medical care appraisal—quality and utilization: a guide to medical care administration,* Volume 2. American Public Health Association, New York (1969).

Goldsmith, S.B. "The status of health status indicators." *Health Services Reports,* 87, no. 2 (March 1972), 212-220.

Harman, Harry H. *Modern Factor Analysis.* Chicago: The University of Chicago Press, 1967.

Kerlinger, Fred N. *Foundations of behavioral research: educational and psychological inquiry.* New York: Holt, Rinehart and Winston, 1966, 544.

Lee, R. I. and Jones, L. W. *The fundamentals of good medical care.* (Publication number 22 of the Committee on the Costs of Medical Care). Chicago: University of Chicago Press, 1933.

Lembcke, P. A. "Evaluation of the medical audit." *Journal of the American Medical Association,* 199, no. 8. (February 20, 1967), 543-550.

Moody, Philip M. and Gray, Robert M. "Social class, social integration, and the use of preventive services," in E. Gartly Jaco (editor), *Patients, physicians and illness: a sourcebook in behavioral science and health.* New York: The Free Press, 1972, 250-261.

North, Robert C., Holsti, Ole R., Zaninovich, M. George and Zinnes, Dina A. *Content analysis: a handbook with applications for the study of international crisis.* Chicago: Northwestern University Press, 1963, 41-45. Peterson, O.L. et al. "An analytical study of North Carolina general practice." *Journal of Medical Education,* 31, no. 12 (December 1965), 1-165.

Roemer, M. I. "Evaluation of health service programs and levels of measurement." *HSMHA Health Reports,* 86, no. 9 (September 1971), 839-848.

Roemer, Milton I. and Shonick, William. "HMO performance: the recent evidence." *Milbank Memorial Fund Quarterly: Health and Society,* 51, no. 3 (Summer 1973), 271-317.

Rummel, R. J. "Understanding factor analysis." *Journal of Conflict Resolution,* 11, no. 4 (December 1967), 444-480.

Shapiro, S. "End result measurements of quality of medical care." *Milbank Memorial Fund Quarterly,* 45, no. 2 (April 1967), 7-30.

Williamson, J. W. "Evaluating quality of patient care: a strategy relating outcome and process assessment." *Journal of the American Medical Association,* 215, no. 4 (January 1971), 564-569.

Zetterberg, Hans L. *On theory and verification in sociology.* New York: The Bedminster Press, 1965, 40-41.

V

Family Medical Expenses

FAMILY MEDICAL EXPENSES INCLUDE payments (or debts) for services not paid for by a third-party agency, as well as insurance premiums or "prepayments." A distinction is made between "out-of-pocket" expenses (non-covered payments) and "total consumer expenses" (non-covered payments plus premiums). Out-of-pocket expense is a subject of widespread interest, but total consumer expenses represent better the consumer's budgetary problems with respect to health expenses.

From the consumer's point of view maintenence of his family's health is but one of many kinds of expense contained in the family budget. He must weigh the relative impacts of the premium and out-of-pocket expenses against some experienced standard regarding the projected health and medical care use patterns of his family. He assumes that the basic risk avoidance of extremely costly care is maintained in insurance policies, no matter what the premium cost. The question then, theoretically, is "given an expected need for health services, would the increased out-of-pocket expenses resulting from an insurance package with less coverage be more than offset by savings in the form of lower premiums?" Some of the answers to this question will be revealed in the comparative "total expense" levels demonstrated by the plans.

All of this rests on an individualistic assumption that those with fewer health care needs should not have to pay so much as those with greater needs. Unfortunately, this assumption leads to greater financial burdens for those who can least afford them, since greater need for health care resides in the lower classes (although greater demand comes from the upper classes). Under a social philosophy that includes medical care as a basic human right the financing of health services would have to be based on distributing financial responsibilities according to financial resources. To a certain extent such a system is in operation in contemporary America, since those who can least afford medical expenses must be supported by the more affluent either by charity or the welfare system. There is much evidence that the system may be less than optimal in its present form.[1]

An analysis across plans of out-of-pocket expenses and premium prices meets with several thorny problems. Out-of-pocket expenses are generated only in part by noncoverage in an insurance package.

---

[1] For instance, Steven Jonas of the Department of Social Medicine, Morrisania City Hospital, New York, says:

> In its January issue, the magazine *Fortune* said, 'American medicine, pride of the nation for many years, stands now on the brink of chaos...much of the U.S. medical care, particularly the everyday business of preventing and treating routine illnesses, is inferior in quality, wastefully dispensed and inequitably financed. Medical manpower and facilities are so maldistributed that large segments of the population, especially the urban poor and those in rural areas, get virtually no care at all. Right now, for all the fresh billions so recently poured into the system (by Medicare and Medicaid) most Americans would still be financially destroyed by a prolonged and serious illness in the family.' In its January 17 issue *Business Week* was saying, 'A lot of Americans would rather die than get seriously sick. For millions, going to the hospital means going broke, or close to it. For many more, good medical care is non-existent.' '...America is a goldmine for the fee-for-service private practitioner, whose income, assuming some basic competence in medicine, is limited solely by his personality and the hours he wants to work. It is also a money-maker for the commercial insurance companies, the proprietary hospitals, the drug and hospital supply companies and the commercial laboratories. For everybody else, most patients and non-fee-for-service health workers alike, it is most unsatisfactory.' (*Lancet,* October 3, 1970, p. 728.)

Consumers themselves may be responsible for out-of-pocket expense through their own preference behaviors. The failure of consumers to convert benefits into claims (or services) may be due to several factors. For those who subscribe to the group practice plans there may be "out-of-plan" retention of a "family doctor" or private specialist where trust and personal confidence in group physicians is not sufficient to meet psychological or perceived medical needs related to serious or intimate health care. Also, out-of-plan use by group plan consumers is sometimes attributable to impatience with bureaucratic procedures, clinic waiting time, or a "charity atmosphere," all of which may be viewed as more expensive (either financially or psychologically) than the non-covered expenses incurred through some medical visits to outside "family doctors."

Conceivably, consumer ignorance about benefits available to them or an ineptness in filing claims results in some proportion of accumulated out-of-pocket expenses. Whenever consumers initiate out-of-plan use despite coverage or fail to initiate appropriate claims, the resulting out-of-pocket expenses may be partially attributed to the plans. We might suppose that out-of-plan use by comprehensive group practice consumers is "caused" by negative features inherent in a large, rigid bureaucracy. For other plan consumers the failure to file claims is due to the plan organizations' inefficiency in keeping their consumers fully informed of their entitlements and equipped with easily managed claims forms.

To put total responsibility for consumer behavior on the health plans is, of course, inappropriate. In reporting out-of-pocket payments, we must caution the reader to keep in mind that the extent to which the data reflect relative inadequacies in the financial arrangements of an insurance plan is influenced by the degree to which out-of-plan use or failure to file claims is prevalent.

The portion of premiums contributed by employers constitutes no direct expense to the consumer. In view of the history of labor-management negotiations for fringe benefits, however, we prefer to include the employer's contribution in the premium expense to the consumer, since the contribution may be conceptually equated to wage earnings.

Other indirect expenses associated with plan use, especially in comparing direct service, group practice plans with open-market plans, may be briefly identified. Time expenses such as traveling time to the physician's office, waiting for appointments, waiting in clinics, time involved in treatment, and length of the recovery period may be interpreted as non-pecuniary (personal inconvenience) or pecuniary (non-paid time off from occupation). Finally, "psychic expenses" such as aggravation related to perceived improper, discourteous, or unsympathetic service may be very real "expenses" to some persons. Although we will not investigate "time" and "psychic" expenses, the reader may speculate about how these expenses may be distributed differentially between comprehensive group practice plans and open-market plans.

PREVIOUS RESEARCH

Studies reviewed earlier in our consideration of use also provide some background information on the topic of expenditures. For instance, the Anderson and Sheatsley study (1961) found that expenses to plan members under H.I.P. (a group practice plan with comprehensive benefits) were appreciably lower than under G.H.I. (private practice, fee-for-service), counting both the insurance premiums paid and out-of-pocket outlays for hospital and physicians' services and drugs. Moreover, a higher proportion of overall costs was met by the insurance plan for H.I.P. members than for G.H.I. members.

The Columbia University study (Trussel, Williams) in 1962 provided confirmation of these findings. They found that the premium paid for the Kaiser Plan benefit package was higher than for the other two, but the out-of-pocket expenditures were so much lower that the aggregate costs per family per year in the three plans were Blue Plan, $259, General Electric Plan, $252, and Kaiser Plan, $224. These differences are not large but are in the same direction as those reported by Anderson and Sheatsley.

Further support is given in the study of California state government employees (Perrott, 1971). Annual out-of-pocket expenditures per person for hospitalization were found to be $47.56 in the Blue plans, $42.72 in the commercials, and $21.66 in the group practice plans. For ambulatory services the expenditures were $17.07, $13.03, and $3.68, respectively. These figures were all adjusted for age and sex composition of the subscribers to each type of plan.

These studies consistently demonstrate a lower level of total consumer expense in the group plans. The differences are considerably more convincing when only out-of-pocket figures are studied than when total expenses are considered, since the prices of the group plan comprehensive benefit packages are generally higher. In our own data we demonstrated in Chapter 2 that the large group plan had the second highest average annual premium, second only to the physician-sponsored plan which includes comprehensive joint contracts with the hospital-sponsored plan. The premium level for the small group plan is lower because some of its contracts do not include hospital benefits.

OUT-OF-POCKET EXPENSES

In this chapter we have the option of using one of two estimates of the dependent variable, similar to those discussed in Chapter 3 (Use of Services).

All consumer respondents were asked the following question concerning their out-of-pocket expenses: "About how much did *you* pay . . . of your total *doctor and hospital bills* for you and your family over the past 12 months?" Respondents were cautioned to include only the expenses of family members covered under the health plan being investigated and not to include health plan premiums. Responses were forced into precoded categories: (a) no expenses, (b) $1-$49, (c) $50-$99, (d) $100-$249, (e) $250-$499, (f) $500-$749, (g) $750-$999, and (h) $1000 or more. We also collected recall information on expenses for drugs (outside the hospital) and dental services, but these will not be dealt with here.

The second source of information was the medical records and claims forms. From the medical records the total volume of care was translated into dollars by applying the CRVS conversion factor supplied in the physician questionnaire. For hospital care the value of the non-physician services was established from the hospital bill or, in the case of the large group practice in which no bill is prepared, from the rates supplied us by the hospitals involved. When claims records were kept and made available to us by the health plans, we were able to find out from them the amount paid by the insurance; when they were not kept (large group and physician portion of the small group plan) or not made available (physician-sponsored plan), the fiscal responsibility of the plans was determined from the benefit packages.

The out-of-pocket expenditures at which we arrived for each of these estimates are not quite the same. In the medical-records estimate all expenses that were not paid by the insurance plan being studied were identified as out-of-pocket. We had no way of knowing whether the amounts over and above that assumed by the study plan were paid by the consumer himself or by another source on his behalf—for instance, workman's compensation or another insurance plan. Data from the consumer questionnaire, however, are more likely to reflect only money that the consumer himself pays. This is the traditional estimate of out-of-pocket expenses.

When means are reported for the consumer recall data, they are derived from taking the midpoints of each of the categories listed above. For the highest category ($1000 or more) the midpoint turned out to be $1200. This use of category midpoints reduces the variances, thus stabilizing the mean because it is not influenced by extreme values.

Variations by Plan

We compared estimates of out-of-pocket expenditures between the questionnaire item and the calculations from medical records and claims. For the total sample of consumer questionnaires we obtained an estimate of $58.91 per person per year for all families in the sample. The per person rate was calculated by using the midpoints of the ranges described previously and dividing by the number of insured people in the family. This was preferred to a "per family" rate, since family size would certainly influence family out-of-pocket expenses, and family size is not consistent across the six plans. The second estimate was also from consumer questionnaires but included only those consumers for whom we also had medical records information. This questionnaire estimate was $56.79 per person—almost identical to that of the total sample. As expected, the estimate obtained from the medical records was higher—$77.02 per person, which we believe reflects the different meaning of "out-of-pocket" involved in calculating the medical records estimate. The differences between the total questionnaire sample estimate and that of the medical records is statistically significant at the .02 level ($t=2.46$, $df=831$).

Although it is logical to explain the difference between the two estimates in this way, there is the further question of the probable accuracy of the respondent recall. We cannot claim to be testing this with the comparison described above, since the two estimates are not of the same parameter. Other studies have indicated that consumer recall for medical expenses is rather more reliable than consumer estimates of use (National Center for Health Statistics, 1963). Comparisons were made in these studies between detailed interview data and data obtained from self-reporting, and there was observed a slight tendency for the latter to result in overestimation. There were apparently no consistent tendencies to over-report or under-report by sex, age, and education level.

We conclude that use of the consumer questionnaire data in this instance is justified and probably provides a reasonable estimate of actual out-of-pocket expenditures.[2] We are further encouraged by examining the differences between questionnaire and medical records estimates for each plan. Statistical tests run on differences in these estimates for each plan show that none of them is significant at the .05 level. Generally we find variances in the medical records data to be very large and Ns relatively small, so that the mean is unstable and differences that appear to be substantial are not reliable. The closest correspondence between estimates is in the two group plans, indicating that we probably did not miss a great many out-of-plan medical records in our medical records study of these plans.

We now turn our attention to the questionnaire data from the total sample and a comparison of the plans on out-of-pocket expenses. Table 5-1 shows the large group practice plan to have the lowest per person figure, followed by the small group plan. Statistical tests of the differences between means reveal that the large group plan has a significantly lower mean than all other plans at the 0.001 level. The highest per person figure is found in the hospital-sponsored plan. Differences among the other plans generally do not attain this level of significance.[3]

A majority of consumers and their families in the large commercial and group plans have spent less than $20 per person out-of-pocket for doctor and hospital bills during a 12-month period. Because the direct service plans offer several contracts providing physicians' services without any deductible or coinsurance, some proportion of their consumers may accumulate no out-of-pocket expenses despite having consumer services. In the large commercial plan, on the other hand, deductibles and coinsurance make it virtually impossible to report no

---

[2] We should again emphasize that the data from the questionnaires probably represent amounts actually paid by the consumer personally. Since it does not include amounts paid on his behalf by some other agency, it does not actually represent the total liability assumed by sources other than the study plan (as do the medical records data).

[3] Statistical significance with samples this large is relatively easy to obtain. This means we are sensitive to rather small differences in contrast to the analysis with the subsample in which only the larger differences were picked up. As a precaution against rejecting the null hypothesis too readily, we look for significance at the 0.001 level.

TABLE 5-1
Annual out-of-pocket expenditures
per insured person for doctor and hospital services,
by plan from 3 sources

	Plan						
	All plans	Large Comm	Small comm	Hosp-spon	Phys-spon	Large group	Small group
Consumer questionnaire: total sample							
None (%)	43.4	47.3	39.6	33.5	27.0	63.7	33.7
\$1 - \$20	15.0	7.1	9.6	9.0	15.0	21.0	23.3
\$20 - \$75	20.4	19.2	22.0	20.3	33.4	11.4	24.0
\$75+	21.2	26.4	28.9	37.2	24.7	3.9	19.0
Mean (\$)	58.91	79.20	68.86	108.14	73.79	13.10	50.02
SD	127.70	182.45	113.23	176.93	122.85	48.25	92.44
N (families)†	2,621	480	483	280	232	584	563
		$F=29.0$, df=5/2615, $p<0.001$					
		$\chi^2=353.3$, df=15, $p<0.001$					
Consumer questionnaire: subsample							
Mean (\$)	56.79	45.72	58.43	99.96	70.16	12.28	60.83
SD	120.38	103.25	93.20	171.84	120.02	68.65	121.12
N (families)	689	113	103	125	94	136	119
		$F=7.74$, df=5/683, $p<0.001$					
Medical records and claims							
Mean (\$)	77.02	84.23	102.78	94.86	138.59	12.44	54.25
SD	203.25	170.78	227.15	150.56	375.17	67.17	139.59
N (families)	689	113	103	125	94	136	119
		$F=5.49$, df=5/683, $p<0.001$					

†Only those in the study year 12 months are included.

out-of-pocket expenses when medical services have been used (except in the special prepaid clinic portion of this plan).

The group practice plans clearly outperform the remaining plans in terms of keeping expenses down for those who use services. In addition to those who had all their bills paid by the group practice plans, around 20% of their consumers paid \$1 to \$49 out-of-pocket. In the commercial plans only about 9% of consumers had out-of-pocket expenditures between \$1 and \$49. Given the prevalence of \$100 deductibles per person in these plans, we may assume that few of these expenditures were accompanied by reimbursements.

Only one-third of the provider-sponsored plans' consumers had no out-of-pocket expenses (i.e., no services). Slightly more of these persons had lower expenses than those in the commercials. Again controls built into open-market type benefit packages indicate that these "small expenses" represent the full charges made for consumed services. On the other hand, small expenses accumulated under the large group plan due to nominal coinsurance fees reflect services that have value well beyond the out-of-pocket expenses reported.

About 11% of consumers in the large group plan had moderately high annual out-of-pocket expenses ($20 to $75). Partial coverage for maternity in many of the contracts certainly contributed to these figures. Only 4% of the large group plan consumers had heavier expenses ($75 or more). We may suspect that some of these expenses were due to out-of-plan use.

The small group practice plan had greater proportions of consumers with both moderate out-of-pocket expenses (24%) and heavy expenses (19%) than reported for the large group plan. The increased expenses associated with the small group plan arise from the open-market type coverage for hospitalization. Extensive benefits for physicians' services in the hospital, however, are responsible for less frequent instances of high out-of-pocket expenses under the small group plan than under the open-market plans. In general the small group plan reduces the risk of very high out-of-pocket expenses below the levels that may be typically expected under the open-market plans.

An emphasis on hospitalization benefits and concomitant deemphasis on benefits for physicians' services, especially with respect to ambulatory care, may be responsible for a substantially higher frequency of high out-of-pocket expenses under the hospital-sponsored plan (37% reporting expenses of more than $75). The hospital-sponsored plan consumers had the largest out-of-pocket expense of all ($108.14). A combination of high-need consumers and limited coverage for out-of-hospital services appears to be a likely determinant.

Of the two commercial plans the small plan reported lower average out-of-pocket expenses ($69 vs. $79 for the large plan). This difference is unexpected, because our large commercial plan sample atypically included some consumers who had comprehensive coverage for physicians' services through a group practice clinic.

In conclusion, our data support the common sense proposition that out-of-pocket expenses will vary directly with the degree to which benefits are extensive and controls restricted. The clearest demarcation between our study plans in terms of insurance coverage is between the large group practice plan and the open-market plans, whether commercial or provider-sponsored. The small group plan strikes a middle ground between the extremes, combining features of the large group plan with respect to benefits for physicians' services and features of the open-market plans with respect to benefits for hospitalization. Out-of-pocket expenses are most clearly interpreted in terms of this trichotomy; expenses are lowest under the large group plan, highest under the open-market plans. Out-of-plan use in the group plans drives up expenses under these plans from what it would be if all care were taken within the plan.

If, for purposes of comparing these data with previous research, we combine the plans into plan types, the following figures for expenses per year are obtained.

Plan type	Mean out-of-pocket per person	Percent spending $75+
Commercials	$76.49	27.0
Provider-sponsored	$96.86	33.1
Group practice	$18.39	6.0

Our study agrees with previous research in that the group practice plans are characterized by the lowest out-of-pocket expenses. But we find that the provider-sponsored plans have significantly higher out-of-pocket expenses than the commercials, in contrast to the study of California state government employees (1971). As to actual levels of expense, our estimates are higher than those reported in the California study for the commercials and provider-sponsored plans but lower for the group plans.

Organizational Determinants

The ranking of plans according to comprehensiveness of benefit packages which was reported in Chapter 2 proves to be a rather accurate predictor of out-of-pocket expenses for the extremes. That is, the two group practice plans ranked as most comprehensive in their benefits and as generating the least out-of-pocket expense; the hospital-sponsored plan ranked least comprehensive and generates the highest out-of-pocket expenses. The small commercial and physician-sponsored plans perform better than expected, whereas the large commercial performs worse, slipping from third ranked under comprehensiveness to fifth under out-of-pocket expenses. The record of the large commercial plan may be due in part to the relatively low level of demand by consumers (on demand indicators discussed in Chapter 2 this plan ranked last).

Out-of-pocket expenses, however, cannot be considered apart from use of medical services. Although it is desirable from the consumer's perspective to have low out-of-pocket expenses, this presumes that he is able to obtain medical care when he needs (or wants) it.

With few exceptions the group plans do not apply deductibles. On the other hand, commercial and provider-sponsored plans require, with few exceptions, a rather substantial deductible. These facts introduce a problem of interpretation to the comparative analysis of out-of-pocket expenses, especially when such expenses are small or moderate in magnitude.

If a family is insured under an open-market plan that applies the common $100 per person deductible, an out-of-pocket expense which totals less than the required deductible may represent the full value of services received. That is, not having satisfied the deductible, the out-of-pocket expense represents an accurate estimate of charges for services received. A family receiving services under a group practice plan, however, may receive a quantity of services valued well beyond the associated out-of-pocket expenses. That is, the reported out-of-pocket expense most probably underrepresents the value of services received.

Identical out-of-pocket expenses accrued under an open-market plan, on the one hand, and under a group practice plan, on the other, are *not equivalent* in terms of the common denominator by which we may assess their economic and health significance. The common denominator, of course, is the quantity or value of services received that is tied to a given out-of-pocket expense. A more penetrating analysis of our data requires that we ascertain for each of the plans what levels of out-of-pocket expenses arise for given degrees of use.

Table 5-2 reports distributions and average out-of-pocket expenditures by health plan and by three categories of use. *Low use* is defined as no reported hospitalization during the preceding 12 months and no doctor visits during the past three months. (We assume that the relative number of doctor visits during a three-month period is somewhat representative of the relative number of doctor visits over a 12-month period.) *Medium use* is defined as no hospitalization during the past 12 months and one or more doctor visits over the past three months. Finally, *high use* is determined by one or more family members hospitalized during the preceding 12 months. (We assume that doctor visits are associated with hospitalizations).

Although the group practice plans are generally responsible for lower out-of-pocket expenses, regardless of use, differences between the large group practice plan and the open-market plans increase drastically with use. A general increase in differences among the plans is reflected in the changes in the chi-square statistic and Gamma from low-use to medium- and high-use categories. When hospitalization is involved, out-of-pocket expenses under the open-market plans (including the small group plan that provides open-market insurance for hospitalization) are four to six times those in the large group plan.

TABLE 5-2
Annual out-of-pocket expenditure per insured person for doctor and hospital services, by plan and level of use

	Plan						
	All plans	Large comm	Small comm	Hosp-spon	Phys-spon	Large group	Small group
Low use							
None (%)	73.2	84.9	72.6	70.2	46.1	78.4	69.5
$1 - $20	8.0	4.8	4.4	2.8	19.6	7.5	18.7
$20 - $75	13.1	7.3	13.5	22.2	17.2	12.9	11.8
$75+	5.7	3.1	9.6	4.8	17.1	1.2	0.0
Mean ($)	17.41	10.03	20.04	24.65	50.42	7.18	5.53
SD	52.27	58.50	49.84	89.41	96.59	23.59	13.41
N	796	185	200	89	84	153	85
	$x2=96.4$, $df=15$, $p<0.001$ ($\gamma=.14$)						
Medium use							
None (%)	34.4	21.9	20.9	22.4	11.1	63.9	30.7
$1 - $20	17.5	7.4	14.7	15.5	16.5	20.1	31.9
$20 - $75	25.8	29.1	29.9	23.2	51.4	14.4	23.4
$75+	22.3	41.6	34.5	38.8	21.0	1.7	14.0
Mean ($)	56.74	88.59	88.44	115.00	56.84	11.02	29.60
SD	91.38	108.93	126.29	195.40	69.80	54.06	44.13
N	891	171	147	92	93	266	122
	$x2=272.5$, $df=15$, $p<0.001$ ($\gamma=.36$)						
High use							
None (%)	22.6	6.1	11.1	11.7	27.7	52.5	3.2
$1 - $20	16.5	15.2	11.8	8.2	3.6	31.5	14.5
$20 - $75	21.3	31.0	24.9	15.1	20.5	4.9	56.8
$75+	39.6	47.8	52.2	64.9	48.2	11.1	25.5
Mean ($)	104.80	133.33	121.01	165.05	150.28	23.22	107.42
SD	130.21	175.59	135.25	165.57	202.24	57.22	134.61
N	523	65	123	92	47	143	53
	$x2=224.3$, $df=15$, $p=0.001$ ($\gamma=.34$)						

These mean dollar differences range from $84 to $142. Plan differentials on out-of-pocket expenses are considerably smaller in the low-use category.

About 11% of the consumer families in the large group plan who have experienced hospitalization reported out-of-pocket expenses of $75 per person or more. Even the relatively small dollar figure for the large group plan in the high-use category appears to be distorted upward by expensive out-of-plan use.

The commercial and physician-sponsored plans exhibit somewhat lower out-of-pocket expenses in medium and high use in terms of average out-of-pocket expense compared with the hospital-sponsored plan. When hospitalization is involved, the hospital-sponsored plan, which emphasizes hospitalization benefits was surprisingly expensive (average expense $165). Nearly 65% of the consumers of the hospital-sponsored plan having one or more family members hospitalized reported out-of-pocket expenses of $75 or more. These findings may reflect not only the limitations of the benefits provided by the plan but also the relatively high hospitalization rates in this consumer population.

Looking at these same data in terms of types of insurance plan, we find the commercial type outperforms the provider-sponsored type at all levels of use. The ranking of plan types reported for all families is thus not altered by introducing a control for use. We should recognize that this result is heavily influenced by the high annual out-of-pocket expenses reported by consumers in the hospital-sponsored plan. The data are as follows:

Plan	Mean out-of-pocket expenses for Low users	Medium users	High users
Commercials	$12.79	$88.56	$128.40
Provider-sponsored	$33.89	$93.24	$161.60
Group	$7.04	$12.39	$28.28

We also note that the superior performance of the "group" plans is mostly due to the large group plan and that the small group plan behaves very much like the other open-market plans when it comes to heavy expenses due to hospitalization.

As we have discussed earlier, one of the important determinants of level of out-of-pocket expense is out-of-plan use. In the group plans this is conceptualized simply as care received from providers not associated with the physician group. In the other plans out-of-plan use is thought of as care received that is insured but, for one reason or another, not claimed. In this study we have not studied the latter type of use, although the data would require information on this topic by careful analysis of the relation between benefit packages and care received.

Out-of-plan use has a particular influence on financial outlays for consumers in the group plans because of the comprehensive nature of the benefit packages. This is true especially in the large group plan, since medical services received within the group would require very little out-of-pocket expense.

By analysis of medical records data we are able to outline a "profile" of the out-of-plan user in both group plans. The results should be regarded as tentative because of the small sample sizes.

In the small group practice plan 15% of the families in the medical records sample (the subsample) had one or more insured members with out-of-plan medical services. The mean per person out-of-pocket expense for these families was $106 for the 12 months, compared with $58 for the remainder of the families who had no out-of-plan use. More medical services were received out-of-plan by families of *high need* than by families of *low need.* Among the indicators of need the best predictor of out-of-plan use was presence of chronic illness in the family. In this plan there was a tendency for families with *low-demand* characteristics to go outside the plan more than the *high-demand* families. The demand indicator of ethnic minority had the highest proportion of medical services outside the plan. Overall, however, the effect of the demand characteristics appears to be much less than the effect of the need indicators. Most of the outside care was received outside the hospital (73%) and none of the care was associated with pregnancy. We thus have a picture of the out-of-plan user in the small group plan as likely to be of minority ethnic status with relatively high medical needs. The reason for out-of-plan use is not evident in these data, since it is not accompanied by highly negative attitudes toward physicians. Organizationally we might suspect access to be a problem for these people, since the small group plan has relatively few clinic locations in the metropolitan areas.

Out-of-plan ambulatory and hospital use was found in 14% of the families in the large group practice plan subsample—almost the same proportion in the small group plan. On the average these families paid $30 per person out-of-pocket for their medical care, compared with $11 for those without out-of-plan use. As in the case of the small group plan, high-need persons in the large group plan contributed more heavily to out-of-plan use than those characterized as low-need. Differences became evident, however, in terms of demand indicators. Persons going outside the large group plan were more likely to be in high status occupation, income, and ethnic categories. Additionally, these people tend to be symptom-hypersensitive and perceive no influence of health insurance on their use of medical services. Of all the demand indicators, *negativity toward physicians* proved to be the best indicator of out-of-plan use in the large group plan; those with three or more complaints about physicians (on the Guttman scale of negativity toward physicians) had much higher rates of out-of-plan use. Again, most of this care was ambulatory, with 64% of the medical care bits (physician encounters) occurring in this setting. Visits for pregnancy were involved to a small degree. The portrait of the out-of-plan user in the large group plan is quite different from that in the small group plan. In the former it appears that the higher status consumers who are hypersensitive and have no serious financial limitations (as evidenced by the attitude toward the influence of insurance on use patterns and their income levels) are most likely to go out of the plan for some of their medical care. Motivations for out-of-plan use are suggested by the negative attitude toward physicians. If one wished to extrapolate from the evidence, it is possible that these people are reacting to the negative attitude of physicians in the large group plan toward "unnecessary" visits (noted in Chapter 3) by turning to private physicians.

Out-of-pocket expenses for the two group plans, therefore, are inflated by out-of-plan use, apparently to a greater extent in the small group plan. The demand characteristics are again shown to be greatly significant in the large group plan. They use more medical services both within and outside the plan. The question naturally arises, what is the proportion of *low-demand* consumers in this plan who are deterred by organizational features from receiving the care they need? The relatively low rate of service to the low-demand consumer noted in Chapter 3 is apparently not attributable to out-of-plan use in the large group plan.

Consumer Characteristics

Consumer expenses are dependent in part on the use of services. Similarly, expenses of the insuring agency are also dependent on the use of services (or claims resulting from charges for the use of services). The consumer (or consumer group) hopes to control expenses by negotiating an insurance contract that provides the most comprehensive coverage for the premium paid. The insuring agency may attempt to reduce its expenses by insuring consumer groups whose use experience constitutes a "low risk" to the insurer.

In Chapter 2 the six plans were compared as to whether they rated by experience and, if so, to what relative degree they were successful in avoiding "high-risk" consumer groups. The group practice plans include the highest proportion of "high-need" families. The hospital-sponsored plan, despite experience rating, covers a considerably greater proportion of high-risk consumers than the remaining open-market plans. The large commercial plan and the physician-sponsored plan were most successful in avoiding "high risks," as measured by need indicators.

The level of consumer need in a plan will influence the distribution of consumer expenses in that plan. The relation between need and consumer expenses is due essentially to differential-use patterns associated with high- and low-need consumer groups. Although out-of-pocket expenses differed by plan in the same order as the extent of benefits provided under those plans, this meaningful relationship between benefits and expenses may be distorted by varying levels of need among memberships in the plans. The relatively small out-of-pocket expenses reported by consumers in the group practice plans, in light of the greater proportion of "high risks" in these plans, indicate even more forcefully their expense-saving advantages, particularly for consumers who are likely to use them heavily.

The large commercial plan and the physician-sponsored plan include fewer "high risks" among their consumers than the other plans. This finding may partially explain why out-of-pocket expenses in these two plans were lower than those reported for the other open-market plans.

Table 5-3 is a direct test of the impact of need on the relation between the scope of benefits and out-of-pocket expenses. In Table 5-3 our most powerful index of need—family members with chronic illnesses—is held constant and out-of-pocket expenses are reported across plans. "High risk" is here defined as "high need."

Regardless of the number of family members who have chronic illnesses, the large group practice plan demonstrates substantially lower levels of out-of-pocket expenses than any of the other plans. This is particularly the case for families with two or more chronically ill members (not shown in Table 5-3). The out-of-pocket expense for consumers in the large group plan in the category of families with chronic illnesses ($16.32 per person) represents "savings" ranging

TABLE 5-3

Annual out-of-pocket expenditures per insured person for doctor and hospital services, by plan and incidence of chronic illness in the family

	Plan						
	All plans	Large comm	Small comm	Hosp-spon	Phys-spon	Large group	Small group
No chronic illnesses							
None (%)	52.3	51.0	53.8	52.0	37.1	57.3	58.0
$1-$20	15.6	7.1	9.7	9.3	16.1	34.5	21.4
$20-$75	18.6	18.8	23.6	21.1	28.6	6.4	15.4
$75+	13.5	23.1	12.9	17.6	18.2	1.7	5.2
Mean ($)	33.86	49.92	34.75	42.01	49.34	8.28	17.64
SD	78.51	98.28	80.10	89.91	84.88	22.61	52.82
N	1,238	303	284	126	137	212	176
	$\chi^2=169.2$, df=15, $p=0.001$ ($\gamma=0.19$)						
One or more chronic illnesses							
None (%)	37.2	41.2	14.4	18.3	11.8	66.5	28.5
$1-$20	13.5	6.9	10.1	8.8	13.3	13.6	24.8
$20-$75	21.9	20.2	20.9	19.7	43.9	14.7	28.6
$75+	27.5	31.8	54.7	53.2	32.0	5.2	18.2
Mean ($)	80.71	130.03	124.67	162.78	83.25	16.32	51.91
SD	159.14	226.34	234.86	209.99	104.59	58.66	92.59
N	1,184	174	188	153	86	361	222
	$\chi^2=369.1$, df=15, $p<0.001$ ($\gamma=0.28$)						

from $36 per person (small group plan) to $147 (hospital-sponsored plan) below the mean out-of-pocket expenses accruing under the other plans. Not surprisingly, such "savings" are much diminished for families with no chronic illness. The proportions of consumers in families with chronically ill family members having small out-of-pocket expenses ($20 or less) over the past 12 months are, again, particularly high in the group practice plans (80% in the large group plan, 53% in the small group plan) relative to the open-market plans (from 48% in the large commercial to 24% in the small commercial). These differences are considerably diminished in the "low-need" consumer category. Finally, comprehensive benefits for physicians' services under the group practice plans resulted in only a slight increase in out-of-pocket expenses for chronically ill consumers. Increases in out-of-pocket expenses for these consumers, however, were substantial in all the open-market plans.

We note that the introduction of a control, this time for chronic illness, has an effect on the overall plan rankings. For families of low need the open-market plans perform quite uniformly without significant differences on out-of-pocket expenditures. In the families with reported chronic illnesses, however, the hospital-sponsored plan has the highest average, as it did for the "heavy" users (see Table 5-2).

When these data are summarized in terms of the types of plan, the following results are obtained:

	Mean out-of-pocket expenses for families	
Plan	with chronic illness	without chronic illness
Commercials	$128.56	$46.16
Provider-sponsored	$142.89	$44.88
Group	$ 19.75	$ 9.46

When "need" is defined as it was in previous chapters (age, chronic illness, short-term illness, and women of child-bearing age), a significant difference is found between low- and high-need for the entire sample on all indicators except "women of child-bearing age." Average per person outlay for the low-need category is $52.15, whereas it is $70.43 for the high-need category. Means on per person outlay for these two categories for each plan are the following:

Plan	High-need families	Low-need families
Large commercial	$112.39	$69.95
Small commercial	$ 96.84	$58.23
Hospital-sponsored	$142.50	$82.73
Physician-sponsored	$ 75.31	$69.83
Large group	$ 12.51	$11.78
Small group	$ 54.81	$37.71

The group plans continue to demonstrate lower out-of-pocket expenses within the low-need category, but the differences are considerably diminished from those observed in the high-need category. For instance, in the latter category the average per person outlay in the hospital-sponsored plan is $129 more than in the large group practice plan; in the low-need families the difference is $71. Differences in out-of-pocket expenses by consumers in the low-need as opposed to the high-need categories within each plan are slightest in the group plans and the physician-sponsored plan.

The most striking statistic in the out-of-pocket expense data with respect to need is the very high amount of money put out by high-need families in the hospital-sponsored plan. To put the figures in perspective it was reported for the year 1967 (which was the second year of the study) that total expenditures per person in the United States—both public and private—for physician and hospital care amounted to $132.25 (California Medical Association, 1968). Out-of-pocket expenses *alone* for these services in the high-need families in the hospital-sponsored plan amount to $142.50 per insured person. Even when low-need families are included, the total in this plan comes to $108.14 (see Table 5-1). If we were to add to this the amount paid in premiums (which we shall do in a later section of this chapter), the total would far exceed the national average.

In addition to health care needs, health plan consumer populations may differ in the degree to which health care is valued or afforded. The *demand* for services results basically from the interaction of self-perceived need for health care and the propensity to seek professional aid. Social definitions of illness as well as scientific knowledge of symptoms and pathologies influence consumers' decisions on health care needs. Values related to the urgency of seeking professional care as well as the financial resources (including insurance) to cover the concomitant expenses motivate consumer illness and health behaviors.

Previous research has abundantly illustrated that knowledge, values, skills, and resources which predispose to greater use of professional health care services are distributed unevenly among the various social strata of society. Generally the demand for services increases with rising social class status. Several intercorrelated measures of social position frequently applied in survey research provide proxies for factors underlying demand. Income may indicate financial ability to afford medical services, life styles that emphasize the role of "family doctor," and access to medical care. Education is an indicator of one's awareness of social alternatives, including the benefits of early diagnosis and treatment by professional medical personnel. Occupation, as is the case with education, provides varying opportunities for exposure to skills and knowledge relevant to one's relation to an often bureaucratic system of delivering and financing health care services. Cultural norms inherent in ethnic strata influence a person's response to symptoms and to the professional services available in the community.

The fact of health insurance itself may constitute a critical stimulation of demand. Significantly, the degree of demand enhancement (termed "moral" hazard by economists) may vary with the scope of benefits and controls constituting the benefit package. The deterrent effect on use of deductibles, coinsurance, and ceilings is illustrated by consumers' perceptions of the impact of insurance coverage on their families' use of services. Consumers in the open-market plans are far less likely to view their insurance as having had a positive impact on their use of medical services than are consumers in the group practice plans. That is, increased demand as an outcome of the former type of insurance coverage is significantly depressed below levels reported for the group practice plans (see Table 2-8).

Since demand factors, along with need factors, influence use, the "risk" composition in a given plan population is affected by the distribution of highly educated, high-income, professional consumers among the plans. An analysis of consumer indicators of demand in Chapter 2 showed the highest demand in the small group practice, small commercial and large group plans (in that order) and demand decreasing from the physician-sponsored through the hospital-sponsored to the large commercial (lowest demand).

Using indicators of demand as we did in previous chapters (income, education, occupation, insurance influence on use, and symptom sensitivity), we find that the large group practice plan has significantly lower out-of-pocket expenses, regardless of whether we consider high- or low-demand categories. For the total sample out-of-pocket expense is about the same for low-demand ($57.91) as for high-demand ($54.77) categories.

Data on per capita outlays for each plan by category of demand are the following:

Plan	High-demand families	Low-demand families
Large commercial	$ 81.73	$ 79.86
Small commercial	$ 81.41	$ 56.32
Hospital-sponsored	$ 129.66	$ 110.51
Physician-sponsored	$ 65.37	$ 68.20
Large group	$ 14.13	$ 13.14
Small group	$ 49.91	$ 51.75

It is interesting to note that for every plan in the sample except the large group plan the per person average for the *high-need* families exceeds the average for the *high-demand* families. It thus appears that demand does not exert as much influence as need on the amount of money the consumer is required to pay out-of-pocket. The slightly higher figure in the large group plan for high-demand families corresponds to the fact that these families tend to go out of plan more frequently for medical services.

The influence of demand factors on financial outlay of consumers can be further studied by examining the relation between changes in out-of-pocket expenses from low- to high-demand categories and changes in the amount of medical services received.

Using doctor's care units to represent an estimate of the volume of care received, we found in Chapter 3 that four of the plans registered increases in volume of service from low- to high-demand categories; the hospital-sponsored and the small group plan registered decreases. Our present statistics indicate, however, that out-of-pocket expenses are higher in the hospital-sponsored plan for the high-demand category. It therefore appears that in this plan the high-demand consumers receive a smaller volume of care but pay a higher price. In the hospital-sponsored plan, the out-of-pocket increase from low- to high-demand categories is 17%, whereas volume of services *decreases* 10%. It seems possible from these estimates that there is a significant price shift in this plan for the high status consumer. The one plan in which out-of-pocket expenses increase from low- to high-demand categories but do not exceed percent increase in the volume of services is the large group plan. Of course, in this plan there are no direct charges by the physician for services received within the plan; increases that are observed must be attributed to out-of-plan use. Another plan in which volume increases at a greater rate than out-of-pocket expenses is the large commercial plan.[4]

We conclude that the tendency for the higher status consumer to incur disproportionately higher out-of-pocket expenses, is most evident in the hospital-sponsored plan.

---

[4] The data in this discussion involve consumer estimates of out-of-pocket expenses from questionnaires in the total sample, and calculations of volume of services from the medical records sample. The astute reader will recognize this comparison might be better made using the same sample for both measures. This was checked, and the data do not lead to different conclusions. There is, however, the further consideration that perhaps the differences discussed might be explained by changes in rates of hospital admission from the low- to the high-demand category, since the measure of volume of services includes only physician services and does not take account of expenses due to hospital day-rate charges. This was also checked, and merely adds further support to the argument. In the hospital-sponsored plan, for instance, hospital admission rates *decrease* markedly from low to high demand categories (39% decrease). This is also true for the physician-sponsored plan (69% decrease). Therefore we conclude that the differences in out-of-pocket expenses for the high-demand people compared with the low-demand people cannot be explained through hospital admission rates.

The key indicator of the demand concept in this instance would seem to be income. Our discussion above, however, suggests that fluctuations in the level of out-of-pocket expenses are not entirely (in some cases, not at all) due to true demand effects. By "true demand effect," we mean higher demand leading to greater consumption of services. This we have shown to be true in Chapter 3, but when speaking of monetary outlays for services there is the possible additional effect of the "sliding scale" of medical fees. This corollary effect of demand characteristics results in greater expenditures for some people, but not necessarily greater services. Until we deal in the next section with total expenses (including premium outlays), we cannot conclude that the higher out-of-pocket expenses for the

TABLE 5-4

Annual out-of-pocket expenses
per insured person for doctor and hospital services,
by plan and family income

	Plan						
	All plans	Large comm	Small comm	Hosp-spon	Phys-spon	Large group	Small group
Less than $11,000							
None (%)	50.5	55.5	42.6	56.3	30.9	69.6	43.3
$1-$20	12.6	6.2	12.0	6.4	19.8	13.7	19.4
$20-$75	19.4	17.6	22.7	16.3	33.1	10.8	22.8
$75+	17.5	20.8	22.7	31.0	16.2	5.9	14.5
Mean ($)	57.66	85.73	57.29	91.08	68.27	14.09	44.94
SD	141.22	216.71	103.04	163.23	134.64	36.74	89.81
N	372	318	208	161	138	283	265
	$\chi^2=142.6$, df=15, $p<0.001$ ($\gamma=0.12$)						
$11,000 *or more*							
None (%)	33.2	31.4	31.9	16.7	19.8	55.8	23.4
$1-$20	18.9	9.2	8.5	13.3	8.0	29.5	28.1
$20-$75	21.3	16.6	23.2	27.5	34.6	12.5	24.1
$75+	26.5	42.9	36.3	36.3	37.6	2.1	24.4
Mean ($)	60.48	72.64	83.95	105.39	82.58	12.87	56.23
SD	107.16	83.56	123.25	161.93	102.90	58.95	96.96
N	1150	141	245	111	92	281	280
	$\chi^2=248.5$, df=15, $p<0.001$ ($\gamma=0.20$)						

high-demand consumers in the hospital-sponsored plan are due to physician charges; they may conceivably be due to less comprehensive benefits purchased by consumers with greater personal financial resources.[5]

Out-of-pocket expenses are examined in Table 5-4 separately for lower and higher income families. Those with family incomes of $11,000 and more spend an average of $61 per person over and above what their insurance pays; those with incomes below the $11,000 level pay $58. Looked at another way, some 18% of those with lower incomes have out-of-pocket expenses of $75 per person or more, compared with 26% of those with higher incomes. Between-plan comparisons for each income category reveal a familiar pattern: highest average expenses are found in the hospital-sponsored plan, regardless of income, and the lowest in the group practice plans. Overall differences among the plans are greater in the upper income brackets as revealed by the increase in size of the statistics χ^2 and γ.

Within-plan comparisons reveal that the "rich" pay more out-of-pocket, except in the large commercial and large group practice plans in which there is very little difference.

Combining the plans into types, we obtain the summary information:

Plan	High-income families	Low-income families
Commercial	$76.92	$80.41
Provider-sponsored	$97.90	$83.43
Group practice	$19.32	$18.42

Ethnicity proves to have an interesting effect on out-of-pocket expenditures, similar to that illustrated above for income. For instance, majority ethnic status families (primarily white North American or North European) in the provider-sponsored plans pay an average of $113.72 out-of-pocket per person, whereas the minority

---

[5] But the general health insurance literature shows that higher income persons have *wider* benefit packages (Anderson and Feldman, National Health Survey, Somers and Somers, etc.).

status families (blacks, Mexican-Americans, South European) pay \$47.87 in those plans. The reverse is true in the commercial plans, in which majority ethnic status persons pay \$66 and minority status persons pay \$106. In the group practice plans the majority status persons also pay more, and this is greatly influenced by the out-of-plan use by these people in the large group plan. Demand characteristics in the provider-sponsored plans seem to lead to greater financial outlays for the people from the upper socioeconomic and cultural strata to a greater extent than in other plans. It seems likely that this is due in part to the acceptance of plan payment as "payment in full" by physician members of the physician-sponsored plan for persons from families below the \$8000 per year income level (Chapter 2).

In summary, we found that families in the large group practice plan paid significantly lower medical costs than families in the other plans. The greatest out-of-pocket expenses were found in the hospital-sponsored plan. In terms of plan types, the group plans had the lowest average expenditures, with the commercial plans next, and the provider-sponsored plans the highest.

Controlling for use of medical services, families reporting both doctor visits and hospitalizations (heavy users) paid one-sixth of the costs if they were in the large group plan. As use of medical services increased, especially with hospitalization, the expenses of consumers in the small group plan rose to resemble those of the open-market plans. The hospital-sponsored plan again had the highest per person costs. By plan type the provider-sponsored plans had the highest averages for all three types of user: light, medium, and heavy.

Out-of-plan use was studied for the group practice plans only, and it was found that approximately 15% of the families in both group plans went outside the plan. The out-of-plan user was generally from a high-need family, but in the large group plan the high-demand families tended to go outside the plan. In the small group plan the *low-demand* families were out-of-plan users. In the large group plan negative attitudes toward physicians were associated with outside use.

High-need families spent more out-of-pocket in all plans. Demand factors were found to have very little influence on out-of-pocket expenses. For every plan the high-need families paid more expenses than the high-demand families. In the hospital-sponsored plan, when out-of-pocket expenses were compared with volume of services received, the high-demand consumers paid more expenses than the low-demand consumers but received fewer medical services.

In the provider-sponsored plans there is an increase in

out-of-pocket expenses for people with higher incomes and persons of minority ethnic backgrounds. This trend is reversed in the commercial plans and may be the result of providers agreeing to accept as full payment the amount paid by the plan for families below a certain income.

TOTAL EXPENSES

In an analysis of consumer expenses particular attention to the total burden of health care expenses on the consumers' family budget is important. Assuming the consumers' perspective, out-of-pocket expenses for medical services, hospital services, and insurance premiums constitute pecuniary losses. Consumers whose families use few services may be especially concerned with the expense of insurance premiums. Consumers whose families use many medical services may be relatively more concerned with expenses over and above the benefits provided by insurance.

Out-of-pocket expenses for drugs and dentistry are other important sources of expense for health maintenance and ideally should be computed as portions of total consumer expenses. In this volume, however, we define total consumer expense in terms of out-of-pocket expenditures only for doctor and hospital services and insurance premiums.[6]

Previously we presented data establishing that lower out-of-pocket expenses are associated with plans whose benefit packages are more comprehensive. Since comprehensiveness usually commands higher premiums, it becomes possible that for certain kinds of consumers the premium price of comprehensive coverage actually inflates consumer expenses beyond what would be expected with less expensive (less comprehensive) benefits. That is, since catastrophic loss would be covered under most benefit arrangements, expensive but broadly comprehensive coverage may in reality reflect "overinsurance" in which such benefits are not likely to be converted to services. On the other hand, certain kinds of consumers may be "well-insured." That is, for a given increment in premium expense, they might recover a much larger portion of their losses due to out-of-pocket expenses.

Total expenses were computed on a per person basis, similar to the computation of the out-of-pocket portion of the figure, as derived

---

[6] Data were collected on dental and drug expenditures and may be reported at another time.

from the estimates in the consumer questionnaire, with averages computed from midpoints of ranges checked. Premium data were not obtained from the questionnaire, since we frequently found that consumers did not know what premium they paid because it was deducted at the source or paid by the employer in total or part. Premium levels, consequently, were obtained from the insurance plan or, when this was not possible, from the literature on employment group benefit packages.

It is recognized that the premium portion of total expenses does not rise in direct proportion to family size. Rather most benefit packages have a single premium rate for families of "three or more," so that additional dependents do not raise the premium. Converting the premium figure to a "per person" rate, therefore, makes plans with the larger families look less expensive because the per capita rate is reduced by the presence of larger insured family units. This operates particularly against the provider-sponsored plans in which average family size is about 2.7 compared with 3.0 or more in the other plans. The influence of family size is documented later.

Variations by Plan

Consumers in the group practice plans pay less for their total medical care than consumers in other plans. At the 0.001 level of significance the large group plan has a lower per person average than all other plans in the study, including the small group plan. At the same level of significance the small group plan is less expensive than all others except the large group and small commercial plans.

The plans follow types on total expenses: the group plans are the lowest, the commercial plans are next, and the provider-sponsored plans are most expensive (with nearly identical means). As we stated above, the large group plan is significantly less expensive overall than the small group plan. Within the commercials, the difference between the large and small plans does not attain significance ($t=2.03$). Between the provider-sponsored plans there is almost no difference.

Out-of-pocket expenses, discussed previously in this chapter, were greatest for the hospital-sponsored plan and lowest for the large group practice plan. Table 5-5 shows that this ranking for these two plans is maintained with the addition of premiums. The figure for the hospital-sponsored plan is almost double that for the large group plan.

In terms of these total expenses it appears that the plans are ranked very similarly to their ranking on comprehensiveness of benefit packages. In Chapter 2 we found that the group practice plans sold the most comprehensive packages; these data reveal that they also are the least expensive in terms of total consumer outlay. Conversely, we also found that the provider-sponsored plans sold the least comprehensive packages; these data reveal that they are the most expensive in total consumer outlay. Our judgment in Chapter 2 that the provider-sponsored plans are "too expensive for what they offer" is substantiated by these data.

TABLE 5-5
Distributions of annual out-of-pocket expenses plus annual premiums (total expenses) per insured person for doctor and hospital services, by plan (percent)

	Plan						
	All plans	Large comm	Small comm	Hosp-spon	Phys-spon	Large group	Small group
Total expenses							
\$1-\$75	17.9	14.8	22.7	7.1	12.4	19.2	22.9
\$75-\$150	46.7	46.6	36.8	34.1	37.8	62.9	48.1
\$150-\$225	16.3	17.3	16.3	26.6	17.4	10.6	15.7
\$225+	19.1	21.3	24.2	32.2	32.4	7.2	13.3
Mean (\$)	166.42	183.32	159.79	234.62	230.42	123.61	141.88
SD	152.95	214.40	124.59	197.64	184.91	69.56	106.59
N (families)	2,621	480	483	280	232	584	563

$\chi^2=233.8$, df=15, p=0.001
F=34.7,df=5/2615, $p<0.001$

Purchasing health insurance under the large group practice plan results in average savings per person of \$18 annually (compared with the small group plan) with \$111 (compared with the hospital-sponsored plan) for the consumer. Nearly one-third of the families in the provider-sponsored plans pay an average of \$225 *or more* per person for physician and hospital services (and insurance). In the large group plan only 7% of the families pay this much.

Previous research, discussed earlier in this chapter, has arrived at very similar conclusions on total expenditures.

It is interesting to compare the figures in Table 5-5 to national statistics on expenditures per person for physician and hospital care. We reported earlier in the chapter that the national average in 1967 was \$132 per person. Our data reveal that the overall average for the insured populations in these six plans is \$166 per person. The difference cannot be explained by heavier than national use of services under these plans, since ambulatory use and hospital use are not greatly different. Much of the difference can be explained in terms of higher costs of services in California, especially in the Los Angeles urban area, and also by the fact that some of our data reflect expenditures in 1968, when prices had risen somewhat from 1967. In the provider-sponsored plans the average per capita expenditure is *double* the national average. In the large group plan the per capita average is lower than the national average—the only plan for which this is true. In a period of steep rises in the price of physician and hospital services the performance of the large group plan in controlling costs is impressive. The inflationary influence of the provider-sponsored plans, on the other hand, provides by contrast a convincing illustration of the ineffectiveness of cost controls in these plans.

As a summary, the data on total expenses per person are collapsed into plan-types, so that generalizations to the performance of plans similar in structure might be ventured.

Plan	Mean total expenses	Percent above $225
Commercial	$177	22%
Provider-sponsored	$233	32%
Group	$126	8%

Organizational Determinants

In our discussion of the structure of the six study plans we noted the tendency of the provider-sponsored and commercial plans to rely on consumer constraints to control costs (through deterrents in benefit packages), whereas the group practice plans concentrate more on provider constraints. Through the mechanism of experience-rating the provider-sponsored and commercial plans are able to adjust premium levels in accordance with risk. Consumers that are likely to use more insured medical services are either excluded altogether or required to pay a higher rate.

We are interested, then, in the effect of *use* on financial outlay (see Table 5-6).

TABLE 5-6
Total expenses per insured person for doctor and hospital services, by plan and level of use

Total expenses	Plan: All plans	Large comm	Small comm	Hosp-spon	Phys-spon	Large group	Small group
Low use							
\$1-\$75	23.6	25.2	35.4	4.6	25.2	13.7	28.1
\$75-\$150	50.7	52.4	39.0	53.4	37.4	67.5	54.2
\$150-\$225	13.3	12.5	15.5	26.6	5.8	5.3	17.7
\$225+	12.5	9.9	10.1	15.2	31.6	13.4	0.0
Mean (\$)	36.24	117.70	115.70	164.66	225.63	133.44	111.93
SD	91.79	99.84	74.27	101.63	195.66	71.71	38.73
N	796	185	200	89	84	153	85
	$\chi^2=112.7$, df=15, $p<0.001$ ($\gamma=0.14$)						
Medium use							
\$1-\$75	16.4	6.1	15.1	13.7	5.8	19.0	36.6
\$75-\$150	47.1	42.6	41.4	28.2	48.5	64.7	35.4
\$150-\$225	18.7	22.5	12.6	31.7	23.7	14.2	17.0
\$225+	17.8	28.8	31.0	26.5	21.9	2.1	11.0
Mean (\$)	160.53	185.17	179.59	228.93	191.28	119.37	117.79
SD	112.25	122.30	133.81	209.54	133.36	69.47	76.07
N	891	171	147	92	93	266	122
	$\chi^2=167.2$, df=15, $p<0.001$ ($\gamma=0.33$)						
High use							
\$1-\$75	13.3	4.8	11.4	3.4	2.2	26.7	18.8
\$75-\$150	35.1	39.2	27.2	22.7	19.2	52.0	38.1
\$150-\$225	20.7	29.3	23.5	22.8	28.2	10.4	21.4
\$225+	30.9	26.7	37.9	51.1	50.4	10.9	21.7
Mean (\$)	204.88	219.05	205.07	287.38	305.62	120.78	181.46
SD	149.61	192.62	149.32	199.74	226.86	70.84	154.60
N	523	65	123	92	47	143	53
	$\chi^2=109.4$, df=15, $p=0.001$ ($\gamma=0.34$)						

A steady climb in consumer outlay for the entire sample at higher levels of use is illustrated. For the "low-use" category (no reported hospitalizations in one year and no reported office visits in three months) the total expenditure per person is \$136.24; for the "medium-use" category (doctor visits reported) it is \$160.53, and for the "high-use" category (doctor visits and hospitalizations) the figure is $204.88 per person. In each instance the figure for both group practice plans is below the average for the total sample.

Considering either out-of-pocket or total expenses at any level of use, the provider-sponsored plans are the most expensive. The fiscal advantages of the group practice plans, however, are not maintained for people who are low users. For them the major portion of their medical expenses are the premiums. These people pay more in the large group practice plan than in any other.

Over-insured is a term often coined for low users who pay more in premiums than they receive in services. The whole point of insurance, however, is that no individual family can expect or anticipate its illness or accident rate in a future year. From the perspective of the insurance plan, the low-risk consumers are helping to meet the cost of those who need more medical care. The total expenditures per person of those who use more care (medium and high users) in the large group plan do not rise as they do in other plans but remain constant (the lower level in the higher use categories cannot be substantiated without knowing the family sizes in these categories). If the low-risk families were to drift away from the group plans to buy less expensive benefit packages, this would eventually load the group plans with even higher risk populations and cause increases in premium levels.

If the data were extended to a national population insured under one of the six plans in this study, it is clear that the group plans would be most economical. For those with relatively few medical needs, however, such a system would be more costly than the present one.

Although we may discuss "over-insurance" for the low-risk category, "under-insurance" is also prevalent for those who need more medical care. For "high-use" patients, for whom expensive hospitalizations are encountered, the advantage of the large group plan is well demonstrated. In the provider-sponsored plans *more than* 50% of the high-use families spend $225 per person or more. The comparable figure in the large group plan is 11%.

There is no doubt that families who are low medical care users can spend too many premium dollars for comprehensive benefits ("over-insured"). Commercial major medical policies insure them against heavy financial loss, and the reductions in premium expenses more than balance out what extra amounts of out-of-pocket expenses they may incur. On the other hand, families with high-use patterns "save" considerably by paying a higher premium for comprehensive benefits under the group plans.

Another view of patient financial outlay and use of service is to calculate the price per unit of medical service in each plan. This involves the doctor's care index used earlier in this chapter in relation to out-of-pocket expenditures. The index converts all physician services, whether received in the home, office, or hospital, into units based on the California Relative Value Studies and conversion factors supplied by physicians in our study. The total expense estimates from the questionnaire answered by families in the medical record study are compared with the actual records. Hospital charges are excluded. If plan types were considered, the group plans appear to offer the "best buy,"followed by the commercials and the provider-sponsored plans.

A valid comparison of prices would include hospital admission rate. Hospital days constitute the most expensive aspect of medical care services. Modifying the price per unit to take account of hospital days may be done by dividing price per unit by hospital days. This reduces the theoretical price-per-unit. The lowest adjusted price occurs in the small commercial plan, which has a heavy liability for hospitalization. The large group plan has the highest adjusted price because of economies associated with a very low average number of hospital days[7]

Plan	Price per unit	Hospital days per person	Adjusted price index
Large commercial	$1.82	0.126	14.4
Small commercial	$1.65	0.194	8.5
Hospital-sponsored	$2.26	0.152	14.9
Physician-sponsored	$2.25	0.150	15.0
Large group	$1.66	0.071	23.4
Small group	$1.35	0.104	12.9

In Chapter 2 the large group plan was estimated to be operating "in the black." According to the adjusted price figures,this is possible because the large group plan drastically reduces hospitalization rates but at the same time charges its consumers the second highest average premium rate of the six study plans. Chapter 3, however, revealed that the lower rates were most evident for the high-need and the low-demand families, suggesting unmet medical needs.[8]

[7] But this analysis, one must emphasize, makes no judgment on the medical or human necessity (justification) for the medical or hospital services rendered.

[8] By the same token, these and other consumers may well be over-serviced in the "free choice" (commercial and provider-sponsored) plans because of well-known fee incentives. Further studies of health status outcome are clearly needed to settle this issue.

Consumer Characteristics

Data on total consumer expenses has been presented in terms of per person rates. Because premiums do not increase linearly with increases in number of insured people in a family unit, the first consumer characteristic we wish to study is *family size.* The per person designation tends to favor the plans with more large families. When family size is controlled, the following data are produced.

Plan	Total expenses ($) per person for Single persons	Couples	Couples and dependents
Large commercial	210	285	138
Small commercial	184	231	150
Hospital-sponsored	194	327	245
Physician-sponsored	387	246	167
Large group	172	153	108
Small group	150	184	146

Earlier analysis revealed that the large group plan has the lowest total consumer expense, except for consumers with low use of medical services. Another exception may now be added to the general finding: for single consumers the large group plan has a higher rate of total expenses per person than the small group plan. Single people spend more on doctor and hospital services in the physician-sponsored plan than in any other plan. This high figure is a combination of both high premiums and high out-of-pocket expenditures; the physician-sponsored plan has the highest out-of-pocket expenses for single persons.

The financial advantage of the group plans begins to be evident in two-person families. Couples in the large group plan, for instance, have "savings" averaging from $31 per person (compared with the small group plan) to $174 per person (compared with the hospital-sponsored plan) in this type of family unit. Again, in larger family units (with dependent children) the large group plan has the lowest per person rate and the hospital-sponsored the highest. In all cases the total expenses per person in the larger families are lower than those in the two-person family—the effect of premium formulation discussed above. In the larger families the only remarkable difference among plan rates is between the large group and the hospital-sponsored; otherwise averages per person are relatively constant.

We conclude from these data that the low total expenses per person recorded for all families in the group plans may be partially explained by the fact that the average family size in those plans is large (3.2) compared with the average in the provider-sponsored plans (2.7). Generally, however, considering plan types, the group plans have a lower total expense average than the other plan-types. The data by plan type confirm this. The ranking of the three plan types is consistent regardless of family size.

	Total expenses ($) per person for		
Plan	Single persons	Couples	Couples and dependents
Commercial	206	274	142
Provider-sponsored	246	297	218
Group	169	158	114

Turning to a consideration of the impact of consumer need on level of total expense, we found for the total sample that the high-need consumers had a higher per person total expenditure ($179) than the low-need families ($163). The most important determinants of level of expense were *age* and presence of *chronic illness.* For instance, when the average family age is 41 years or more, total expenditures averaged $222 per person compared with $145 per person for the younger families. Regardless of level of need as measured by our indicators, the two group plans maintained a lower level of consumer expense than the other four plans.

The combined influence of comprehensive benefit packages and constant premiums regardless of risk, is demonstrated for the large group plan by within-plan comparisons between the low-need and high-need categories as follow:

Plan	High-need families	Low-need families
Large commercial	$219	$175
Small commercial	$190	$149
Hospital-sponsored	$268	$205
Physician-sponsored	$240	$230
Large group	$124	$125
Small group	$144	$131

For every plan in the study except the large group plan the total expenses of the families with greater medical need are higher than families with less medical need. In the large group plan the averages per person from one category to the other are almost identical. This "softened" financial liability in the large group plan perhaps in large measure explains why this plan attracts the largest proportion of families defined as "high-need." This was established in Chapter 2 by measures on a number of indicators of need or "insurance risk." The small group plan ranked second on the need index. Financial outlays, as reflected in the above figures, suggest that high-need consumers selecting either of the group plans are, indeed, making a "rational" choice.

The greatest financial liabilities for the high-need families fall on those selecting the hospital-sponsored plan. A great many high-need consumers select this plan, however, since it ranks third behind the group plans in terms of the need measures employed in Chapter 2. The reasons for this "irrational" choice on the part of families with high medical needs might be found in the hospital-sponsored plan's "experiment" with community-rating.[9] This plan was forced to abandon community rating because of the drift of high-risk families into and low-risk families out of the plan. The result was a population that was difficult to insure at competitive rates. We speculate that the abandoning of the community-rating system has not yet resulted in a reversal of this drift. Our data indicate that the high-need families would do better financially in any other plan in the sample—but particularly well in the large group practice plan. Of course, it is not logical to assume that the fiscal situation between the plans would remain constant if the risk composition within the plans were to change radically.

Another influence on rationality of choice is the requirement that alternative plans were to be offered along with the group practice plans. Thus, when such a choice is available, the consumer has the option of taking a group practice plan or some other alternative—a situation that encourages selection according to medical need. In other situations no such requirement for alternatives exists, and consumers therefore may become "assigned" by employers or even trust funds to the health insurance plan chosen for the consumer group as a whole. It might be predicted that such assignment—particularly in the instance of high-need families assigned to one of the provider-sponsored plans—will result in relatively high consumer dissatisfaction with financial protection. We will study this in the next chapter.

We found earlier that *demand* did not have much influence on out-of-pocket expenses for the sample as a whole. In relation to total expenses, however, we find that the low-demand category has a significantly higher level of expense ($169 per person) than the high-demand category ($154 per person). This relationship is maintained for all plans except the small commercial, for which the high-demand consumers pay more. The influence of demand characteristics is shown by the following data on total expenses per person:

---

[9] Moreover, many employment groups have no choice about the plan in which they are to be enrolled. The decision is made by the employer or even a labor-management trust fund.

Plan	High-demand families	Low-demand families
Large commercial	$181	$183
Small commercial	$167	$155
Hospital-sponsored	$236	$240
Physician-sponsored	$204	$230
Large group	$121	$131
Small group	$140	$145

Each of the demand indicators related to socioeconomic status demonstrated greater expenditures for the lower status families (income, education,and occupation). Since the demand effect was generally not found in relation to out-of-pocket expenses alone, the influence of total expenditures comes primarily from the premium structure, responding to greater medical risks in the lower socioeconomic classes. Those with fewer financial resources, therefore, are usually required to pay more for their doctor and hospital services than the more well-to-do.

A more detailed examination of the relation between total expenses and family income shows that the impact of medical expenses on the lower income category (less than $11,000 per year) is greatest in the hospital-sponsored plan. In this plan people in this stratum pay more than those with better incomes ($232 per person average vs. $206 average). At the other extreme, as usual, is the large group plan, in which expenditures for doctor and hospital care in the lower incomes amount to $129 per person. It is in this income bracket that total expenditures are perhaps the most important, since here we find the greatest medical need combined with the lowest personal financial resources. Because of methods of deriving premiums, and a relatively low level of comprehensiveness of benefits, the hospital-sponsored plan aids the low-income people the least in avoiding high expenses. Consumers in the physician-sponsored plan do not fare much better, since the low-income people here pay an average of $221 per year. In the commercial plans there is a considerable lessening of the financial squeeze (i. e. high medical expenses combined with low incomes). Of the two commercial plans, the small plan average is lower for the low income-category: $144 per person compared with $195 per person in the large plan. Expenses are reduced sufficiently in the small commercial plan that they compare very favorably with those in the small group plan in which we found the low income consumers paying an average of $140 per person.

If total expenditures are calculated for plan types, the ranking of the types is very clear for the low-income consumers. These consumers in group plans pay an average of \$131, compared with \$186 in the commercials and \$229 in the provider-sponsored plans.

Another way of viewing the impact of medical expenses on low-income families is to calculate the percent of families in each plan who incur very heavy expenses—that is, \$225 or more per person per year. Use of this measure does not change the general conclusion that the group plans result in the greatest savings and the provider-sponsored plans result in the greatest financial burdens. But within these types we note that the small group plan has the smallest percent of families incurring heavy expenses: 11.8%. In contrast to this the hospital-sponsored plan has 33% in this category among the low-income families.

Our discussion centers on the relation between total expenditures for medical care in the various plans and total personal financial resources. This relationship may be examined more precisely by calculating a *per capita income* for each family in the study and relating to this the *per capita expenditures* for medical care.[10] We found that families paid out an average of 5% of their per capita incomes for doctor and hospital expenses (out-of-pocket plus insurance premiums). For each plan in the study the percents were as follows:

	Percent of per capita income spent on medical care		
Plan	All families	Low income	High users
Large commercial	6.6	7.8	10.7
Small commercial	4.4	5.1	16.9
Hospital-sponsored	7.1	9.2	8.7
Physician-sponsored	6.3	8.1	12.2
Large group	3.8	5.5	5.9
Small group	3.8	4.4	6.3

[10] Family income is derived from the consumer questionnaire. The question was worded, "what was your total *family* income *before taxes* for (study year)? Include in the total your spouse's income, income from rentals, investments or other jobs"? This was followed by 10 categories ranging from "\$0-\$4999" to "\$30,000 and over—please specify."Per capita income for the family was calcuated by dividing the mid-point of the range checked (or, in the case of the open-ended category, the mid-point assigned from frequency distributions of answers was \$55,000) by the number of members in the family.

The largest percentage of family income under conditions of heavy use (involving hospitalization) is taken by the small commercial plan, no doubt because of its very high premium rate and concomitant weak benefit structure. Under conditions of least family financial resources the hospital-sponsored plan is most expensive to the consumer.

Overall it appears that the best buy in health insurance among the six plans from a financial perspective is either of the group plans, followed by the small commercial plan. A low-income family, however, will find total expenses under the large group plan heavier than in either the small group plan or small commercial plan across the board. The greatest control over heavy expenses due to use of medical services is demonstrated by the large group plan, although these figures do not show the savings to the consumer to be remarkably greater than either the small group or the small commercial plan.[11]

In summary, families paid, on the average, 5% of their per capita income for medical and insurance services. The lowest percent (3.8%) was in the group practice plans, and the highest (7.1%) in the hospital-sponsored plan. The 2 group plans have the lowest per person total expenses, followed by the commercials and the provider-sponsored plans in that order. This ranking follows the earlier ranking given for comprehensiveness of benefits. Under conditions of low use (not predictable, of course, in advance) medical services in the large group plan are more expensive than in the small group plan or either commercial plan. The greatest advantage of the large group plan is under conditions that result in high use of medical services. In the provider-sponsored plans total health expenses were double the national average.

In terms of price paid vs. services received, the large group plan is the most expensive and the small commercial the least expensive.[12] This is caused mainly by adjustment for hospital days and thus indicates that the major economy achieved by the large group plan is by gross reduction in hospitalization.

The influence of community rating in setting premiums (whereby no adjustments are made for risk) has no effect in the large group plan in which no differences between high-need and low-need families are exhibited. In all other plans people with greater medical needs pay more.

---

[11] In offering these judgments it must be emphasized that a high proportion (usually more than 50%) of health insurance premiums in most employment groups is paid by the employer.

[12] No judgment is made on the medical necessity of the doctor and hospital services rendered. Indeed, other studies suggest much over servicing, particularly for elective surgery, in the open-market fee-for-service plans.

For low-income families the "best buy" from a financial perspective is the small group or small commercial plan. For families who are heavy users of medical care the best buy is the large group plan. The most expensive plan for this category of consumer is the physician-sponsored plan.

CONCLUSIONS

Out-of-pocket expenses and total consumer expenses were lower in the group practice plans (particularly the large group plan) than in the commercial or provider-sponsored plans. This relationship was evident despite the greater proportional representation of consumers with "high-need" and "high-demand" characteristics in the group practice plans.

Discrepancies in consumer expenses between the group practice plans and the "free choice" plans were related to use patterns. Families using relatively few services "saved" considerably less through group practice plan membership than did families using greater quantities of services. Although "savings" in the form of diminished out-of-pocket expenses characterized the experience of consumers in the group practice plans, upward distortion of the reported out-of-pocket expenses in these plans due to out-of-plan use may have under-represented savings that actually occur. This may be particularly pertinent in the case of high-need or high-demand families who tend most often to incur high out-of-pocket expenses under the large group plan, through out-of-plan care both in and out of the hospital.

Out-of-pocket and total consumer expenses under the small group plan were substantially higher than such expenses incurred under the large group plan. These differences were not significantly altered by statistical control for "need."

The hospital-sponsored plan exhibited the highest total expenses. This was most evident with respect to total consumer expenses when high premiums were added to generally high out-of-pocket expenses.

Perhaps the most crucial indicator of health plan performance is its impact on total expenses for medical services, especially for families whose personal financial situation is most vulnerable to high medical expenses. Among the low-income families the small group plan performs very well in showing the lowest portion of family income going to pay for medical services—whether the payment be direct, as in out-of-pocket expenditure, or indirect through insurance premiums. But when families use medical services heavily the advantage of the large group plan is evident. It must be observed, however, that "heavy users" among the large group plan families are still relatively light users of expensive hospital facilities. It is here, with costs and expenses related to hospitalization, that the large group plan effects its most telling economies. That these economies appear to be associated with lower hospital use rates among the low-demand (especially low-educated) families in the large group plan suggests the possibility of "under-servicing." This provides a promising area for further research into the effects on use and expenses of large, bureaucratically organized, prepaid group practices.

REFERENCES

Anderson, Odin and Sheatsley, Paul B. "Comprehensive medical insurance: a study of costs, use and attitudes under two plans." Research series No.9, Health Information Foundation, New York (1961).

California Medical Association. "Recent patterns of total and personal health care expenditures in the United States." *Socioeconomic Report,* 8, no. 10 (September 1968).

Columbia University School of Public Health and Administrative Medicine. "Family medical care under three types of health insurance." Foundation on Employee Health, Medical Care and Welfare, New York (1962).

National Center for Health Statistics. "Measurement of personal health expenditures." *Vital and Health Statistics,* 2, no. 12 (June 1963).

Perrott, George S. *Federal employees' health benefit program: enrollment and utilization of health services 1961-1968.* Washington, D.C.: Public Health Service, Health Services and Mental Health Administration, 1971. See also: Perrott, George S. "Federal employees health benefits program: utilization of hospital services." *American Journal of Public Health,* 56, no. 1 (January 1966), 57-64.

VI

Consumer Opinions

CURRENT NATIONAL DEBATES accompanying social change in the financing and delivery of health care services often devolve on the effects of increasingly bureaucratized or, as maintained in some circles, "socialized" structures on the quality of medical care. Spreading risks across broad-based populations and "prepayment" for direct services are viewed by liberals, on the one hand, as effective means for providing increased financial access to professional medical care for large numbers of Americans whose budgets and insurance are inadequate to meet the soaring costs of care. Moreover, shared facilities and knowledge are seen as facilitating both quality medical care and efficiency.

Conservatives, on the other hand, argue that efficiencies attributed to large group practice operations at best, or to nationalized insurance and health care at worst, are in practice enormous wastes which inevitably plague bureaucracies. Instead of increased access to care, it is argued that long waiting lists for attention, cumbersome and frustrating clinic procedures, and few opportunities to establish "family doctor" relationships result in decreased use. Moreover, for those who receive services negative incentives built into bureaucratic systems reduce the physician's interest in his patients and ultimately the quality of care given.

Although the considered opinions of professionals have been expressed publicly, consumers whose welfare is the center of interest have not often been surveyed properly as to their opinions. That is, consumers whose health care experiences have occurred within the entrepreneurial solo practice context and the quasi-"socialized" group practice system have not been adequately compared as to their feelings about such matters. In this chapter such comparisons are pursued with respect to two opinions: (1) satisfaction with the extent of *financial coverage* for medical and hospital expenses and (2) satisfaction with *medical care* received.

Previous research on consumer opinions of their plans has generally concluded that greater satisfaction with financial coverage is found in the group practice plans, but this is accompanied by less satisfaction with medical care in these plans (Anderson and Sheatsley, 1961; Medical Advisory Council to the California Public Employees Retirement System, 1971). This literature on consumer satisfaction, although instructive, has failed to define standards by which plans may be compared. The use of highly generalized, forced-choice questionnaire items or open-ended semistructured interviews has led to inadequate specification of consumer complaints. Nonspecific survey questions have elicited uniformly high levels of consumer satisfaction which are difficult to interpret because of an unwieldy array of possible points of reference for response. In-depth interviewing has produced rich detail in consumer criticisms and expressed need, but without standardized responses.

The degree to which expressions of satisfaction (or dissatisfaction) reflect objective features of services or subjective factors such as pre-enrollment attitudes and knowledge of the plan has not been systematically explored. As a consequence, the significance of measured consumer satisfaction as a criterion for assessing the quality of services has remained equivocal.

In this chapter a somewhat more flexible method for measuring and reporting satisfaction together with some initial attempts at relating satisfaction to specific frames of reference may constitute a step forward in the interpretation of consumer opinions about health insurance plans.

SATISFACTION WITH FINANCIAL COVERAGE

A questionnaire item served as our source of data for analysis of consumer opinions of financial coverage presented in this chapter. The question asked was "how satisfied are you with the extent of *financial coverage* for medical and hospital expenses?"

Responses to this question were registered in the form of check marks along a visual line scale whose endpoints were labeled "highly satisfied" and "highly dissatisfied," respectively. Seven hashmarks symmetrically spaced between the endpoints were provided to facilitate spatial judgments by respondents and to allow the analyst greater flexibility in post hoc assignment of categories than is permitted with the conventional pre coded forced-choice format (agree-disagree-no opinion).

A review of the frequency distributions of responses suggested the following optimally interpretable categories: (1) *highly satisfied,* including checked responses between the appropriate endpoint of the scale and the first hashmark to the right; (2) *highly dissatisfied,* including checkmarks between the "highly dissatisfied" endpoint and the first hashmark to the left; (3) *uncertain,* including everything between the extremes. These groupings have the admitted disadvantage of including a great degree of variation within the "uncertain" category. But we thought separating out the extreme attitudes would provide clarity that would be lost by a more nearly equal division of the scale. We feel quite certain that those we have classified in the extreme categories are unreservedly "for" and "against" the insurance plan in question, whereas those between the extremes probably have less stable evaluations.

Variations by Plan

Percentages of consumers who reported varying degrees of satisfaction with financial coverage under the six plans are presented

TABLE 6-1

Opinion of financial coverage by plan (percent of respondents)

Opinion of financial coverage	Plan						
	All plans	Large comm	Small comm	Hosp-spon	Phys-spon	Large group	Small group
Satisfied (%)	22.1	23.6	1.7	19.1	5.7	46.3	15.9
	17.8	17.1	14.5	10.3	19.8	24.8	17.9
	10.9	6.4	9.8	5.9	11.7	13.9	14.6
	8.7	9.2	9.8	7.1	16.9	4.2	8.9
	17.5	24.1	17.6	19.1	18.7	4.3	23.0
	5.9	2.0	14.8	4.8	6.9	0.8	5.8
	6.5	5.5	8.2	8.9	12.3	1.0	7.3
	3.5	2.5	7.1	4.9	2.5	1.8	2.1
Dissatisfied	7.2	9.5	6.6	20.0	5.6	2.9	4.5
N	2750	473	560	293	242	565	616

$\chi^2=671$, df=40, $p<0.001$ ($\gamma=0.14$)

in Table 6-1. For purposes of the initial examination of variations by plan we have not collapsed the original categories used in the questionnaire. Subsequent analysis will use the collapsed categories.

Among the study plans the large group practice plan clearly stands out in terms of the favorableness with which its consumers view financial coverage. Nearly half the consumers in this plan register extreme satisfaction, and this is more than twice the proportion found in this category in the closest competitor, the hospital-sponsored plan. The large group practice plan evokes a substantially greater percentage of very satisfied persons as well as the lowest percentage of the very dissatisfied.

Thus opinions on financial coverage expressed by consumers in this plan appear to reflect measured advantages in the scope of coverage provided and consequent consumer expenses. Further exploration of the origins of these opinions is pursued later in this chapter.

The small group plan compares generally well with the open-market plans on opinions of financial coverage. Differences between this plan and the open-market plans are not so substantial as they are in the large group practice plan nor always positive. The percentage of small group practice plan consumers reporting highest satisfaction was greater than all but the hospital-sponsored plan. The rate of high *dissatisfaction* in this plan was lower than recorded for any of the open market plans.

The *large commercial plan,* apparently in accordance with its general ranking on coverage provisions, secures the greatest percentage of persons who express highest satisfaction with their financial coverage among the open-market plans. Combining the top two categories (as we will do in subsequent tables), high satisfaction is expressed by 41% of the consumers in the large commercial plan, compared with 29% in its closest open-market competitor—which is, surprisingly, the hospital-sponsored plan. If consumer opinions, however, are gauged by *dissatisfaction* rather than *satisfaction,* a different picture obtains. Fully one-fifth of the consumers in the hospital-sponsored plan express extreme dissatisfaction with their financial coverage. This is more than twice the rate found in the large commercial plan which has the second highest percent of highly dissatisfied customers. It is interesting that the two provider-sponsored plans each have nearly equivalent percents of consumers in the extreme categories. In all other plans there is a considerable propensity for consumers to register extreme satisfaction rather than extreme dissatisfaction.

There appear to be two striking truths revealed by the data in Table 6-1. First, we observe a much higher rate of extreme satisfaction among consumers in the large group practice plan and a corresponding low rate of disenchantment. Second, the greatest rate of dissatisfaction with coverage is in the hospital-sponsored plan.

Other than these major differences, consumer opinions are not remarkably different among the plans.

As for the tendency found in other studies of consumers to be satisfied rather than critical, we can report similar trends. Looking at "all plans" in Table 6-1, we find a preponderance of respondents in the first four categories (60%), which are "satisfaction" categories, and an additional 18% who could not decide whether they were satisfied. In view of health plan experiences we have documented in earlier chapters, one might expect a somewhat more critical consumer evaluation. This raises the suspicion, suggested at the outset of this chapter, that consumer opinion is influenced by factors other than accurate evaluation of objective merits of the health insurance plan.

If the study plans are collapsed into three types, there is a consistent ordering of types regardless of whether we use extreme satisfaction or extreme dissatisfaction as the ranking criterion. The group type elicits the most satisfaction (41%) and the least dissatisfaction (3%). Commercial plans rank second according to the consumers, with 20% satisfied and 9% dissatisfied. The least satisfactory type of health plan is the provider-sponsored, with as many consumers dissatisfied as satisfied (15%).

We thus conclude that there are differences among the study plans in consumer opinion of financial coverage.[1] The greatest difference in satisfaction is between the large group practice plan and all other plans and in dissatisfaction between the hospital-sponsored plan and all other plans.

Organizational Determinants

A patient's opinion of his financial coverage will vary according to the comprehensiveness of his health insurance plan. The large group practice plan which provides the most financial coverage would therefore be expected to have a higher percentage of satisfied enrollees.[2]

When plans are ranked according to comprehensiveness of coverage, out-of-pocket expenses incurred, and expressed

---

[1] The χ^2 and γ statistics in Table 6-1 suggest that the relationship between plan and opinion is significant but not strong. Under conditions of collapsed opinion or plan categories, the χ^2 statistic remains significant at <0.001 whereas G increases from 0.14 reported in Table 6-1 to 0.46 for the crosstab of *plan type* by collapsed opinion categories.

[2] The measures highly satisfied and highly dissatisfied are referred to as satisfied and dissatisfied to simplify the discussion.

dissatisfaction with financial coverage, the large group practice plan ranks first on all three criteria. This plan has the best coverage, results in the lowest expenses, and has fewest dissatisfied customers. In second place is the small group practice plan and in last place, the hospital-sponsored plan.

Beyond these consistencies the plans tend to shift their order, depending on the measure used. For instance, in the physician-sponsored plan the benefit packages ranked next to the lowest in comprehensiveness. Out-of-pocket expenses reflected the scantiness of the coverage. Table 6-1, however, indicates a relatively small degree of consumer dissatisfaction with the coverage. The physician-sponsored plan ranks close to the small group practice plan on this measure. Apparently the low incidence of dissatisfaction in the physician-sponsored plan is related to factors other than the financial coverage.

Although there seems to be some correspondence between consumer opinions of financial coverage and objective reality, the fit does not occur uniformly. There are factors that contributed to subjective perception of each plan's performance, such as characteristics of the perceiver, and the nature of the relationship between organization and the customer.

Consumers who have had more experience with a health insurance plan would probably be more aware of shortcomings in financial coverage. Accordingly, the rates of all consumers in each plan are compared with rates of dissatisfaction expressed by those in the "high-experience" categories. Three categories of "high experience" were use of both physician and hospital services in the preceding year, report of high out-of-pocket expenses, and report of high total expenses. Dissatisfaction was calculated as the sum of the last two levels in Table 6-1.

The plans ranking highest on comprehensive coverage (the two group practice plans and the large commercial plan) registered decreasing rates of dissatisfaction with more use. The less comprehensive plans, however, registered increasing dissatisfaction. Although the shifts in percentages were not great, the largest changes occurred in the large group plan and the physician-sponsored plan—in opposite directions, of course. In the large group practice plan there was a drop from 5 to 1%, and the physician-sponsored plan experienced an increase from 8 to 14%.

Out-of-pocket expense tests a different influence on consumer opinion. Dissatisfaction with financial coverage that does not change with increases in out-of-pocket expense indicates a form of tolerance for the health plan. Origins of this tolerance are not necessarily the same in each plan. In one plan it may derive from accurate knowledge of coverage and the opportunity to select a health plan. In another tolerance might be attributable to a value-position of the consumer vis-a-vis his insuring organization.

The effect of high out-of-pocket expenses on dissatisfaction was tested in the plan types rather than as separate plans to preserve adequate cell sizes and also because value-associations were thought to be as relevant to types of organization as to each plan. Results were as follows:

Plan type	Percent dissatisfied	
	No expense	High expense
Commercial	4.8	12.8
Provider-sponsored	10.8	30.4
Group practice	4.4	5.5

Dissatisfaction with the open-market plans is apparently generated by adverse financial experiences, but the same effect is not demonstrated in the group practice plans. Of further interest is the relatively high percent of dissatisfied consumers in the provider-sponsored plans who have "no expenses." This may indicate a predisposition toward dissatisfaction that developed from adverse personal experience in the past.

In the third criterion, total expenses, the same tendencies are observed as those just discussed. The percent of dissatisfied consumers in all plans, however, was greater for those with low total expenses than it was for those not having out-of-pocket expenses. The effect is particularly noticed in the group practice plans in which the percent of dissatisfied consumers rises to 10 for those with the lowest total expenses. This may be caused by coinsurance charges against certain items in the plans' less comprehensive packages. [3]

Consumer opinions may be influenced by prejudice or knowledge about the health plan coverage. The first orientation to be considered is a consumer's preenrollment attitude about the benefit packages. Each consumer was asked whether his favorable assessment of coverage provided by the plan was a major consideration in his having selected the plan. The second orientation is the person's current knowledge about his plan's coverage. A list of 10 benefit items ranging from ambulatory to in-hospital care was given to each person in the study, who then checked those items he believed were covered by his plan.

In the open-market plans dissatisfaction was strikingly less frequent

[3] In the insurance industry some plans labeled "comprehensive" are actually less comprehensive than others.

in consumers whose preenrollment attitudes were both highly favorable and instrumental in the selection of their plans. This effect is not found in the group plans. Consequently, for consumers with positive preenrollment attitudes toward coverage the variation in percent of dissatisfaction among the plans is reduced. Since the effect is not observed in the group practice plans, a great deal of dissatisfaction in the open-market plans may be due to assignment of consumers to insurance plans selected by their employers or unions.

The data show that opinions of financial coverage are associated with consumers perceptions of that coverage. If a person believed he had more coverage than he actually had, his satisfaction was greater. A person who thought he had less coverage was more dissatisfied. People who accurately described their coverage fell in between the two extremes. The most striking differences in satisfaction occurred around the extreme poles of the opinion scale. The very satisfied were those consumers with very high expectations and the very dissatisfied were those with low expectations. This pattern was observable in all plans.

Consumer Characteristics

As in previous chapters, we will study the impact of *need* and *demand* factors on the dependent variable. Considering characteristics indicative of need first, we feel that with decreasing health status the perceived salience of insurance coverage may be expected to increase. Expenses for medical services associated with declining health status may be expected to increase and insurance coverage thus become more important.

Increased family health care needs should have varying impacts on consumers' opinions of financial coverage according to plan. The group plans, which provide nearly complete coverage for medical and surgical services, should experience positive (if any) change in the level of satisfaction in which, for instance, chronically ill family members heighten the demand for physicians' services.

The commercial plans provide more coverage for ambulatory services than do the provider-sponsored plans, although physician services in hospital and charges are somewhat better covered in the provider-sponsored plans. In either case consumers with chronically ill family members, for instance, may be more consciously disturbed about expenses arising from cost-sharing mechanisms and relatively limited insurance coverage than consumers whose families have less medical need. Such feelings may be reflected in decreasing satisfaction with financial coverage or with increasing numbers of chronically ill family members for both the commercial and provider-sponsored plans.

financial coverage. This suggests a tendency for serious illness to polarize consumer opinion, which is consonant with the salience argument advanced above. But the percent shifts are not large. For families with chronic illnesses the ordering of plans according to percent dissatisfied reveals a familiar pattern. The provider-sponsored plans generate the most dissatisfaction under these conditions, followed by the commercial plans, with the least dissatisfaction again in the group practice plans.

Changes in opinions within plans from the "no chronic illness" to the "chronic illness" categories do not follow the pattern predicted. The most dramatic changes appear in the physician-sponsored and group practice plans. In the former plan, as we expected, chronic illness is associated with a drop in the percent satisfied and a large increase in dissatisfaction (from 3 to 17%), but, contrary to

A test of this proposition is available in the data presented in Table 6-2. Taken as a whole, consumers from families with chronic illnesses display slightly more satisfaction *and* dissatisfaction with expectations, the same pattern is observed in the large group practice plan: consumers from families with chronic illness are much more likely than others to express uncertainty about financial coverage or outright dissatisfction. The small group practice plan registers

TABLE 6-2

Opinion of financial coverage by plan by presence of chronic illness in the family

Opinions of coverage	Plan: All plans	Large comm	Small comm	Hosp-spon	Phys-spon	Large group	Small group
No chronic illness							
Satisfied (%)	39.6	38.5	26.5	28.4	30.3	81.2	31.6
Uncertain	50.0	50.3	58.4	46.0	67.1	17.7	60.7
Dissatisfied	10.4	11.1	15.2	25.6	2.6	1.1	7.7
N	1299	293	317	128	148	215	198
	$\chi^2=244$, df=10, $p<.001$ ($\gamma=.18$)						
One or more chronic illnesses							
Satisfied (%)	42.4	45.0	22.5	30.2	17.6	64.1	46.0
Uncertain	45.8	42.0	65.2	45.5	65.1	28.7	47.3
Dissatisfied	11.8	13.0	12.3	24.3	17.3	7.2	6.7
N	1247	176	231	164	87	339	251
	$\chi^2=162$, df=10, $p<.001$ ($\gamma=.27$)						

expected gains in satisfaction with the occurrence of chronic illness, accompanied by decreases in dissatisfaction. The consequence of this for the relationship between the group practice plans is that the small group practice plan replaces the large group practice plan in terms of lowest expressed dissatisfaction under conditions of chronic illness. Considering the superiority of coverage under the large group practice plan, this shift cannot be attributed to differences in product between the two organizations. In the other plans changes are small. Opinions in the hospital-sponsored plans appear to be impervious to influence by this particular variable, with both satisfaction and dissatisfaction remaining almost constant and nearly equivalent.

The vagaries of the data cannot be adequately explained at this level of analysis. Continuity with previous data interpretation is found regarding the influence of experience on opinion—namely that increased experience with an insurance plan leads to more accurate judgments on the part of the consumer concerning his financial coverage (we have previously observed a relationship between presence of chronic illness and use of medical services). Beyond this, however, the similarity in opinion shifts between the physician-sponsored and the large group plan, and the dissimilarity between the group practice plans, cannot be interpreted in terms of benefit package or incidence of chronic illnesses.

At a more general level of analysis a composite percent dissatisfaction for each plan for high-need and low-need families is calculated. The composite figure is an average of percent dissatisfied in each of four categories reflecting high and low need. For instance, an average was calculated from figures for families with mean age over 40, families reporting chronic illnesses, those reporting short-term illnesses, and families with females in the child-bearing years. The average of these four figures is reported as the percent of dissatisfaction in "high-need" families. The converse was done for "low-need" families. The resulting rates of dissatisfaction by plan are (percents dissatisfied) the following:

Plan	High-need families	Low-need families
Large commercial	12.3	11.8
Small commercial	11.4	13.0
Hospital-sponsored	29.4	22.8
Physician-sponsored	13.2	5.0
Large group	5.6	2.4
Small group	5.8	7.0

For the entire sample 11% of the high-need consumers and 10% of the low-need consumers expressed dissatisfaction with financial coverage. Increased dissatisfaction with increased need is found in both provider-sponsored plans (which are the plans with the least comprehensive coverage), but a shift in the same direction is found in the large group practice plan.

Regardless of need, there is the least complaint in the large group practice plan and the most in the hospital-sponsored plan. The appeal of the large group practice plan, however, is not specified by need as one might expect. Its advantage, as measured by consumer opinion, is greater in the low-need category. This is in contrast with the small group practice plan, in which the expected decline in dissatisfaction takes place with increased need. One must bear in mind that the consumers in the large group practice plan complain relatively little about financial coverage; this is almost a tautological statement: since there is literally nothing to complain about in the coverage in this plan, the interpretation of dissatisfaction must involve some type of halo effect. That is, the consumer expressing dissatisfaction with nearly totally comprehensive coverage must be projecting other dissatisfactions onto his opinions about monetary protection.

Concluding our discussion of the impact of consumer need on opinion, it is clear that the group practice plans generate the least dissatisfaction among the most needy families and the hospital-sponsored plan generates the most.

We turn now to a consideration of *demand* factors.

Demand, defined sociologically in this volume as propensity to engage health care services, is contingent on psychological factors which may be importantly influenced by the fact of insurance coverage and the nature of the plan. Reluctance to seek out health care services may be in large part an expression of fears of unaffordable economic loss and of medical procedures such as surgery and hospitalization. For persons who have health insurance such fears may be allayed to a greater or lesser degree, depending on the type of plan. When psychological inhibitions exist, insured consumers may find expression for their reluctance to engage health care services in the form of dissatisfaction with their plans. Such dissatisfaction may be directed toward financial coverage, medical care, or both.

Differences between the plans with respect to levels of dissatisfaction may thus be interpreted as indications of the degree to which plan characteristics (i.e., coverage, cost-sharing mechanisms, organization of medical services) alleviate or reinforce psychological barriers to demand. Since persons in lower social strata have demonstrated in previous research a tendency toward low demand, we may examine our opinion data particularly for evidence of social class differences in levels of dissatisfaction. The relative degree of reduction in social class disparities in dissatisfaction recorded for a given plan may be viewed as the relative degree of success that a plan has had in equalizing demand factors inherent in social class distinctions.

Table 6-3 reports consumers' opinions on financial coverage by two income classes across the six study plans. Lower income consumers appear more likely than higher income consumers to have definite opinions on financial coverage. As suggested above, financial burdens are bound to have greater meaning for those with less money. Increases in percent dissatisfied and percent satisfied are observed with lower incomes. The rise in dissatisfaction is more pronounced, with 14% of the lower income people counted among the disgruntled compared with 7% of the upper income consumers. The income shift in dissatisfaction is greatest in the commercial and hospital-sponsored plans. Every plan except the physician-sponsored shows more dissatisfied low-income than high-income consumers. The policy of doctors in the physician-sponsored plan of recognizing plan reimbursements as payments in full no doubt has some influence on consumer opinions in the lower income category.

Again we note that regardless of income the large group practice and hospital-sponsored plans demonstrate the least and the most dissatisfaction, respectively. For the upper income consumers, however, there is not much difference among five of the six plans; the

TABLE 6-3
Opinion of financial coverage by plan by family income

Opinion of coverage	Plan						
	All plans	Large comm	Small comm	Hosp-spon	Phy-spon	Large group	Small group
Less than $11,000							
Satisfied (%)	41.8	49.6	14.4	31.8	33.0	77.2	35.3
Uncertain	44.7	37.2	64.5	40.8	59.3	17.2	55.6
Dissatisfied	13.5	13.2	21.1	27.4	7.7	5.6	9.0
N	1477	338	259	170	143	266	302
	$\chi^2=283$, df=10, $p<0.001$ ($\gamma=0.11$)						
$11,000 *or more*							
Satisfied (%)	34.5	18.5	28.3	26.6	14.1	64.1	27.8
Uncertain	58.4	74.3	63.7	55.8	77.3	31.8	67.7
Dissatisfied	7.1	7.2	8.0	17.6	8.5	4.1	4.5
N	1172	127	258	114	95	286	293
	$\chi^2=178$, df=10, $p<0.001$ ($\gamma=0.21$)						

only plan at a perceptible disadvantage in this market is the hospital-sponsored plan which has more than twice as much dissatisfaction as any other plan. This relatively high rate for these consumers may be due to the tendency noted in Chapter 5 for out-of-pocket expenses to rise with income for equivalent amounts of medical services.

For low-income consumers, for whom the effects of insurance is certainly most important, the large group practice plan has the best record in terms of both satisfaction and dissatisfaction. Consumer dissatisfaction with coverage is not remarkably lower in this plan compared with the small group or the physician-sponsored plan, but high satisfaction is expressed by more than twice the consumers in the former plan.

Thus, using income as a measure of demand, we find that the rate of dissatisfaction between high- and low-demand categories is held relatively low and constant in the group and physician-sponsored plans, but discrepancies favoring the high income consumer are in the other three plans. In either case the large group plan continues to be most satisfactory in consumer opinion.

A second indicator of demand is *education* .Our data indicate that education of head of household has almost no effect on level of dissatisfaction with financial coverage in any plan. College-educated consumers, however, are much less likely to express high satisfaction than those with less education. This finding is consistent across all plans in the study. For the high-demand consumer (indicated by high education) the effect of this more critical attitude is found mostly in the physician-sponsored and small commercial plans. In each case the percent of consumers with high satisfaction drops from about 40 to 13% from the lower educated to the higher educated categories. The large group practice plan exhibits the least change (drop of only 3%) and consequently stands out in terms of high satisfaction in educated consumers.

We tested for the simultaneous effect of education and use of medical services on opinion of financial coverage. Since higher education is associated with a more critical attitude, we expected that the combination of high education and heavy use of medical services would intensify the tendency for expression of less satisfaction.

Plans were combined into types to attain adequate cell sizes. Support for the hypothesis was found. In all three plan types fewer college-educated, high-use consumers expressed satisfaction, and more expressed dissatisfaction than college-educated consumers with no use of services in the preceding 12 months. Thus dissatisfactions that are perceived by some are felt by more under conditions of immediate experience with the plans. Unexpectedly, a large drop in percent satisfied in the college-educated category is found in the group practice plans: from 63% of those without medical services to 38% of high users (doctor and hospital experience in the previous year). Separate figures by plan show the small group practice plan dropping off more sharply than the large group, but the large group practice plan shows significant change (24%). The erosion of appeal for the educated with rising use is experienced by all plans, regardless of extent of coverage.

In the low-education category the picture is somewhat altered. First, under conditions of no medical experience in the previous year the level of satisfaction for all three plan types is about equivalent (40%), but *dissatisfaction* in the group type is twice as great as with other types. This dissatisfaction is almost entirely due to that expressed by large group practice plan consumers—20% are highly dissatisfied. In contrast, consumers with college educations expressed no dissatisfaction in either group practice plan. The dissatisfaction of consumers with high school or less education appears to be due to something more than paying high premiums and consuming no medical services because the dissatisfaction of the same type of consumer in the high-premium physician-sponsored plan is very low. We speculate on the basis of this and data discussed in earlier chapters that the large group practice plan consumer is expressing dissatisfaction with paying high premiums and being *unable* to obtain needed medical services because of real or perceived inaccessibility. When the low-educated consumer receives medical services in this plan, dissatisfaction disappears and satisfaction is expressed by 96% of the respondents.

The critical nature of the college-educated consumer is nowhere better demonstrated than in contrast with the consumers of lower education when both are heavy users of medical care. In all three plan types both highly and lower educated consumers with heavy use of services agree on the supremacy of the group plans, followed in order by the commercials and provider-sponsored types. In all cases it appears that the consumer with less education is more pleased with whatever payment is made by his insurance plan than the college-educated consumer.

Two points have been established. First, high satisfaction with financial coverage is least likely to be expressed by college-educated consumers who have experience with doctor and hospital services. Second, consumers with low education and no recent medical experience are most likely to express extreme dissatisfaction with coverage in the group practice plans—particularly the large group practice plan.

Demand indicators were combined in the same manner as in previous chapters to yield measures of the dependent variable for "high-demand" and "low-demand" categories. Percent dissatisfaction was used as the measure of consumer opinion in this case. This combination of indicators of demand (income, occupation, education, opinion of the influence of insurance on use of services, and symptom-sensitivity) produced the following figures (% dissatisfied).

Plan	High-demand families	Low-demand families
Large commercial	13.1	14.8
Small commercial	15.1	12.8
Hospital-sponsored	24.1	25.7
Physician-sponsored	13.8	10.7
Large group	2.9	7.9
Small group	7.3	5.8

Differences in expressed dissatisfaction between the two demand categories are not great. Among the high-demand consumers we find the familiar pattern of large group and hospital-sponsored plans at the opposite extremes. Within the low-demand category the small group practice plan elicits the least dissatisfaction. This change in the relative positions of the two group practice plans is due in large measure to a steep increase in dissatisfaction with the large group practice plan from the symptom-hypersensitive to less sensitive categories.

Demand as a whole, like need, does not have much impact on opinion of financial coverage. Under all conditions tested, separately and in combination, the hospital-sponsored plan remains the least satisfactory, whereas the small group practice plan in some instances shows less dissatisfaction than the large group (i.e., under conditions of low demand).

In summary, consumer opinions most accurately reflect actual benefit structures under conditions of greater experience with the plan, and overestimation of coverage leads to higher expressed satisfaction in all plans.

The large group practice plan is remarkable for its high percent of satisfied (71%) and few dissatisfied consumers (5%). One-fourth of the hospital-sponsored plan's consumers were highly dissatisfied with their financial coverage—by far the highest rate of all the plans.

Chronic illness in the family polarizes opinions about coverage. The least comprehensive plans register increased dissatisfaction with increased need—but so does the large group practice plan. Differences among plans in dissatisfaction are less for high-income consumers in five of the six plans. Only the hospital-sponsored plan is at a decided disadvantage in this market. For low-income people the large group practice plan is the most satisfactory. In the more highly educated consumers there is an erosion of satisfaction with coverage as use of medical services increases. This remains true even in the most comprehensive plans. Dissatisfaction with financial coverage is highest for consumers with less education and no recent medical experience in the large group plan. Also, these consumers across all plan types give roughly equivalent satisfaction ratings. In contrast to the above point, when the lower educated consumer becomes a high user, satisfaction with the group practice plans skyrockets (96%), but in the other plans there is little change. Regardless of demand, consumers continue to evaluate the large group plan coverage as best and hospital-sponsored plan coverage as least satisfactory.

The above discussion tends to indicate that consumer opinion of benefits is greatly affected by their personal frames of reference. We have demonstrated the importance of some of the factors defining such frames of reference; there are undoubtedly others. It seems important to recognize that people tend to be most satisfied with plans they have voluntarily chosen on the basis of coverage offered. In evaluating the public acceptability of a plan, it is well to take into account the socioeconomic status (especially education) of the consumers as well as their experience with the plan.

SATISFACTION WITH MEDICAL CARE

It is commonly held that consumers are more likely to receive better *technical* medical care in group practice settings, although they are likely to receive greater *personal interest* from physicians in individual private practices. Better technical care appears to be interpreted primarily in terms of laboratory facilities, paramedical personnel, and availability of specialists. Personal interest or sensitivity to the needs of the patient, however, distinguished from technical competence, is not readily divorced from the notion of quality medical care in the minds of consumers. Convenience (physical and temporal access) of medical care may also be elements in consumers' views about their medical care.

To the degree that opinions about the medical care received under a plan are sensitive to personal interest and convenience factors, we expect that consumer opinions would tend to be more favorable in those plans in which individual practices predominate. That is, free choice of physicians together with entrepreneurial incentives encouraging physicians to establish themselves as the "family doctor" to all their patients should influence opinions in a positive direction. Although some choice of physician is permitted within the group practice context and many consumers are successful in establishing effective personal relationships with group practice physicians, a relative lack of continuity in patient-physician relationships, rationalized and bureaucratized office procedures, and incentives for screening patients on the basis of objective needs appear to be common occurrences, leading often to displeasure with medical care experience.

Greater thoroughness of examination procedures and history notations in the group practice plans is documented in Chapter 4. Moreover, the frequency and range of preventive care is greater under the group plans than under the others (see Chapter 4). These objective differences between the group practice and open-market practice delivery systems with respect to the range of preventive and diagnostic procedures may be suggestive of quality differences to which consumers' opinions might be sensitive. Although preventive examinations, history taking, and diagnostic procedures are technical aspects of medical care, patients can nevertheless be heavily influenced by their perceptions of the thoroughness and honesty with which these procedures are performed. To the extent that opinions are sensitive to these technical aspects of medical care, we expect satisfaction with medical care to be higher in the group plans than in the open-market plans.

As with opinion of financial coverage, opinion of medical care was measured by a questionnaire item constructed as a visual continuum from "very dissatisfied" to "very satisfied."The same conventions for grouping scale categories are adopted for this portion of the analysis.

Variations by Plan

Table 6-4 presents distributions of consumer opinion about medical care in their extended form.

If we look only at the very extreme category of satisfaction, there is little choice among the large group, large commercial, and hospital-sponsored plans which have the highest percent of satisfied customers. Combining the first two categories of satisfaction, as we do in subsequent tables, there is a great similarity in five of the six plans, but the small group practice plan falls short with only 30% compared with about 45% in the other plans. Turning to rates of expressed dissatisfaction with medical care, at the extreme end of the scale, we find that the highest percent of dissatisfied consumers are in the hospital-sponsored plan and the lowest in the group practice plans and the physician-sponsored plan. Combining the two extreme categories of dissatisfaction, the hospital-sponsored plan remains the most unsatisfactory, whereas the large group practice plan has the smallest percent of dissatisfaction.

Favorable opinions of medical care registered for the large group practice plan suggest that greater technical competence outweighs whatever negative influence a relatively less personal interest by

TABLE 6-4
Opinion of medical care by plan
(percent of respondents)

	Plan						
Opinion of medical care	All plans	Large comm	Small comm	Hosp-spon	Phy spon	Large group	Small group
Satisfied (%)	20.9	26.4	17.2	31.7	12.5	27.3	13.4
	20.5	21.8	25.4	14.5	30.2	17.8	16.1
	17.1	6.4	21.5	3.7	3.7	32.7	32.1
	8.1	7.1	4.7	8.3	8.4	7.3	12.4
	18.1	20.7	17.7	20.1	18.6	14.8	18.8
	5.9	4.8	8.5	2.0	8.1	2.3	8.4
	2.5	1.5	1.4	2.5	10.1	1.3	2.3
	2.3	5.3	1.1	2.2	2.4	0.5	3.0
Dissatisfied	4.6	5.7	6.4	11.8	2.7	2.6	2.1
N	2702	442	564	247	245	576	627

$\chi^2=399$, df=40, $p<0.001$ ($\gamma=-0.01$)

physicians and patient inconvenience exert on consumers in this plan. Small group practice plan consumers are considerably more likely to be moderately satisfied than are consumers in the open-market plans but, at the same time, they are much less likely to be *very* satisfied. The proportion of very dissatisfied subscribers in the small group practice plan is somewhat smaller than in the open market plans. Small group consumers demonstrate considerably less pronounced satisfaction than is expressed in the large group practice plan, raising questions of the differences in technical and psychological factors of medical care delivery in the two group practice plans.

As should be expected, differences of opinion on medical care among the open-market plans are slight. All of these plans provide insurance that is consistent with entrepreneurial medical care practices and free choice of physician. We have taken note, however, that high dissatisfaction with medical care is somewhat more frequently recorded in the hospital-sponsored plan. This finding may reflect a greater tendency for physicians to recommend hospitalization, in which such care may be discretionary, because of the relatively few benefit provisions for ambulatory care under this plan. Patients often feel that all possible routes should be considered, hospitalization being a last resort. Thus more frequent discretionary hospitalization may indeed be the source of consumer complaints about medical care. The data presented in Chapter 3 on hospital admissions revealed that the hospital-sponsored plan has the highest rate of all six plans. This was particularly true for the high-need families, and one must assume that either these families have more grave ailments in the hospital-sponsored plan than in other plans or that there is a propensity for in-hospital treatment in this plan.

Taken as a whole, 41% of the total sample expressed satisfaction with medical care received (combining the two extreme categories in Table 6-4) and 7% expressed dissatisfaction (combining the two lower categories). Thus the other half of the sample equivocates on the question. This uncertain population is concentrated in the small group practice plan (65%). Rhetorical objections to "bureaucratized medicine" which are often expressed in public debate are not realized in this particular opinion study. The most bureaucratized medicine is provided in the large group practice plan and dissatisfaction is lowest in its customers, whereas satisfaction compared favorably to that found in the open market plans. Other aspects of group practice medicine may raise more objection by consumers, however, and we pursue some of them presently.

As a summary device the plan type analysis is once again offered. Combining the two upper and two lower categories of satisfaction, the only appreciable differences are in the very dissatisfied consumers, where the group practice plan type registers 4% and the other two types register 10%. All three types have between 40 and 45% satisfied customers. In the group type the low figure on dissatisfaction is primarily due to the influence of the large group practice plan, whereas the high figure in the other plans is mainly due to high dissatisfaction in hospital-sponsored and large commercial plan consumers. In contrast with opinions of financial coverage, opinions of medical care do not demonstrate large differences among plans or plan types. The Gamma statistic in all cases (opinion by plan or plan type) does not exceed 0.09.

Organizational Determinants

We have pointed out that no differential impact on medical care per se is expected among the open-market plans. They disavow any interest in controlling the manner in which care is delivered, and generally concern themselves with quality of care only when there is strong consumer complaint or where there is evidence that a provider is unusually interested in profits. Consequently, major interest lies in differences between the group practice plans and all others.

We first wish to explore the effect of experience on attitudes toward medical care. Are levels of opinion altered by immediate experience with health services? If there are perceived disadvantages in the group mode of delivery, they might be more readily observed by those with extensive experience.

The data show that of the large group practice plan consumers without recent care 40% are very satisfied with medical care (presumably on the basis of previous experience or perhaps conjecture) and 3% are very dissatisfied. There are no appreciable differences within this category between the large group and the open-market plans. The small group practice plan shows lower rates of satisfaction, but *no* dissatisfaction. For consumers with extensive immediate experience (doctor and hospital care in the past year) the group practice plans both begin to emerge as more satisfying. For instance, high satisfaction with medical care is expressed by 49% of the experienced large group consumers, an improvement of 9%; there is a concomitant drop in the dissatisfied ranks to 1%. The record of the small group practice plan is impressive, showing an increase in high satisfaction of 32% from the "no experience" category and still demonstrating no extreme dissatisfaction. The open market plans taken together show a small percentage gain in high satisfaction with increased use, but more dramatically show a rise in dissatisfaction from 3% for those without recent care to 11% for the experienced consumers.

To the extent that opinions of medical care reflect organization of services, these data show a more satisfactory experience for high users in the group practice plans than in the other plans.

In passing we note the relationship between opinion of medical care and high out-of-pocket expenses in the large group practice plan. The argument is not that high expenses influence opinions but exactly the reverse: when there is dissatisfaction with medical care expressed by consumers, we expect it to result in high expenses due to out-of-plan use. The data lend support to this. In the large group practice plan we observe a steady erosion of satisfaction with medical care as out-of-pocket expenses rise. Four levels of expense were tested, and satisfaction was expressed by 52, 39, 35, and 18% as expenses increased. A similar deterioration was not found in the small group practice plan. This suggests that out-of-plan use in the large group practice plan is linked to disenchantment with in-plan medical care.

What is the correspondence, if any, between characteristics of medical care and consumer opinion of medical care? In Chapter 4 we developed four measures of *range of services* describing in quantifiable terms the characteristics of care usually associated with the concept of quality. In order to study the covariation of scores on the four dimensions and consumer opinion of medical care, we turn to the medical record subsample. Further, in order to ensure the most direct association possible between opinion expressed and care received, we used only characteristics of care received by the person filling out the questionnaire. This removes the necessity for assuming that opinion will adequately reflect care received by all insured members of the consumer's family. The sample is consequently much reduced (n=367), rendering detailed analysis or analysis by other than group-nongroup distinctions unreliable.

We considered the "high" and the "low" categories on each of the four "factors" (refer to Chapter 4 for score-cutting points). For the total sample the percent highly satisfied was greater for those with high factor scores than for those with low scores on three of the four factors. For instance, 39% of those with high prevention scores were highly satisfied with their medical care; 31% of those with low scores were highly satisfied. Similarly, high scores on rationality and continuity were associated with a slightly higher percent of satisfied consumers. The other factor—verification—demonstrated an inverse relationship with consumer opinion. Thus 32% of those with high scores on this factor expressed enthusiasm about their medical care, compared with 50% of those with low scores. We noted in Chapter 4 that the verification measure appeared to be indicative of frequent routine lab and radiology testing. The current data indicate that consumers are reacting negatively to routine procedures which they may feel are nonspecific to their problem and which the physician does as a matter of course (most physicians, especially in the group practice plans, did not make notes in their records of the results of these tests).

There is some evidence therefore that consumers tend to be perceptive of distinctions in their medical care reflected by the range of services indices. Is there a differential response to characteristics of care between the group practice plans and others? If there is any basis in medical care folklore, consumers in the group practice plans should reflect technical considerations primarily in their opinions, whereas other consumers find comfort in the more personal aspects of the doctor-patient relationship. Although the sample is too small to draw definitive conclusions, there is some suggestion that this reasoning is correct. The largest increase in percent satisfaction in the group practice plan consumers occurs between those with low rationality scores and those with high scores on this factor; the change is 32 percentage points, from 23% satisfied to 55%. Conversely, in the open-market plans the change is in the opposite direction, so that fewer consumers with *high* rationality scores are satisfied with their medical care. This is also a substantial shift, involving 27 percentage points. Since rationality scores are tied to level of seriousness of complaints, one suspects that these diverse responses to similar physician behaviors are related to fiscal insecurities arising from a combination of high physician charges in time of serious illness and limited insurance coverage in the open-market plans. Whatever the reason, there does appear to be a differential response by consumers to increased rationality of medical procedures. [4]

If to some extent the strength of a doctor-patient relationship is reflected in the continuity factor scores, there is little evidence to support the contention that consumers in the open-market plans are more sensitive to this "personal" aspect of care than those in the group practice plans. Satisfaction with medical care doubles in the group practice plans when continuity scores rise from low to high; scarcely any effect is demonstrated in the open-market plans. As for verification, considerably fewer consumers express satisfaction in the group practice plans when verification scores are high—when routine lab and radiology are frequently performed. The group practice doctor ordering numerous tests may substitute them for giving personal time to his patient. Again in the other plans shifts in verification scores have almost no effect on percent satisfaction with medical care. All consumers, whether in the group or other plans, are sensitive to rises in the prevention score. More preventive procedures are associated with greater expressed satisfaction with medical care. For equivalent prevention factor scores the level of satisfaction is higher in the open-market plans (55%) than in the group practice plans (31%). This heightened "appreciation" in the former plans may be due to lack of insurance coverage (and therefore total consumer fiscal liability) for preventive services.

In summary, more consumers are pleased with care when it is characterized by prevention, rationality, and continuity. Verification

---

[4] The data reported here involve rather small cell sizes and conclusions are consequently tentative. The association between rationality and opinion of care, however, was further investigated by using the entire medical record subsample, and essentially the same findings can be reported. The problem with the total subsample data is that one must assume that the respondent's opinions of medical care adequately reflect care received by all insured members of the family. Whichever shortcoming the reader would rather tolerate (small sample or this assumption), roughly the same conclusions may be drawn.

procedures, involving routine lab and radiology work, are associated with a large drop in satisfaction. Satisfaction in the group practice plans is sensitive mainly to rationality (positively) and verification (negatively). Satisfaction in the open-market plans appears mainly to reflect prevention (positively) and rationality (negatively).

The problem of *access* to medical care is frequently discussed in relation to the group mode of delivery of services. Included in the consumer questionnaire were two opinion items designed to elicit responses on *clinic procedures* in the large group practice plan,[5] and *availability of doctors* when they are needed.

Although consumers in the large group plan are for the most part satisfied with their financial coverage and medical care, dissatisfaction with the medical clinic operations is substantial. Nearly 15% of these consumers are highly dissatisfied. That bureaucratic impasses in large-scale organization and full capacity enrollment can generate dissatisafaction among substantial numbers of plan members is not surprising. Such dissatisfaction may represent the Achilles' heel of large group practice.

In contrast to the proportion of consumers who have expressed dissatisfaction with the clinic setup, 30% indicate very high satisfaction. We further note that 32% express *some* dissatisfaction; conversely, 68% express some satisfaction. The high percentage of families having used some ambulatory service at the large group clinic indicates that inconveniences associated with clinic medical care do not substantially interfere with consumers' use of services.

Discretionary use and out-of-plan use may, however, be importantly affected by clinic inconvenience factors, especially when they produce dissatisfaction. More importantly, however, access differentially affects various social categories of consumers. Some are more able to deal readily with obstacles which to others are insurmountable. To the extent that clinic inconvenience is expressed as dissatisfaction and dissatisfaction influences "demand" for services,

---

[5] The decision to include this question was not made in time for it to appear in the questionnaire for consumers in the small group practice plan (mailed first). Thus comparative data are not available. In future explorations of the data, however, comparisons can be made on responses from consumers in the large group practice plan who received care in clinics of various sizes.

the large group plan may be able to exercise control over use through appropriate construction and manipulation of clinic inconvenience factors. *This may be an effective alternative to copayment controls* and, although the method is episodically irritiating, the consumer retains full insurance coverage.

The other measure of access used was opinion about the availability of physicians when they are needed. The data emerge much as expected, with rates of dissatisfaction in the large group practice plan the highest (10%), followed by the small group (7%), and the open-market plans (6%). High satisfaction figures tend to present the same picture, though differences are not so large as one might expect on this item. This might be due to varying interpretations by the respondent of "availability."

Briefly, then, we have found a rather high rate of dissatisfaction with clinic procedures in consumers in the large group practice plan. Also, compared with other plans, more of these consumers express high dissatisfaction with availability of physicians.

Consumer Characteristics

We have argued that the salience of physician behavior and medical practice is greater for those whose medical care needs are more intense. The foregoing discussion demonstrated that less dissatisfaction with medical care is found in the group practice plans when need is translated into high use of services. We also found that group consumers reacted positively to greater rationality in medical services in the group practice plans but negatively in other plans. On the basis of these findings we expected high-need consumers in the group practice plans to express less dissatisfaction with medical care than low-need consumers, as well as less dissatisfaction than similar consumers in the other plans. Data on the influence of need on dissatisfaction with medical care are presented as follows:

Plan	High-need families	Low-need families
Large commercial	9.2	13.8
Small commercial	6.6	7.0
Hospital-sponsored	13.9	14.7
Physician-sponsored	4.6	4.5
Large group	4.3	1.8
Small group	2.9	3.8

There is a slight overall shift toward less dissatisfaction in the high-need as compared with the low-need consumers. The difference is very small, however. Most of the plans tend to follow this overall tendency. If we compute an overall average for the open-market plans, 10% of the low-need families have serious reservations about medical care received, compared with 8.6% of the high-need families. The small group plan follows this trend also, but there is a reversal in the large group practice plan that we did not expect. The advantage (by this measure) of the large group plan medical care is most evident for the low-need families, less than 2% of which have serious objections; this is the lowest rate of all plans. In the high-need families the rate of dissatisfaction is lowest in the small group practice plan, and the large group does not differ significantly from the physician-sponsored and small commercial plans.

A possible reason for the above findings is found in the nature of the association between need and use of medical services. Previous discussion on the impact of salience on opinions dealt with actual use of services (experience measures and measures of range of services). Need, however, does not bear a perfect relationship to use, and in some plans the correspondence is better than in others. Chapter 3 indicated that for the high-need families doctor visits per person were higher in some of the open-market plans and in the small group practice plan than in the large group practice plan. For low-need families, however, the visitation rate in the large group practice plan was the highest. Dissatisfaction with medical care in the large group practice plan being more common among high-need families may indicate that these consumers feel they require more care than they actually receive.

On all four measures of the need concept more high-need consumers in the large group practice plan express extreme dissatifaction with care than low-need consumers. This is not the general case in all plans; it is usually the reverse. This increase in dissatisfaction in large group practice plan consumers is mainly because of a change from 2 to 7% discontents due to the presence of short-term illness in the family. In contrast, the reverse occurs in the small group practice plan on this indicator: dissatisfaction drops from 6% to zero. Although the 7% rate in the large group practice plan is not high, it is higher than in any other plan but the hospital-sponsored. Data on rates of high satisfaction related to this measure indicate a concomitant decrease (15 percentage points) with the incidence of recent short-term illness.

All of this suggests, at a general level, that medical care delivery systems which involve large group practices tend to generate greater consumer dissatisfactions with medical care in the most needy because access is problematic for those with short-term, relatively minor complaints and those with more serious illnesses may feel that they are not seen frequently enough. These extrapolations from the data should be regarded cautiously, since much more study is required to take them beyond the status of hypotheses. Certain support for the first point is found in the data on "opinion of clinic procedures." For consumers reporting short-term illnesses complaint about clinic procedures in the large group practice plan rises to 20% (combining the two most extreme categories as we have done previously). Thus there is evidence that dissatisfaction with medical care and clinic procedures is maximized in families reporting short-term illnesses in this plan.

Turning to a consideration of the association between *demand* factors and opinion of medical care, we might expect on the basis of previous data that the more highly educated consumers would be more critical than those with lesser educations. At the outset of this section data showed very little difference among five of the six plans on opinion of medical care. Percent highly satisfied in each of these plans varied between a low of 43% and a high of 46%. Only the small group plan exhibited an appreciably lower level of satisfaction at 30%.

When plans were combined into types, nearly all variation in satisfaction was lost, with just below 50% in all three types endorsing their medical care. With these figures in mind, we are now ready to examine the impact of *educational level*.

If we examine the percent of consumers satisfied with their medical care shown in Table 6-5, it is evident in every plan that the college-educated are more critical than those with lesser educations. Satisfaction with medical care is least affected by education in the large group practice plan, in which there is only 1% difference between the two educational categories. In the other plans there is considerable impact. The difference between educational levels in the hospital-sponsored plan, for instance, is 23 percentage points.

For the most critical consumers (i.e., the college-educated), the large group plan holds an edge over every other plan on this measure. In the lower educational category the open-market plans all have a greater percent of satisfied customers. In both categories the small group practice plan has the lowest proportion of consumers highly satisfied with their medical care.

If the data are collapsed into a group-nongroup dichotomy, group practice holds a 39 to 35% edge in satisfaction for the college-educated, while falling behind the predominantly solo-practice plans 44 to 52% for people with high school educations or less. It is possible that these differences in response to medical care in different practice settings are influenced by the difficulty of managing the bureaucracy associated with large group practice. As we

TABLE 6-5

Opinion of medical care
by plan by education of head-of-household

Opinion of care	Plan: All plans	Large comm	Small comm	Hosp spon	Phy spon	Large group	Small group
High school or less							
Satisfied (%)	46.8	47.9	50.5	52.8	55.8	44.9	37.3
Uncertain	45.3	38.6	40.9	28.0	38.5	52.9	59.5
Dissatisfied	7.9	13.5	8.6	19.2	5.7	2.2	3.1
N	1378	254	264	156	115	314	276
	$\chi^2=97$, df=10, $p<0.001$ ($\gamma=$ -0.06)						
Some college							
Satisfied (%)	33.0	42.7	33.3	30.1	34.1	44.1	21.5
Uncertain	61.3	47.8	60.1	64.3	62.7	54.6	71.6
Dissatisfied	5.7	9.5	6.6	5.6	3.2	1.2	6.9
N	1178	155	286	85	88	226	339
	$\chi^2=53$, df=10, $p<0.001$ ($\gamma=$-0.11)						

have mentioned before, the more highly educated are perhaps more able to "work the system." Another interpretation is that the better educated are more sensitive in their opinions to technical aspects of care, whereas others are more sensitive to elements of a continuing doctor-patient relationship.

How does education interact with experience to influence opinion of medical care? We again tested for the simultaneous effect of education and use of services. The resulting data are presented as follows in terms of percent highly satisfied:

	Some college		High school or less	
Plan	*No care*	*High use*	*No care*	*High use*
Large commercial	36	40	58	65
Small commercial	42	33	54	64
Hospital-sponsored	34	41	52	63
Physician-sponsored	38	25	54	79
Large group	48	29	34	55
Small group	20	51	42	68

For every plan, the highest percent of satisfied consumers is found in those with high school or lower education who have been heavy users of medical care in the past 12 months (doctor and hospital experience reported). The large group practice plan has the lowest percent satisfied in this consumer category. College-educated consumers who have had recent use of doctor and hospital services are universally less likely to be satisfied with their care than those with less education. For these college people the open-market plans (with the exception of the physician-sponsored plan) and the small group practice plan generate more satisfaction than the large group practice plan. Thus two points are evident. First, consumers with recent heavy use of services are less satisfied with medical care in the large group practice plan than in the other plans, regardless of education. Second, for the heavy users those with less education are more satisfied with their care than others, regardless of plan. Thus in the heavy users the college-educated are least satisfied with their medical care and the large group practice plan is least popular.

Considering those who have not had recent medical experience, both group practice plans have a smaller percent satisfied than other plans for the people with less education. The large group practice plan has the highest percent satisfied only for its college-educated consumers who have not had recent medical care. In this category of consumer the small group practice plan does least well, with only 20% satisfied consumers.

These data illustrate the importance of considering personal *frames of reference* in interpreting opinion responses. The combination of the educational and experience frames of reference shakes up the overall distribution of opinion about medical care. For instance, the low proportion of satisfied consumers in the small group plan in the overall distribution is maintained only for college-educated consumers without recent use of medical services. Some may argue that public acceptability of medical care under different forms of delivery and financing should take into account opinions of those with the greatest and most recent experience. Under these conditions the large group practice plan is satisfactory to the smallest proportion of the people. In this case it appears that "familiarity breeds contempt" to a certain extent.

By way of summation we may collapse the plans into group and nongroup in terms of predominant mode of delivery and examine the percent of satisfaction under varying conditions of consumer education and experience. The group practice plans record the highest rate of satisfaction with medical care for college-educated consumers without recent medical care (43% vs. 37%). For all other categories the nongroup practice plans have a higher rate. For both types of delivery system the highest percent of satisfaction is found for those with lower educations and high recent use of medical care.

An examination of the effect of income on these opinions reveals almost the same result as education. High-income consumers are universally less likely to be highly satisfied with care than low-income consumers. There is virtually no difference in satisfaction between group and nongroup plans for those with annual incomes of more than $11,000. For those with family incomes below this level the open-market plans are most satisfactory.

Finally, combining five indicators of demand as we have done previously, the following data on percent *dissatisfaction* with medical care are obtained.

Plan	High-demand families	Low-demand families
Large commercial	12.1	9.4
Small commercial	6.2	6.1
hospital-sponsored	11.0	15.8
Physician-sponsored	6.4	5.6
Large group	2.0	2.2
Small group	6.3	4.0
All	6.0	6.0

Overall the percent dissatisfaction between high- and low-demand categories is the same—6%. In both categories fewer consumers express extreme dissatisfaction with the large group practice plan than with any other. High dissatisfaction in large group plan consumers is negligible, remaining at about 2% for all categories of the demand indicators (5% for high-income consumers). This should be borne in mind in relation to the data on *satisfaction* presented previously. The most dissatisfaction, found in the hospital-sponsored plan, reaches a high of 23% in the lower occupational categories.

Physician Determinants

A consumer's opinion of medical care may depend on the type of physician he sees. In this section the association between the consumer's opinion of his care, his doctor's characteristics, and his complaints about his doctor will be explored.

In three of the open-market plans a patient's satisfaction was associated with office waiting periods. If a person encountered long waits, even when he had an appointment, he was, of course, more dissatisfied. People in the group plans, however, did not register this complaint. In the open-market plans people probably expected better service, whereas in the group practice plans the fewer complaints may reflect a resignation to a *modus operandi.* Inconvenient clinic procedures seemed to be an accepted means toward obtaining group practice medical services.[6]

Consumers in three of the open-market plans also complained about their doctors' concern for profit, and in these plans dissatisfaction levels were higher. This complaint was not encountered in the group plans. The issue of home visitation was considered, but it does not appear to affect patient's opinions. There was some resentment, however, among consumers in the open-market plans.

The last item considered was how a patient felt about his doctor's bedside manner. For consumers in the large group plan complaints about the lack of individual attention from physicians most clearly predicts dissatisfaction with medical care. Similar but much smaller differences in intense satisfaction were reported for four of the five other plans. The hospital-sponsored plan was the exception. Dissatisfaction, then, with medical care in the open-market plans is related to consumer complaints about waiting periods and physician profit motives. In the group practice plans dissatisfaction is related to the patients' feeling that their doctors do not give them enough time and attention.

The relationship between physician characteristics and a patient's satisfaction with medical care was studied by matching each person with the medical care he received in a 12-month period with the

---

[6] In actual fact it is not clear that waits are longer in group practice clinics.

characteristics of his physician.[7] Physician characteristics are organized according to the concepts of *limiting, qualifying, facilitating,* and *motivating* (see Chapters 1 and 4).

Limiting features of a physician are age, father's socioeconomic level, country of medical training, and ratio of student applications/admissions in the medical school attended. "High" limitation amounted to a physician being over 40, from a lower socioeconomic background (Hollingshead classes 4 and 5), educated in a medical school located in a country other than the United States, Canada, Great Britain, or Scandinavia with a relatively low student application/admission ratio. "Low" limitation is the reverse.

Consumers were categorized as patients of physicians who were predominantly one or the other. Opinion of medical care received.[8] is presented as percent of consumers who were very satisfied with their care according to the high or low limitation of their physicians.

Plan	High limitations	Low limitations
Large commercial	64	46
Small commercial	51	44
Hospital-sponsored	46	48
Physician-sponsored	51	50
Large group	39	31
Small group	32	31

Consumers were more satisfied with care from physicians who rated high on limitation. Forty-two percent of the consumers were satisfied compared to 37% of those who received care from physicians rated as low on limitation. A physician's age in relation to his patient's satisfaction with the medical care seems to be very influential. In the case of age a patient might respond positively to an older physician because of his greater experience.

[7] This statement is subject to limitations of physician response and to the fact that only physicians seen in ambulatory settings are included here. The number of physicians seen in hospitals is small enough, and there is sufficient overlap with ambulatory doctors so that this latter limitation is probably not too important. Physician nonresponse is reduced in importance due to the fact that we usually succeeded in obtaining a questionnaire from at least the "primary physician" for the family, which means the physician who provided the most care during the year and who therefore should have created the greatest impression on the patient.

[8] We are now dealing only with persons who had some medical care in the past year and are included in the medical records study.

Age is an indicator that is easily observed by the patient and thus has influence on his evaluation of his medical care. In all the plans, except the small commercial plan, age has a definite influence. Its influence is more noticeable in the large group practice plan than in the small group or in the open-market plans taken as a whole. In the large group practice plan 11% more patients are satisfied when they receive care from predominantly older physicians. The effect may be linked to the seriousness of the illness, since the older physicians of the plan see the more difficult cases. In the hospital-sponored plan those who have visited primarily older physicians have one of the highest rates of dissatisfaction. In this case the rate rises to 50%, and is not paralleled in any other plan.

Another of these easily observed indicators is the socioeconomic background of the physician. As noted in Chapter 2, there are no significant differences among the plans in the SES backgrounds of their physicians. There are notable differences, however, among the patients. The consumers in the small group plan have the highest SES, whereas those in the hospital-sponsored plan have the lowest (Hollingshead Two-Factor Index). People in all plans were more satisfied with care from physicians who had lower class backgrounds, but in the hospital-sponsored plan this was most pronounced (61% vs. 38%) and reversed in the small group practice plan (29% vs. 34%).

In an earlier discussion we discredited the myth that group practice plans recruit more physicians who are trained abroad. There is a sharp drop in satisfaction in these plans, however, when patients receive care from physicians who were trained in countries other than the United States, Canada, Great Britain, or Scandinavia. Satisfaction drops to 19% for these consumers—the lowest level yet encountered in our analysis of opinion of medical care. In all other plans this finding is reversed. Further study is needed to understand this phenomenon, but one explanation may be that patients expect the group plans to harbor physicians who cannot make it on their own in the community, and the stigma may become more exaggerated when a physician is from another country.

The *qualifying* indicators of a physician are specialty certification and continuing medical education. These characteristics are not easily perceived by patients unless they are sensitive to the technical aspects of care.

Satisfaction of consumers seeing predominantly highly qualified physicians is 43% compared with 35% for the other consumers. Within plans there appears to be a uniform effect of physician qualification. For the open-market 51% of the patients visiting highly qualified physicians were satisfied with the care they received, and 42% visiting less-qualified physicians were satisfied. The shift in attitude in the large group practice plan is 7% and 5% in the small group practice plan in the same direction. Whatever the reason for the effect, it is apparently not specific to mode of delivery or financing of medical care.

Of the indicators of the *facilitating* (behavioral) dimension, the one most directly relevant to consumer opinion is physician patient load. In the open-market plans consumers complained of long waiting periods, whereas in the group practice plans they complained of the lack of individual attention. Both are related to the number of patients a physician sees. In all plans there is a drop in rates of satisfaction with medical care as physician patient-load increases from four patients or fewer per hour to five or more. The drop is not large: 42 to 37%. There is a significant rise, however, in dissatisfaction. This rate goes from 3 to 19%. Patient loads might be expected to reduce satisfaction with medical care in all types of plans.

The data show an overall drop in rates of high satisfaction with medical care as physician patient loads increase from four or less per hour to five or more.[9] The increased dissatisfaction is most noticeable in the open-market plans.

Plan type	Low patient load	High patient load
Commercial	3.7	14.8
Provider-sponsored	7.2	34.1
Group practice	0.9	1.4

The effect of the complaint that physicians do not give enough individual attention is not observed in the data. The complaint probably is voiced by those who have not received recent medical care—and it may be one reason why they have not. The data just reported is for those who have received care in the last year, whereas the dissatisfaction rate was found in data taken from the total consumer sample in each plan. Lack of individual attention in the

[9] Patient loads were estimated from the physician questionnaire. The physician provided information on the number of patients he ordinarily sees on a regular complete working day and the number of hours ordinarily worked. A patient-per-hour estimate was derived from these data and the dichotomy used here was decided on the basis of the resulting frequency distribution for the entire sample of physicians.

group practice plans is heavily affected by opinions of those who have not received recent medical care.

In summary, 41% of the people in the total sample were satisfied with their medical care and 7% were dissatisfied. The lowest proportion of highly satisfied consumers was found in the small group practice plan, but proportions in the other plans were comparable. Lowest dissatisfaction was in the large group practice plan and highest in the hospital-sponsored plan. No significant differences are observed in satisfaction with medical care when plans are collapsed into types, but the group practice plans have only 4% dissatisfied compared with 10% in other plans.[10]

Out-of-plan use in the large group practice plan, as reflected by high out-of-pocket expense, is associated with lowered satisfaction. This does not appear to be the case in the small group practice plan. In all plans satisfaction with medical care is greater for medical services characterized as preventive, rational, and continuous (as measured by the range of services indices). Large declines in satisfaction are noted for care scoring high on the verification index (routine lab and radiology). In the range of service measures rationality (positively) and verification (negatively) have major effects in the group practice plans. In the other plans prevention (positively) and rationality (negatively) are the major influences. The negative effect of rationality is thought to be related to level of seriousness of illness involved and the "halo" effect of increased medical care expenses for the consumer in the less comprehensive open-market plans. A high rate of dissatisfaction (15%) with clinic procedures is expressed by consumers in the large group practice plan. Also, relative to the other plans, these consumers complain more about unavailability of physicians when needed. Both are thought to reflect problems of *access* in this plan.

Dissatisfaction with medical care tends to be less for high-need families, for it is higher in the large group practice plan. For consumers with both high education and recent, extensive medical care the large group practice plan elicits the least satisfaction of all plans.

More satisfaction with medical care is reported for patients visiting predominantly older physicians. Patients of physicians from lower

---

[10] The scaling of "satisfaction" and "dissatisfaction" in this final report is done somewhat differently from that in the preliminary report on "Health Insurance Effect," although the relationships by either method are essentially similar.

socioeconomic backgrounds are more satisfied with their care, especially in the hospital-sponsored plan, in which patients are predominantly of lower socioeconomic status. Uniformly higher satisfaction is expressed by consumers treated by highly qualified physicians (specialty certified, with recent continuing medical education). The lowest rate of satisfaction is for consumers in the large group practice plan whose physicians were trained abroad. This effect is not observed in other plans.

Satisfaction with medical care in the open-market plans is associated with consumer complaint about waiting periods and physician profit motives. In the group practice plans the relationship is to complaints about lack of individual attention.

CONCLUSIONS

In every plan in this study more consumers express outright dissatisfaction with their financial coverage than they do with the medical care received. Satisfaction in both instances does not vary greatly, being about 40% for financial coverage and medical care; dissatisfaction, however, is 11% for coverage and 7% for medical care.

When opinions of financial coverage are broken down by plan, there is a general correspondence between consumer evaluations and the objective reality of benefit levels. The highest percent of satisfied consumers and the smallest number of dissatisfied are found in the large group practice plan, which has the most comprehensive product. The hospital-sponsored plan, on the other hand, being the least comprehensive, evokes the least satisfaction and the most dissatisfaction on this measure. These major distinctions remain generally true under various controls for consumer *need* and *demand.*

The large group practice plan does best in the opinions of the low-need, high-demand families—a fact that is somewhat disturbing, and has raised questions throughout this book. Dissatisfaction with financial coverage rises for consumers in this plan with lower educational levels and no use of medical services in the previous 12 months. This dissatisfaction, although at a low level, perhaps reflects a larger problem toward which our data have been pointing. This is the problem of differential *access* in a highly bureaucratized system. The high-need family pays a higher premium rate in this plan for services received (Chapter 5), and opinion may be indicating dissatisfaction with high financial inputs for little or no services to families in the high-need category.

Another consideration in interpreting the opinion data is the effect of self-selection. We found, reasonably, that people in the open-market plans who had the option of choosing the plan they thought best suited to their needs, and who chose on the basis of evaluations of coverage, were less likely to be dissatisfied with that coverage. Under conditions of the voluntary option the lower rates of dissatisfaction in the group plans cannot be demonstrated. Antecedent attitudes (pre enrollment) are thus seen to affect current opinions. Further multivariate analyses are called for to determine the extent to which such antecedent attitudes can "explain" differences in opinions among plans.

Consumer satisfaction with medical care does not vary greatly among the plans, although it is somewhat depressed in the small group practice plan. More interestingly, less dissatisfaction is found in the group practice plans—especially the large group practice plan. This is impressive, considering popular (though waning) rhetoric about the disadvantages of care delivered in the large group practice mode. Consumers, however, do complain about items related to bureaucratic characteristics: clinic procedures and availability of physicians. Again, such complaints tend to concentrate in the high-need consumers and among those who report short-term illness. Consumers thus seem to approve of the medical care they receive in the group clinics, but the attendant inconveniences provoke objections. In the community private practices a higher rate of dissatisfaction with the care itself is reported.

Some initial attempts were made to identify the objective referents for expressed opinions of medical care between aspects of the care itself and characteristics of the provider. The range of service measures were found to relate to consumer opinion, so that care characterized as highly preventive, rational, and continuous evoked greater consumer approval, whereas dissatisfaction rose with increases in verification scores. There are suggestions, however, that these associations are intermingled with financial considerations. For instance, there is a differential response to rationality between comprehensive plans and others, and we have speculated that this is due to the relation between rationality, seriousness of illness, and expense. Prevention is another example. All plans show an increase in satisfaction for more preventive care, but it is most evident in the open-market plans in which the consumer gets only what he pays for out-of-pocket. Thus, although economic factors appear to occupy a central position in consumer judgments of care, when these factors are largely obliterated (as in the large group practice plan), we are still able to observe rises in satisfaction with rises in range of service scores (or decreases, as in the case of verification).

Other "nontechnical" aspects of medical care enter into consumer judgments, such as perceptions of physician characteristics. Consumers in the open-market plans react negatively to physicians they feel are profit-oriented; consumers in the group practice plans react to lack of individual attention by physicians treating a large and constantly changing clientele. These are certainly aspects of the much-revered doctor-patient relationship. The erosion of this relationship, however, does not appear to be best illustrated in the group practices but rather in the predominantly solo community practices. In the latter setting there is a significant rise in dissatisfaction with medical care with increasing patient loads. This is certainly not logically divorced from the complaint about the profit motive by consumers in the open-market plans. Of further interest is the impact of socioeconomic congruence on the doctor-patient relationship. Some evidence has been presented that indicates higher rates of satisfaction for patients seeing physicians from lower socioeconomic backgrounds. Since the total consumer sample is predominantly middle and lower-middle class, one suspects that similarity in class backgrounds is instrumental in facilitating doctor-patient communication and in shaping consumer evaluations of experience in the doctor's office. One suspects the effect referred to here would be much more evident in a consumer sample more representative of persons at the extreme opposite end of the socioeconomic continuum from that of the average physician.

REFERENCES

Anderson, Odin W. and Sheatsley, Paul B. "Comprehensive medical insurance: a study of costs, use and attitudes under two plans." Research series #9, Health Information Foundation, New York (1961).

Hollingshead, A. B. "Two-factor index of social position." New Haven, Connecticut, 1957. (Monograph)

Medical advisory council to the board of administration of the Public Employees' Retirement System. "Final report on the survey of consumer experience under the State of California employees' hospital and medical care act." Sacramento, 1971. (Monograph)

VII

Conclusions

AMERICA IS DOMINATED by health plans that are commercial, provider-sponsored, and group practice types of organization. What these plans promise and how they actually perform was the basis of this inquiry.

Conducted within Los Angeles County, the UCLA based study sought representatives of these national types. Two of each, one large and one small, were approached. Eventually they all contributed, with varying degrees of helpfulness, to this work. Each plan is a social system unto itself. The health insurance agency, the consumers who subscribe to its products, and the physicians who serve them are components of the system. Each interacted with the others and influenced or controlled the outcome.

Information was gathered from each component of the six social systems. Board of director members, managers, and technical people in the agencies were interviewed or sent questionnaires. Plan literature and reports were perused for plan goals and perspectives.

People who bought benefit packages from the agencies were selected randomly and sent questionnaires on their experiences with their health insurance. From these people a smaller random sample was selected. Families in this group were asked for permission to photocopy their medical and insurance claim records. Every physician serving anyone who gave permission for the medical record study was sent a questionnaire or interviewed.

The overwhelming mass of data collected from these sources was sorted into manageable units that could be analyzed. The variations of each plan on consumer use of medical services, quality of care, family medical expenses, and consumer opinions of medical care and financial coverage were studied. The variations were then analyzed according to their relation with plan characteristics. The extent to which these variations are influenced by consumer and physician characteristics was also explored. Finally, the behavior of the plan types (commercial, provider-sponsored, and group) was studied.

THE HEALTH INSURING AGENCY

Board of Directors

The commercial plans were founded as life insurance companies, with board members who represented mostly industrial and legal interests. The established health professions founded the provider-sponsored plans, and their boards are dominated by physician and hospital representatives. Group practice plans began through the interaction of employer and consumer groups and the initiative of a few physicians, with board members representing the medical profession and industry. Consumer representation was almost nonexistent.

Plan goals as perceived by organization personnel, consumers, and physicians were measured. The commercial plans ranked highest on the importance of profit in relation to service. The provider-sponsored plans were second in profit orientation, followed by the group practice plans. The division, however, between the large commercial plan and the provider plans is not distinct. Measuring *loss ratio* (amount of premium dollar returned to consumer in benefits), the group plans have the lowest percent of families to whom 50% or less of the premium dollar was returned in benefits. The large commercial has the highest percent, but the distinction among the commercial and provider plans does not follow types. Dollar figures for loss ratios, although of limited usefulness because of small Ns and large variances, show that three plans operated "in the black" in the year of study: large commercial, hospital-sponsored, and large group.

Regulation

Commercial and hospital-sponsored plans fall under the legal jurisdiction of the state insurance commissioner, but the latter plan is subject to much more lenient regulation because of its status as a "nonprofit hospital service plan." The remaining three plans are regulated by the office of the attorney general. The stiffest laws apply to the commercial plans, but are written vaguely. Physician-sponsored and group practice plans are largely self-regulated. The extent to which organizations are responsive to public influence, either through laws or other mechanisms, is termed *permeability.* On measures of consumer satisfaction with action on complaints, consumer knowledge of benefits, and physician satisfaction with effective representation in the plans, the provider-sponsored plans are least permeable. The evidence is that the health insurance industry, as represented in this study, is largely unregulated and only slightly responsive to the consumer.

Management

Physicians in the group practice plans are largely on salary, although many in the small group plan also have individual private practices. Physicians who are members of the physician-sponsored plan are under an agreement to accept plan payment as payment-in-full for patients below a certain income level. Other open-market plans exert only indirect influence on physician charges. Conversion factors for care in the six plans showed the highest charges in the commercial and hospital-sponsored plans, physician-sponsored next, then small group, and finally large group with the lowest rate. Control over hospital charges is exerted only in the large group and hospital-sponsored plans and very minimally in the latter.

Two types of administration are control over providers and control over consumers. The former is best illustrated in the large group practice, whereas the latter is emphasized in the commercial plans. Provider plans have characteristics of both. Estimates of the portion of the premium dollars used for administration show the provider and small commercial plans to be highest, large group the lowest.

Technical Level

Benefit package controls over the consumer measured by eight items are most numerous in the provider-sponsored plans and least in the group practice plans. The group practice plans pay a much higher percent of family medical expenses than any other plan.

A combination of consumer and physician evaluations shows that most respondents feel that the group practice plans sell the most comprehensive benefit packages and the provider-sponsored plans the least comprehensive.

Benefit packages are most expensive in the physician-sponsored and large group practice plans. They are least expensive in the small group plan (the average, however, included several packages written without financial liability for hospitalization). A comparison of comprehensiveness and average price indicates that the provider-sponsored plans are over priced, the small group plan, under priced.

CONSUMERS

"Risk" is the measure of a family's propensity to use medical services.Insurance companies, especially the open-market ones, categorize potential subscribers according to "high risk" or "low risk,"and set premiums accordingly. In our study risk involves the concepts of *need* and *demand.*

Need indicators for this study are age, family size, prevalence of chronic illness, incidence of short-term illness, and percent of women of child-bearing age. Summation of plan ranks on each indicator shows the group plans to have consumers with the highest need, whreas the physician-sponsored plan has consumers with the lowest need.

Demand indicators are income, education, occupation, ethnicity, negativity toward doctors, perceived influence of health insurance on use of medical services, and symptom-sensitivity. Highest demand is found in the small group plan and the lowest in the large commercial.

PHYSICIANS

Large group, small group, and other physicians seen by people in the consumer sample are compared on dimensions of limiting, qualifying, facilitating, and motivating factors.

Limiting factors are measures of age, years since M.D., fathers' socioeconomic status, location of medical school attended, and applicants per position for the school attended. On the average small group physicians are older and large group physicians are younger. No other significant differences were found.

Qualifying factors measure specialty board status, nature of specialty, continuing medical education (formal courses), and professional journals read. Use of specialists is highest in the large group plan, but surgeons are used much less frequently. Use of board-certified physicians is lowest in the small group plan. Group practice physicians receive less "formal" continuing medical education than others.

Facilitating factors include structural and behavioral components. The structural component is doctor/paramedical ratio, access to laboratory in an emergency, and characteristics of hospitals used. Paramedical-to- doctor ratio is lowest in the small group plan and highest in the large group plan. Fastest return on emergency laboratory orders and highest hospital occupancy rates are found in the large group plan the behavioral component is patients seen in the office per hour, consultation rate, meetings among physicians, and fee conversion factors. Small group physicians see fewer patients per hour than all others. Large group physicians interact more on medical problems.

Motivating factors are measures of attitudes toward preventive examination, negativity toward patients, and attitude toward medical record keeping. Significantly fewer large group physicians agree with the necessity of the annual examination (despite performing more). They are also more negative toward patients than their colleagues in the other plans. Their most frequent complaint was about patients making unnecessary visits. No significant differences were found in attitude toward records and reported behavior in record keeping.

Generalizing about Health Maintenance Organizations as they are represented in this study (the group plans) is dangerous. Both plans studied are characterized by group practice and prepayment but are considerably different in structure and operation. The larger of the two has salaried physicians who are not allowed practices outside the plan, plan ownership of all facilities including hospitals, comprehensive coverage with few options and negligible copayment and cost sharing, fast lab service and sufficient paramedical support. The small group plan's administration is very different. Many of the newly formed health plans of the HMO variety, moreover, differ from the two study plans in still other ways.

An apparent lack of distinction emerges among the commercials and the provider-sponsored plans. Representatives of these plan types frequently change positions in the rankings on various measures of structure and performance.

Interestingly, the plan providing the most comprehensive coverage and perceived as having a primary emphasis on service makes a profit. The commercial plans either make less money or lose money on their group health insurance offerings. The commercial insurers readily admit they do not regard group health insurance as profitable but rather as a feature to attract customers to life insurance policies. The "money maker" of the study, the large group practice plan, returns only 60 cents per dollar received in premiums—though its construction of facilities must not be overlooked.

When consumers are ranked on six indicators of medical need, the group practice plans are found to serve the most people who are high-need. The screening of prospective members according to medical history and high-risk occupational groups leaves the large commercial and physician-sponsored plans with the fewest high-need consumers.

USE OF SERVICES

Ambulatory Care

The people in the six study plans made a little over four visits to the doctor during the study year. Subscribers to the large group plan made more visits than those in other plans and those in the large commercial plan made the fewest.

Out-of-plan use is an issue in the group plans, where patients may feel they prefer the attention received from a private doctor or perhaps feel that the group plans' system is too difficult to cope with during an illness. In the small group plan 6.9% of the subscribers chose to use outside care, and in the large group plan 10.5% made this decision during the year. This is a relatively minor proportion of the care received and does not indicate that the problem is so significant as critics of the group-practice plans contend.

A frequent argument against a national health plan offering comprehensive benefits and few or no copayments is that people would overuse medical care. Some indication of this was found in the group practice plans in this study. The greatest use of doctors' services was not by the typical "welfare type," but by people from higher socioeconomic backgrounds with apparent lower need for medical care. The comprehensive benefit packages only increased the probability that somebody from low-income families would visit a doctor at least once during the year. Low-educated families in the large group plan made significantly fewer visits to doctors than did the higher educated families. These findings are reversed in the other plans. It is the low-need people in the large group plan who have inflated doctor-use figures, perhaps because of the use of preventive services. This may not be "unnecessary" use of services, but spokesmen (and practicing physicians) for this plan would like to see most preventive services used by high-risk plan members.

The large group practice plan has a complex bureaucracy that may create deterrents for some people. This "bureaucratic effect" consists of centralized services (sometimes requiring long trips to a clinic), bureaucratic procedures that cause long waits (and long periods away from work), and waiting lists for routine appointments (long delays before a patient can see a doctor). These elements cause difficulties among lower educated people, since they frequently have inflexible work schedules, poorer access to transportation, and less ability to "make the system work." The better educated people, however, are not so easily stymied by the system and can take more advantage of the comprehensive benefits.

In terms of volume of services delivered, greater need leads to greater volume across all plans. Higher income is also related to more services in plans that have less comprehensive benefit packages. The group practice plans and the physician-sponsored plan deliver the lowest volume of services for those who receive care, the large group practice plan delivering the lowest.

The group practice plans provide more laboratory testing than other plans but pay less attention to their results. Physicians in the provider and commercial plans more frequently complain about the limitations placed on laboratory and radiology testing outside the hospital.

Hospital Care

The annual rate of hospitalization in this study was 132 admissions per 1000 insured persons. The rate was significantly lower in the large group plan and next lowest in the small group plan. Features that may explain the differences in rates among the plans are the group plans' more comprehensive benefits for ambulatory care and the large group plan's limited supply of hospital beds.

High-need families had a higher hospital admission rate than low-need families in all plans, but in the large group plan the rate was very low for high-need families. High income leads to high hospital rates in the provider-sponsored plans and the small commercial plan, but the reverse is true in the other plans. Lower education is related to lower hospital admission rates in the large group plan. People in occupations of lower status had higher rates of hospitalization in every plan.

This study confirms again the lower hospitalization rates of the large group practice plan, but the effect is due mostly to very low rates among families with high apparent medical needs and low educations.

The overall days per hospitalization was 0.96 per year per insured person. This is in agreement with rates reported in California as a whole. The days per admission show that the large group practice plan has rates that are nearly equivalent to those of the commercial plans. The small group and provider plans are much higher.

Five of the six insurance plans did not differ significantly from state figures for days per person per year, but the large group plan was much lower. The performance of the large group plan on this measurement is caused then by the low rate of admissions. The low rate of admissions, however, is the result of people with high needs but low education not being admitted as often as others. This again may be a result of "bureaucratic effect."

QUALITY OF CARE AND RANGE OF SERVICES

Quality of care as studied here concentrates on a range of services that have been objectively and unobtrusively determined. This is a different approach than any taken previously, as the estimation of dimensions of quality was accomplished with nonmedical personnel abstracting objective information from medical records. This method is currently relevant to proposed monitoring of care by Professional Standards Review Organizations (PSROs), since information was derived from medical records. In the coding no judgments were made of good or bad, adequate or inadequate. The procedures were either in the record or not.

Procedures thus identified were clustered into four dimensions by factor analysis. These dimensions were prevention, rationality, verification, and continuity.

The *prevention* factor included annual checkup, physical examination, rectal examination, and Pap smear and pelvic examination for women. On each of these indicators taken separately one or both of the group plans had higher scores. When the indicators are combined into a prevention factor score, both group practice plans have higher averages per person per visit than all other plans. In the group practice plans, however, the people who receive the care appear to be those who need it least. In the other plans high-need persons receive more preventive care than the low-need persons. High-demand persons receive more preventive care in five of the six plans, but low-demand persons receive more in the large group plan.

The *rationality* factor is based on physical examination, medical history, chief complaint, diagnosis, and progress notes. The large group practice plan performed better than any other plan on these indicators. As a plan type the group practice plans had a higher average; however, the two plans do not perform equally well on this measure. In all plans persons classified as high-need have higher rationality scores. The difference, though, between the large group practice plan and the others is the greatest for high-need patients. Demand indicators had little influence on the rationality scores, but income did have a significant effect in the large group practice plan. In this plan higher income persons had higher factor scores.

Indicators of *verification* were complete blood count, urinalysis, serology, and chest X-ray. Thus the verification factor mainly reflects administration of routine procedures. The large group practice plan makes more extensive use of all types of laboratory and radiology testing than any other plan. Since the patient is not financially liable, this may be the reason for higher rates of routine work. The physicians in this plan, however, do not make note of the results as frequently as their colleagues in private practice. Overall, less than 50% of the "medical care bits" contained reports of laboratory or radiology tests. In every plan need is inversely related to the verification factor score. This factor score evidently reflects laboratory and radiology work for minor complaints. The low-need patients have higher verification scores in the group practice plans. Demand does not influence verification, except in the large group plan in which an inverse relationship occurs.

The major *continuity* factor indicators are followup visit and followup visit requested. Continuity of medical personnel is measured by the frequency with which a patient sees the same physician from one visit to the next or sees a doctor to whom he has been referred. Followup visits and the rate of request for followup visits did vary greatly from one plan to another. The large group practice plan has the highest rate of referral to specialists. Continuity of medical personnel is lowest in the group practice plans. This has often been a criticism of the group practice plan type. The hospital-sponsored plan has the highest rate of continuity. As the need for medical care increases, so does the rate of continuity. Among the low-need consumers the gap between the group practice plans and the others was the greatest. Education and symptom-sensitivity affected the continuity rate in the large group practice but not in the others. In this plan, then, patients who were better educated and more symptom-sensitive received greater continuity of medical care.

The factor scores also give insight into physician performance and a patient's opinion of that performance. The physician characteristics (limiting, qualifying, facilitating, and motivating) were compared on the four quality dimensions.

On the prevention factor patients visiting physicians who had attended much sought-after medical schools received significantly higher prevention scores. Physicians who were better qualified in terms of specialty certification and continuing medical education also provided more preventive services, except in the group practice plans in which qualification had no impact. Physicians who were rated "high" on facilitation also provided more preventive services. Physicians with a heavy patient load (five or more patients per hour on the average) provided less preventive services. The motivating factor had no impact in all plans except the group plans. In these plans a positive relationship was found between opinion of annual checkup, level of preventive services, and complaints about patients making unnecessary visits. This is probably a reaction to the high use of preventive services by low-need people.

The high rationality scores of the large group plan seem to be due to an organizational structure that encourages ongoing peer review and opportunities for continuing medical education. Physician record keeping had a direct influence on the rationality scores, but good and bad record keepers were evenly distributed among all the plans. Younger physicians tended to provide more thorough care. Qualifying characteristics had positive but not statistically significant impact on the factor scores. The high rationality factor scores in the large group practice plan are maintained only for physicians with low patient loads. Increased patient load has a direct effect on quality of care, and in our study there was no evidence that group practice and high ratios of medical/paramedical personnel avoid the detrimental effects of large patient loads. Doctors who complain that patients make unnecessary visits provide less thorough care than others in the large group practice plan. This is not true in the other plans.

Patients with high verification scores were those who visited physicians who were 40 years of age or younger, graduated from a medical school in a country other than the United States, Canada, Great Britain, or Scandinavia, were not certified, without continuing medical education courses in the preceding 12 months, with short turn-around time from their laboratories, and a positive orientation toward their patients.

Physicians with more limited backgrounds and those with negative attitudes toward patients generated the lowest factor scores. Consumers are sensitive to continuity of their medical care. Those who had higher scores on this factor had fewer complaints about their physicians.

FAMILY EXPENSES

Out-of-pocket

From estimates based on the survey questionnaire, families in the large group practice plan had significantly lower out-of-pocket expenses per person than families in all other plans. The greatest out-of-pocket expenses were found in the hospital-sponsored plan.

Out-of-plan use was studied for the group practice plans only. Approximately 15% of the families in both group plans went outside the plan for medical services, according to data from the medical records subsample. Profiles of the out-of-plan user revealed that in both plans high-need families used more out-of-plan services. In the large group plan the *high-demand* families tended to go outside the plan, whereas while in the small group plan the *low-demand* families did. Out-of-plan use in the large group plan was associated with negative attitudes toward physicians.

High-need families spent more out-of-pocket than low-need families in all plans. The differences among the plans—especially between the large group plan and the others—was greatest among the high-need families. For both high-need and low-need families the hospital-sponsored plan had highest per person expenses.

Demand factors were found to have very little influence on out-of-pocket expenses. For every plan high-need families had a higher average expenditure than the high-demand families. A study of out-of-pocket expenses in relation to volume of services revealed that in the hospital-sponsored plan the high-demand consumers paid more in out-of-pocket expenses than the low-demand consumers but received fewer medical services.

When plans are collapsed into types, the provider-sponsored plans reveal an increase in out-of-pocket expenses for the higher income, ethnic majority patient (it is reversed in the commercial plans). The effect may be due to agreement by providers in these plans to accept as payment in full the amount paid by the plan for families below a certain income.

Total Expenses

Total expenses are out-of-pocket expenses plus health insurance premiums. The former is derived from mid-points of categories checked in the consumer questionnaire, the latter is from data provided by the health plan or the consumer employment groups. All data are presented per person for the study year.

The two group plans proved to have the lowest per person total expenses, followed by the commercials and the provider-sponsored plans. The ranking on costs corresponds to the ranking on comprehensiveness of benefits. In the provider-sponsored plans the total expenditure is double the national average. Total expenses in the large group plan averaged $129 per person (1968), whereas the comparable figure for hospital-sponsored plan was $234 per person.

Under conditions of low use of medical services the large group plan is more expensive than the small group plan or either of the commercial plans. The greatest advantage of the large group plan is under conditions of heavy use of medical services.

On price paid in relation to services received the large group plan shows up as the most expensive and the small commercial the least expensive. This is due to adjustment for hospital days and thus indicates that the major economy achieved by the large group plan is in gross reductions in hospitalization. For the large group practice plan reductions are affected among high-need consumers.

Controlling for family size, we find that the group plans consistently have the lowest total expenses per person and the provider-sponsored, the highest. The influence of experience rating in setting premiums (whereby adjustments are made for risk) is felt in all plans except the large group plan. The result in the former plans is that high-need persons pay more.

We found that families paid an average of 5% of their per capita incomes for medical services and insurance premiums. The lowest percent was in the group plans (3.8%) and the highest in the hospital-sponsored plan (7.1%).

For low-income families the "best buy" in terms of percent of per capita income is the small group or small commercial plan. For families who are heavy users of medical care the best buy is the large group plan. The most expensive plan for this category of consumer is the physician-sponsored plan.

Considering volume of services (California Relative Value Study units for doctor services and hospital days), the consumer in the large group practice plan pays the most per unit of service and the consumer in the small commercial plan pays the least.

OPINIONS

Satisfaction with Financial Coverage

Consumer satisfaction with financial coverage was measured by a questionnaire item involving a nine-point scale. Responses falling between the first two and the last two marks on the scale were defined as *highly satisfied* and *highly dissatisfied* .

The large group practice plan had the highest percent satisfied (71%) and a very low percent dissatisfied (5%). The hospital-sponsored plan had the highest rate of dissatisfied consumers (25%).

Consumer satisfaction was influenced by several demographic factors and attitudes toward medical care. For instance, presence of chronic illness in a family tended to polarize opinions about health care coverage. High-income persons were generally more satisfied with the large group practice plan. Among the highly educated consumers satisfaction decreased as use of medical services increased, regardless of plan. Lower educated persons without recent medical care experience were dissatisfied with the financial coverage in the group practice plans. For these people satisfaction with plan coverage is equivalent in all the plans. In contrast, lower educated people who had recent medical care experience became more satisfied (96%) in the group practice plans, but in the other plans there is little change. Regardless of demand, consumers evaluate the large group plan coverage as best and the hospital-sponsored plan coverage as least satisfactory.

Consumers who overestimated their coverage expressed higher satisfaction in all plans. In the least comprehensive plans consumer dissatisfaction increased with increased need.

Satisfaction with Medical Care

Satisfaction with medical care was expressed by 41% of the sample, dissatisfaction by 7%. The lowest proportion of highly satisfied consumers was found in the small group practice plan, and rates in the other plans were comparable. Lowest dissatisfaction was in the large group practice plan, and in the hospital-sponsored plan. Collapsing plans into plan types, no differences are observed for rates of satisfaction with medical care, but the group practice plans have only 4% dissatisfied compared with 10% in the other plans.

Out-of-plan use in the large group practice plan, as reflected by high out-of-pocket expense, is associated with lowered satisfaction with medical care received within the plan. This does not appear to be the case in the small group practice plan.

Satisfaction with medical care for the entire sample is greater for medical services characterized as more preventive, rational, and continuous (as measured by the range of services indices). Large declines in satisfaction are noted for care scoring high on the verification index (routine lab and radiology). Among the range of service measures rationality (positively) and verification (negatively) have major effects in the group practice plans on satisfaction. In the other plans prevention (positively) and rationality (negatively) are the major influences. The negative effect of rationality is thought to be related to level of seriousness of illness involved and the "halo" effect of increased medical care expenses for the consumer in the less comprehensive open-market plans.

A relatively high rate of dissatisfaction (15%) with clinic procedures is expressed by consumers in the large group practice plan. Also, in relation to the other plans, these consumers complain more about unavailability of physicians when needed. Both are thought to reflect problems of *access* in this plan.

Dissatisfaction with medical care tends to be less among high-need families but not in the large group practice plan. Dissatisfaction in this plan is highest for those with short-term illnesses. Among consumers with both high education and recent extensive medical care the large group practice plan elicits the least satisfaction of all plans. The group plans have higher proportions of satisfied consumers among the college educated than other plans. Among those with less education medical care in predominantly solo-practice settings is most popular.

Satisfaction with medical care in the open-market plans is associated with consumer complaint about waiting periods and physician profit motives. In the group practice plans the relationship is to complaints about lack of individual attention.

More satisfaction with medical care is reported for patients visiting predominantly older physicians. The effect is most pronounced in the large group practice plans. Higher rates of satisfaction are observed for patients of physicians from lower socioeconomic backgrounds.

This is particularly true in the hospital-sponsored plan, in which consumers are predominantly of lower socioeconomic status, but it is not true in the small group practice plan in which the average SES score of consumers is highest of all the plans.

The lowest rate of satisfaction found among all variables is for consumers in the large group practice plan who have primarily been treated by physicians who have trained in a country other than the United States, Canada, Great Britain, or Scandinavia. The effect is not observed in other plans.

Uniformly higher rates of satisfaction are expressed by consumers treated by highly qualified physicians (specialty certified, with recent continuing medical education). Very large increases in patient dissatisfaction are associated in the open-market plans with increased physician patient load. There are also substantial decreases in satisfaction in these plans. Virtually no such effect is found in the group practice plans.

A LOOK AT PLAN TYPES

The danger of generalizing study results in terms of plan types is that the two representatives of each type vary greatly in structure and output. Nevertheless, popular thought and much of the medical care literature concentrate on the advantages and disadvantages of these types and public policy tends to treat them as the major variants in the marketplace. Consequently, one of the analytic objectives of our study was to examine performance of the plans across the the three types.

Membership compositions of the three types of health insurance plan were compared on measures of risk. The commercial plans enroll persons with the lowest risk of illness, whether measured by age levels, symptom-sensitivity, or presence of chronic illnesses. The last is especially low. The next level of risk is found among persons enrolled in the provider-sponsored plans. The group practice plan consumers are characterized as having the highest level of illness risk.

Ambulatory service use is relatively similar in all plan types. The greatest emphasis on ambulatory services is in the group practice plans, and consequently the highest rate of use occurs in this plan type. The next highest is in the provider-sponsored plans, the lowest in the commercial plans. In the last plan type the low-risk consumer population and the heavy cost-sharing results in nearly one-half of the enrolled families not seeing a doctor once during the three-month test period, compared with about one-third of the families in the other two plan types. Across all plan types doctor visits are higher for upper class families and lower for high-risk families.[1]

The aggregate measure of doctor's care (office or clinic, home, or hospital) is the volume of service. The highest per capita volume is rendered in the provider-sponsored plans, followed by the group practice and the commercial plans. This relationship prevails under various sociodemographic breakdowns, except that in lower class families the volume of service is about as high in the group practice as in the provider plans.[2]

Hospital utilization rates differ markedly among the three plan types. Admission rates are highest in the provider-sponsored plans and lowest in the group plans. Hospital days *per admission* does not indicate any advantage for the group plans. Differences in the aggregate hospital days per insured person per year are due to lower admission rates, and lower admission rates are mainly determined by the large group practice plan which has low rates of admission among the high-need category of consumer.

Out-of-plan use—long considered a hidden deficiency of the group practice plans—was found to be negligible in this study. About 8% of the ambulatory visits and 7% of the hospitalizations occurred outside the plans.

Factor score measures of quality of medical care (range of services) demonstrate more preventive care in the group plans, more care with "rational" characteristics, but less continuity.

Family medical expenses include both out-of-pocket expenses and insurance premiums. Out-of-pocket expenses for doctor and hospital services during a year are lowest in the group practice plans and highest in the provider-sponsored plans. The relationship prevails in all sociodemographic breakdowns. Premiums are highest in the group practice plans (associated with their wider range of benefits and greater proportion of high-risk members) and lowest in the

---

[1] It is important to recognize that data for plan types is weighted according to the relative size (i. e., consumer enrollments) of the representative plans. Thus in the data for group plans, for instance, the contribution of the small group plan is one-sixth that of the large group plan.

[2] These figures are based on the total consumer population. When only those who receive some care are considered, the group plans deliver the lowest volume of care per patient seen, with the large group practice plan having the lowest figure.

commercial plans (offering a narrow range of benefits, greatest cost-sharing features, and smallest proportion of high-risk members).

Combining these cost elements, the lowest costs are found in the group practice plans and the highest costs are found in the provider-sponsored plans, with the commercial plans in between. This is true for both upper and lower social class families and for families with or without a history of chronic illness. The lowest medical care costs are found in the commercial plans for low-income families. The lowest percent of income paid for medical services and insurance premiums was in the group plans, the highest in the provider plans.

The consumers' attitudes toward financial protection and medical care received under the three plan types differ greatly. Consumer satisfaction with financial protection is highest in the group practice plans, regardless of the demographic characteristics. In contrast, the provider-sponsored plans had many highly dissatisfied members. Regarding medical care received, there were no significant differences in satisfaction among the plan types but significantly less frank dissatisfaction in the group plans.

IMPLICATIONS

The current American power structure provides the consumer with very little leverage in the medical care system. Health plans need to become more permeable to consumer influence by providing greater consumer representation on boards of directors and enforceable legal regulations and making adequate provision for responding to complaints. With greater consumer input, more attention would be given to control over provider prices rather than to control over consumer use of services. Plan-management structures might be simplified to reduce administrative overhead and consumer confusion. Consumers might also influence composition of benefit packages so that adequate medical care is available in all plans.

Control over consumers, whether by benefit exclusions, cost sharing, or avoidance of high-risk persons is misplaced or perhaps even unnecessary. As evidenced by the large group practice plan, the overload on the medical care system under comprehensive coverage does not come from the "welfare types,"but from well-educated, middle- and upper class people. They understand what "comprehensive coverage" means, perceive the possible value of preventive care, and have little trouble negotiating the bureaucratic maze. For them the institution of controls over consumption means giving up the optional niceties; for others it can mean severe financial hardship to obtain even the most needed medical care.

The experiences of the high-need, low-income families are mixed but are generally better in the large group practice plan. Yet the high-need families in this plan make fewer visits to their doctors than similar families make in the other plans. They also receive the lowest volume of care. Nor is this plan that much less expensive for the high-need families. When family expenses for medical care are calculated as percent of per capita income, the large group plan ranks third lowest. Considering expenses in relation to volume of services actually received, it is the most expensive.

The organization of the group-practice plans emphasizes convenience for the provider more than the consumer. Such a *bureaucratic effect* reduces access to the high-need patient, drives him to use some out-of-plan services, and increases use some by those most able to handle large organizations. The large group practice plan may have replaced control over consumers via the benefit package with the constraints of bureaucratic inaccessibility.

A major issue in the national health insurance controversy is control of quality. The PSRO surveillance mechanism is dependent on medical record information. This study has demonstrated an objective set of measures based on the medical record and involving nonmedical abstractors. This or a similar method should be studied further for general application. Traditional methods of peer review have had many difficulties and have not always yielded valid or reliable results.

Quality, as we measured it, is adversely affected by patient load. What of the question of preventive medicine? Some currently feel it should be concentrated on the high-risk populations; in our study these people did not receive the most preventive care.

A primary concern in any national health insurance scheme is *price.* In a time of rocketing inflation it is of interest that the large group practice consumer pays only 4% of his income for total health expenses—much lower than consumers in other plans. But is the economy achieved by this plan real?[3] Moreover, we have noted that percent of per capita income paid out by the lower income families is not lowest in this plan.

Studies of health insurance do not always take into account the

---

[3] For example, should hospital construction have to be financed by these plan members, in contrast to the community support of capital costs in other plans?

experience of the physician. Physicians have a keen interest in the topic of this research, and we found them to be highly cooperative in filling out questionnaires and in facilitating access (with proper patient clearance) to medical records. The physicians were by no means of one opinion on most major issues, and many voluntary comments indicated that the "spokesmen" for the medical profession do not always represent the variety of viewpoints found among practicing physicians.

The physicians were concerned about the "leveling" effect of peer surveillance found in the group practice plans. The impact of the individual provider is reduced and there is an implication of limited individual freedom and initiative.

The concept of adequate paramedical support in a group practice system reducing the effect of the patient load on quality of care was not supported by our findings. The doctor who sees five or more patients per hour provides less preventive and less rational care. We have much yet to learn about effective use of paramedical personnel in teams.

Preventive medicine is an ongoing consideration. The large group practice physicians, who have had the most experience with preventive care, argue for selective application with emphasis on patients in the higher risk categories. In spite of higher risks in the large group practice plan, the one indicator of health outcome we had—days lost from work due to illness—showed no significant differences among the plans.[4] Effective preventive medicine requires the intelligent cooperation of physician and patient and perhaps neither is currently adequately educated in this area.

Continuing physician education did not seem to be advantageous. Perhaps as one fee-for-service physician said, "Continuing education can only yield a magnification of the initial physician, not a correction of basic defects." Physicians were often in favor of continuing education as a regular part of practice rather than the one-shot formal courses. In our study this occurred in the large group practice plan in which persistent interaction with colleagues took place.

More research is needed to relate physician education and characteristics to performance in practice. Very little is known about this connection. Performance analyzed by process measures such as

---

[4] The data were taken from a question in the consumer questionnaire which asked for the number of days of work missed due to illness during the previous 12 months. These were not analyzed in detail because of the recall problems involved.

our factor scores is a beginning, but the impact on consumer health must, at some point, be understood.

Physicians, consumers, and plan officials were all asked their opinions about "the best way for people to pay their *doctor's bills.*" Response to categories ran from tax-sponsored national health insurance to "everybody pays his own bills." About 7% of the physicians and 7% of the consumers favored the tax-supported scheme, and almost none of the plan officials favored this alternative. The most popular response was "through voluntary plans, with the government paying for those below a certain income level." This was further supported by the consumer satisfaction data, in which voluntary choice of plan was demonstrated to be closely related to satisfaction.

Evaluation is stressed today as a means of providing objective information on competing human services programs. It is hoped that scientific data will replace value judgments and political decisions as the main criteria for judging relative worth of alternate approaches. As this study illustrates, evaluation is a difficult and complex procedure. There are no simple answers to the question, "Which program works best?" However, data in this study add to the growing knowledge of performance of the major competing types of health care delivery and financing systems in America and will hopefully move policy makers closer to decisions that will result in improved health care for all Americans.

APPENDIX A

METHODOLOGY

DEVELOPING THE QUESTIONNAIRES

Insuring Agencies

Three types of information were required from the insuring agencies:

- Information from board, management, and supervisory personnel, which described their perceptions of organizational goals and the manner in which their activities and training contributed to attainment of those goals.
- Information from knowledgeable persons within the organization regarding structure and procedures.
- Information from available sources on history, goals, and legal environment.

A pretest of the proposed data collection methods was conducted in 1966. Questionnaires and interview schedules were developed and tested on the personnel of a large mutual insurance company home-based in Los Angeles County.[1] This company was very cooperative and the company executive working with us offered many helpful suggestions for improvements in our research procedures. Descriptive information on administrative procedures and product (benefit packages) was easily obtained through interviews and a wide range of manuals, articles, and organization charts.

Problem areas were pinpointed during the pretest; for instance, financial resource and allocation information was difficult to collect. The data were sometimes not available in the forms we needed and required considerable effort and expense to obtain. Descriptive rather than "hard" data seemed to be more appropriate for this purpose in the subsequent research. Another problem was that although information on the product was readily available it was difficult to summarize—a problem that has appeared in previous research. The pretest emphasized the need in a study that compared a number of agencies with diversified products to summarize product characteristics across a few important dimensions. Finally, the pretest showed that legal training was needed so that laws regulating the operation of health insuring agencies could be understood and correctly interpreted. A final-year law student specializing in corporate law at UCLA was assigned to work with this part of the study.

Consumers

Two sources of information on consumer experience were defined:

- Background and subjective information from questionnaires.
- Objective information from medical records and claim forms.

The first source of information, the questionnaire, was designed to provide data on independent (organization, physician, and consumer

---

[1] Information from this research was not included in the final study, but was the subject of a separate report (Parsons, 1972).

characteristics) and dependent (use of medical services, family expenses, and consumer attitudes) variables. Questions were developed as indicators of *need* and *demand* (independent) and of *use of medical services, expenditures,* and *satisfaction* (dependent). The questionnaire indicators of need, a concept involving an objective appraisal of health status, were proxy measures. On the dependent variables we tried to reduce recall error by asking for information on ambulatory care for only three months and establishing broad categories for response on expenditures.

The questionnaire was pretested in 1966 on 311 employees of the Federal Aviation Agency in Los Angeles who were enrolled in three health insurance plans corresponding to our commercial, provider-, and consumer-sponsored types. From the pretest several important aspects of the study were clarified; for example, the pretest question on consumer satisfaction covered only two dimensions—satisfaction with financial coverage and with physicians' services. The revised version included four dimensions of satisfaction—financial coverage, medical care, availability of physicians, and claims procedures.

The final questionnaire consisted of 33 questions (mostly closed-end, check-off types) that required 30 minutes to an hour to complete.

The second source of information, medical records and claims, required a legal release form. This form was designed with the help of the UCLA School of Law. It was one page in length, contained four sections, and provided spaces for the signatures of the respondent and spouse (when applicable) and date of signing. The sections asked for a list of all physicians used by the subscriber or his insured dependents during the preceding 12 months, a list of all hospitals used during the same period, a list of all family members covered by the insurance plan during the 12-month study period, and provided a statement authorizing the health plan under study to release to UCLA Health Insurance Research all details of claims for care received in the 12-month period.

Physicians

The physician pretest was conducted in 1966 on a sample of 116 physicians selected from those who provided medical service during a

12-month period to members of a relatively small consumer-sponsored health insurance plan which allowed free choice of private doctor (the Los Angeles Firemen's group health plan). A major purpose of the pretest was to ensure that the questions asked were meaningful to practicing physicians and to convert open-end into more convenient closed-end questions. Thirty-eight physicians were interviewed, at which time the various content areas of the questionnaire, defined by the general model (see Chapter 1, Figure A-1), were explored.

Another concern was the anticipated difficulty of having physicians complete lengthy questionnaires (the final version was 16 pages, 29 questions long, requiring anywhere from 20 to 60 minutes to complete). The pretest assured us that physicians were sufficiently interested in the subjects to answer: 78% responded to the pretest.

SAMPLING

Insuring Agency Personnel

Plans were selected to represent the three principal types of health insurance identified in our plan typology: commercial-solo, provider-solo, and consumer group. In order to represent the plan types across a range of sizes, one large and one small of each of the three types were studied. Selection was restricted to plans with a reputation of merit and having a range of group enrollment contracts within Los Angeles County, where the study was to be centered.

The study design involved research into each health insuring agency's history, resources, goals, benefit offerings, hierarchy, division of labor, and communication. To accomplish this interviews were held with members of the boards of directors and questionnaires were given to supervisors, managers, and top officials. Because time and the release of information normally considered confidential were involved, obtaining plan cooperation was understandably difficult.

Four commercial-solo companies were approached. The first company declined to cooperate, the second agreed only to the pretest, the third agreed to participate. This last company later imposed limitations on interviews with board members, restricting contacts with those who were not company employees. The fourth plan, a relatively small commercial agency, agreed unconditionally to the terms of the research design. The two commercial plans included in the study are identified as *large commercial* and *small commercial*, and have a size ratio of 3:1.

The two provider-sponsored agencies we planned to include declined cooperation, and the data concerning them were gathered without their assistance. Toward the end of the research the hospital-sponsored plan granted a single interview with a member of the management level which yielded some information on the company's general operation. This plan also gave us access to claims information. The physician-sponsored plan provided no information. These plans are designated *hospital-sponsored* and *physician-sponsored* throughout the book. Their size ratio is about 2:1.

The two group-practice service plans that were selected agreed to cooperate with the study. The large plan eventually refused interviews with its board of directors and the small plan did not provide certain financial information. These two plans are identified as *large group* and *small group plans.* Their size ratio is 6:1.

In each of the four cooperating plans interviews were held with six to eight key persons, at least one of whom was a member of the board of directors. If interviews with board members were not permitted, a management level person, who understood the board's mode of operation, was interviewed instead. These interviews helped us to understand the board's composition, who was represented, communication among board members and management personnel, generation of policy changes, motivation of change, and the organization's history. Interviews with supervisors and managers focused on restrictions and regulations imposed by local, state, and federal government, that affect the plan and tax structure, investment programs, and claims procedures. Management personnel also provided information on how the company's goals were implemented. Managers who were responsible for the operation of group contracts received questionnaires. Response to the questionnaire was 96.4%.

The participating insurance agencies assigned staff members to assist us with the data collection. These people, who were knowledgeable about their organizations, served as intermediary consultants. They were very helpful in clarifying interview and questionnaire material and in directing us to printed sources of information.

Consumers

The study was limited to people in group enrollment contracts sponsored by the six plans. Ideally the consumers participating in the survey would statistically represent all subscribers to group contracts in the six study plans. A strictly random sample, however, was not possible because the plans, with the exception of the small group plan, did not keep consumer lists. In five of the plans membership groups were selected randomly in size strata; the consumers were then chosen at random from these groups. The contracts were selected in different sizes to account for the impact of size on the premiums and benefits.

The principle applied to the plan selection was applied to contract selection within each plan. The contract groups were classified by size into three subdivisions. At least two membership groups were chosen from each subdivision. The group contracts selected for classification were those with a majority of their members living in Los Angeles County.

The method of selecting consumer groups varied according to the amount of cooperation received from each insuring agency. The large commercial plan presented a problem of defining groups with members living in Los Angeles County. The plan provided a list of identification numbers and contract sizes for 170 group policies accounting for at least 85% of the company's group health insurance business in the county.

After the population was divided into three strata, according to group size (i.e., the number of subscribers who consitituted the base on which the benefit packages and premiums were determined), we discovered that the contract size estimates provided by the plan were in error and the actual subscriber distributions were not equal. Table A-1 displays the distribution according to the corrected population estimates.

Groups were randomly selected from the three strata and their policy numbers were submitted to plan officials. The officials called on each group's broker or company administrator to cooperate with the study. Refusal to participate could come from the insuring agency, the broker, or the company administrator. This process was very time consuming and many groups had to be replaced.

When the sample groups were finalized, their names were released. Representation of subscribers in each stratum resulted in 76% for stratum A, 21% for stratum B, and 3% for stratum C. Obtaining clearance from enough groups in strata B and C to make the

TABLE A-1
Characteristics of strata in sampling of contracts

Plans and Strata	Strata Limits (Families)	Total Contracts	Total Families		Contracts Sampled	Families Sampled		Families Drawn	
			(N)	(%)		(N)	(%)	(N)	(%)
Large commercial									
All		170	101,974	100.0	17	43,213	100.0	1,498	100.0
A	10,000+	2	32,836	32.2	2	32,836	76.0	471	31.4
B	285 - 9,999	19	56,188	55.1	5	9,075	21.0	611	40.8
C	284 or less	149	12,950	12.7	10	1,302	3.0	416	27.8
Small commercial									
All		176	16,663	100.0	35	7,887	100.0	1,740	100.0
A	2,083+	2	5,047	30.3	2	5,047	164.0	635	36.5
B	257 - 2,082	12	6,208	37.2	3	1,821	23.1	578	33.2
C	256 or less	162	5,408	32.4	30	1,019	12.9	527	30.3
Hospital-sponsored									
All		...	...	100.0	10	48,524	100.0	758	100.0
A	3,651+	...	...	33.0†	2	36,393	175.0	351	46.3
B	366 - 3,650	...	...	26.0†	3	10,675	22.0	198	26.1
C	351 or less	...	...	41.0†	5	1,456	3.0		
Physician-sponsored									
All		...	...	100.0	13	...††	...	647	100.0
A	3,509+	...	...	33.0†	2	...††	...	221	34.2
B	352 - 3,508	...	...	26.0†	3	...††	...	226	34.9
C	351 or less	...	...	41.0†	8	...††	...	200	30.9
Large group									
All		329	156,039	100.0	137	68,396	100.0	1,531	100.0
A	10,000+	4	56,919	36.4	2	34,946	51.1	523	34.2
B	2,800 - 9,999	11	47,344	30.3	4	15,599	22.8	522	34.1
C	2,799 or less	314	51,776	33.2	131	17,851	26.1	486	31.7
Small group									
All		103	29,079	100.0				1,510	100.0
A	5,290+	2	11,091	38.1	All	All		507	33.6
B	1,239 - 5,289	5	8,532	29.4				377	25.0
C	1,238 or less	96	9,456	32.5				626	41.4

†Based on figures from another large American metropolitan area.
††Estimates of contract size for large contracts beyond the local area were not reliable.

distribution in the sample resemble that in the overall plan population would have required an impossible amount of time, and statistical adjustments were made to compensate for the misrepresentation.

The small commercial plan's group contract memberships were not limited to Los Angeles County residents. Again we relied on plan officials to provide a list of groups that had a majority of their members living in the county. These groups (176) were then stratified by contract size. The total subscriber population was consequently divided into relatively equal proportions (see Table A-1). Stratum A had only two membership groups and both were included. Groups representing strata B and C were selected at random, the number being determined by the need to minimize tactical problems of obtaining clearances and to represent the range of groups adequately. Stratum B was represented by three groups and the small group stratum, C, contained 30 groups. Once the groups had been selected clearance had to be obtained from both the insuring agency and the groups. If the group officials did not agree to cooperate, or if the group canceled its policy sometime between being drawn for the study and the mailing of the questionnaires, the group was replaced by a random selection of another group from the same stratum. Enrollment group cooperation in this plan was very high.

The provider-sponsored plans declined to participate, giving us a final refusal after three years of encouraging negotiation and at a point when data collection in the other plans was nearly completed. Because we did not want to exclude these plans, and because there was so little time, we decided to study them on a smaller scale. In order to obtain a representative sample of subscribers to group contracts in Los Angeles County, we were faced with the problem of finding a list of these groups. This was obtained primarily in the 1966 edition of the *Business Directory* for Los Angeles and Orange Counties (Los Angeles Chamber of Commerce, 1966). Every employer with 20 or more employees is listed in this document. We also obtained lists of unions with 1000 or more members from the California State Department of Labor Statistics. City, county, state, and federal government agencies were also included.

We selected 10 groups for each of the two plans, distributed across three strata, two from the large groups, three from the medium-sized groups, and five from the small groups.

All groups listed were arranged alphabetically. A random starting point and a sampling interval were established according to the number of groups in the population and the number of groups to be drawn. Representatives of each group selected were approached by telephone and asked if they had a group health policy with either or both of the provider-sponsored plans. If the group did have such a policy, it was added to the appropriate stratum and became part of the sample. This was continued until we had the desired number of groups.

Union members who were covered under a union or trust-fund policy rather than a policy at their places of employment were counted as members of the union. If they were encountered in any of the companies we called, the company was deleted. Contracts involving both provider-sponsored plans were assigned arbitrarily to the physician-sponsored plan.

We were able to select exactly 10 groups for the hospital-sponsored plan in accordance with the design. For the physician-sponsored plan we had to select 13 groups because stratum C required more than the designated five groups to establish a sufficient sample.

Population estimates could not be obtained from either of these plans. Assuming that the relative sizes across the strata would not be radically different for Los Angeles, compared with another large American metropolitan area, we obtained consumer population distribution figures for both plans from such an area. Estimates thus obtained indicated that 33% of the population were likely to be found in the large groups, 26% in the medium-sized groups, and 41% in the smaller groups. We concluded that this estimate of size was better than arbitrarily making the sizes equal across all three strata.

The large group practice plan did not have a complete list of group contract subscribers, and in several instances membership lists were filed with the employment group. For these reasons, and because of the large number of group contracts (329), the plan officials asked that we select groups as the first stage of our sampling and that they make the initial contact with the groups we selected to inform them of the plan's cooperation with the study.

We selected at random 137 of the 329 group enrollment contracts.

The number of contracts selected for each stratum was determined by having at least two contracts in each stratum and the proportion of sampled contracts to the total being roughly equal to the proportions in the sampling universe; for instance, in stratum A (10,000 or more subscribers) there were 4/329 groups in the universe; in the sample of groups for stratum A there were 2/137. The proportion in both cases is about 1/100.

The small group practice plan gave us access to a set of files containing one card for each member of the group contracts in Los Angeles County. The cards were divided by employment group. Because the plan placed no restrictions on the groups, all 103 were included. The majority of the members in each group lived in Los Angeles County.

Reaching the consumers

The steps taken to question the people insured by the six companies in our study can be illustrated as:

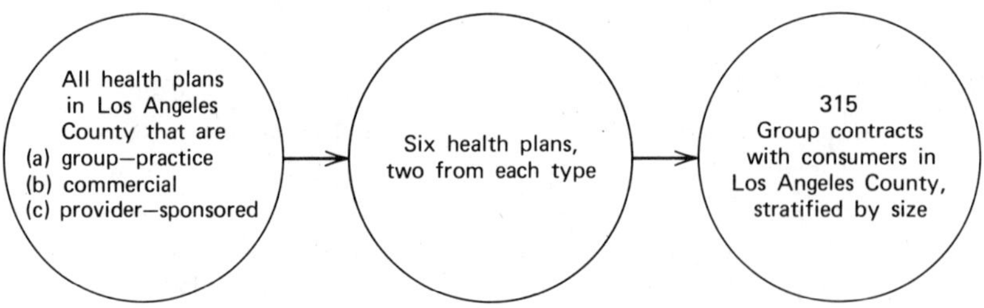

The number of desired responses from each plan was set at 600, a number that would yield statistically sufficient cases of hospital use, the least frequently occurring medical care event. A sample of 600 subscribers and their families calculated on an average of three persons per family would provide approximately 1800 persons per plan. The annual rate of hospitalization was estimated at around 10% of the total plan population, which would yield about 180 hospitalizations per plan. In the provider-sponsored plans lack of time and finances forced us to aim for 300 family units.

Response to mailed questionnaires is related to the length of the questionnaire, sponsorship, interest in the topic, etc. (Hetherington, Rogson, and Buxbaum, 1969). Because we anticipated about a 50% response, the number of consumers to whom we sent the questionnaire was twice the number of responses desired.

Drawing the names

For each plan the goal was to reach 1200 members in order to be assured of 600 responses, with about 200 in each of the three strata. The people were to be drawn from the second-stage sampling of the contracts in proportion to the contract's entire Los Angeles County membership. This posed some difficulty because the plan administrations did not have good estimates of the proportion of consumers living in the county. Occasionally employers and union officials were also unable to provide accurate estimates. The result was a sampling interval set according to insufficient information and requiring resampling to fill quotas. Once estimates were obtained it was a simple matter to determine for each group the number needed in a sample, establish a sampling interval, select a random starting point, and proceed to draw names and addresses.

Consumers defined as eligible for sampling were those under 65 years of age living in Los Angeles County at the time of the study. The age ceiling was necessary because persons 65 and older were under the Medicare program.

The medical and claim records subsample

The design specified an intensive analysis of medical records and claims belonging to a smaller but still representative subsample. The people chosen for this study were taken from those already identified and consisted of one of four consumers in the commercial and group practice plans. In the provider-sponsored plans the ratio to the major sample was 1:2, so that the same number of medical records would be analyzed. Each plan was thus represented by an equal number of subsample consumers.

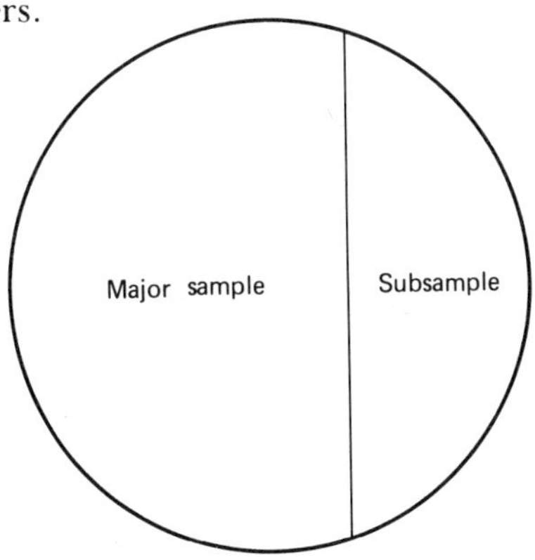

Mailing the questionnaires

Consumers in the major sample were mailed a questionnaire; those in the subsample were mailed a questionnaire and an authorization form. The authorization form, properly completed and signed, provided legal access to medical records and claim forms for all care received by insured family members for the 12 months predating receipt of the questionnaire.

The response from these mailings resulted in another division in the consumer sample: *respondents* and *nonrespondents* .

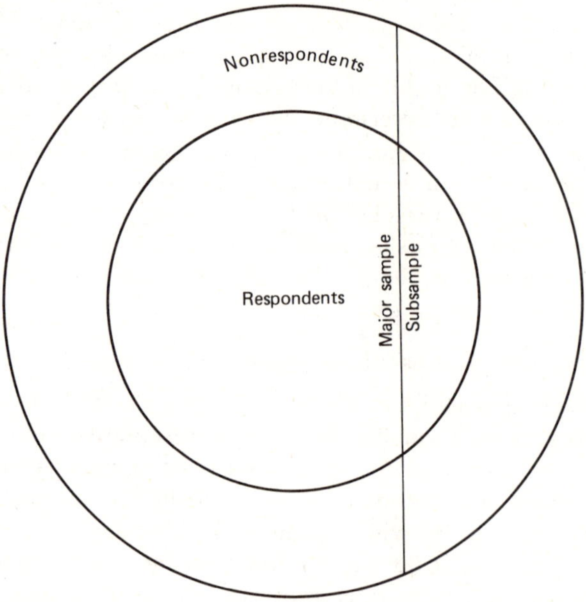

Non respondents

In order to estimate the extent to which the respondent data were biased because of response patterns, it was necessary to find out about those who did not respond. The respondents were expected to have a middle-class bias because in past studies middle-class persons have responded more readily to lengthy questionnaires concerning relatively esoteric subjects (Vincent, 1964). (b) We selected a small random sample (5-15%) of those not answering our questionnaire with the idea of having 85% or more of these people participate. We decided on a small sample because of the time and expense required to get a high rate of return. An abbreviated version of the questionnaire was devised for household interviews. The interviewing work was contracted to a survey research agency.

TABLE A-2

Sample size and response rates
consumer study and medical records study

	Total Study		Respondents			Nonrespondents					
							Contacts				
	Sample	Response (%)	Returns (N)	Contacts/ Resp	Response (%)	Nonrespondents	(N)	(%)	Returns (N)	Contacts/ Resp	Response (%)
Total Sample											
All plans	6,195	48.3	2,912†	1.6	47.0	3,283	287	8.7	218†	3.7	76.0
Lge comm	1,379	42.9	580	1.9	42.1	799	59	7.4	37	4.0	67.2
Sml comm	1,418	46.2	644	1.8	45.4	799	47	6.1	33	4.0	70.2
Hosp-spon	561	50.7	272	1.5	48.5	289	44	15.2	35	3.0	79.5
Phys-spon	546	45.7	233	1.6	42.7	313	41	13.1	35	3.1	85.4
Lge group	1,265	46.3	574	1.3	45.4	691	47	6.8	34	4.8	72.3
Sml group	1,026	60.7	609	1.3	59.4	417	49	11.8	44	3.5	89.8
Major Sample											
All plans	4,172	51.6	2,151†	1.6	51.6	2,021	16	0.8	12†	3.3	75.0
Lge comm	962	43.7	419	1.9	43.6	543	3	0.6	3	3.0	100.0
Sml comm	1,064	48.0	510	1.8	47.9	554	1	0.2	1	3.0	100.0
Hosp-spon	283	53.4	151	1.5	53.4	132	0	0.0	0	...	...
Phys-spon	275	46.7	129	1.5	46.9	146	1	0.7	0	3.0	0.0
Lge group	792	55.7	441	1.3	55.7	351	0	0.0	0	...	...
Sml group	796	63.1	501	1.3	62.9	295	11	3.7	8	3.4	72.7
Subsample											
All plans	2,023	30.7	652†	1.7	32.2	1,371	271	19.8	153†	3.7	56.5
Lge comm	417	30.7	121	2.1	29.0	296	56	18.9	24	4.1	42.9
Sml comm	354	36.3	121	2.0	34.2	233	46	19.7	24	4.0	52.2
Hosp-spon	278	41.6	108	1.6	38.8	170	44	25.9	26	3.0	59.1
Phys-spon	271	37.0	86	1.7	31.7	185	40	21.6	29	3.1	72.5
Lge group	473	26.9	115	1.4	24.3	358	47	13.1	25	4.8	53.2
Sml group	230	47.0	101	1.3	43.9	129	38	29.5	25	3.5	65.8

†Major sample and subsample not equal to total sample in these columns because some of those approached for both questionnaire and authorization responded only to the questionnaire, and were counted as refusals in the subsample figures but respondents in the overall figures.

Even though the nonrespondent sample was drawn from both the major sample and the subsample, all nonrespondents were asked to sign the medical record and claims authorization. This was done because we felt the subsample needed bolstering in size.

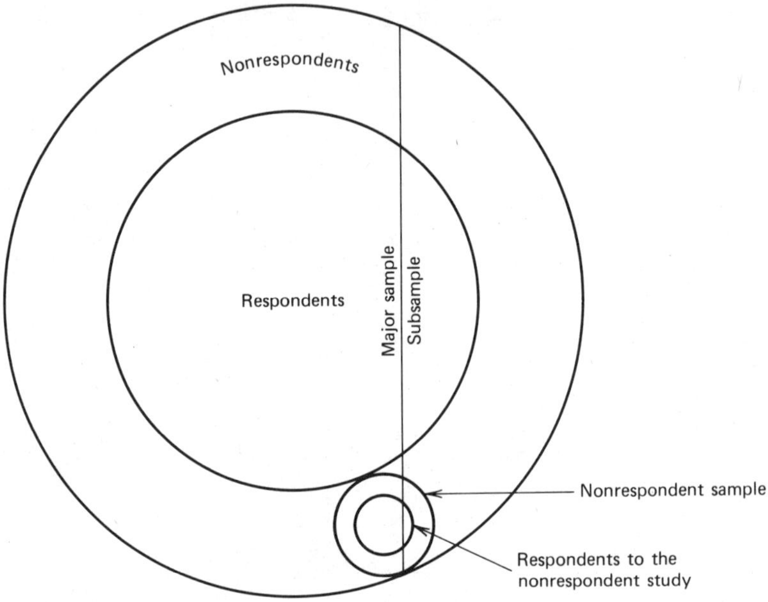

Responses

The response rate for the major sample was fairly close to the 50% we had anticipated. Table A-2 shows the variation in responses from plan to plan. The response rate from the subsample is consistently lower because of the request for release of claims and medical information. The subsample response rates reflect those persons who returned both the questionnaire and the authorization: those who returned just the questionnaire are counted as returns for the major sample only. The difference in the response rate between the two types of request is 13.2%. In all, we received 3130 questionnaires from the 6195 consumers in the sample, including returns from the nonrespondent study. In the sample requesting authorization to study claims and medical care 805 authorizations were received from 2023 families approached.

Generally we wished to define respondents as those who returned the materials after one or two contacts. In practice, however, "respondent" came to mean the first 600 consumers who responded (or 300 in the case of the smaller provider-plan samples), regardless of the number of contacts. As Table A-2 indicates, the number of contacts for respondents varied according to plan. The problem is best illustrated by the large commercial plan which had a response rate, after two mailings, much lower than 50%. We chose to approach the consumers a second time, rather than drawing new names, because of the time and cooperation required.

For the nonrespondent consumers a response rate of 85% was reached in only the small group practice plan (89.9%) and the physician-sponsored plan (85.4%). Again, the response from the large commercial plan consumers, the lowest, caused us to have the least confidence in estimates of nonrespondent characteristics for that plan.

Comparing the respondents and nonrespondents

The high percentage of nonresponse in this research led to a substantial investment in the study of the nonrespondent sample. Comparisons between respondents and nonrespondents were made on major control variables that were used throughout the analysis:

- Subscriber characteristics
  - Age
  - Sex
  - Religion
  - National and racial background
- Characteristics of head of household
  - Education
  - Occupation
  - Socioeconomic status
- Family characteristics
  - Income
  - Marital status and dependents (family structure)
  - Chronic illnesses.

Response rate studies in the past have demonstrated that social survey studies in America frequently have a "nice middle-class bias" caused by higher response from the more educated people. We expected that the major bias would be an overrepresentation of people with higher incomes, education, occupational level, and socioeconomic status. In some of the plan samples this expectation was confirmed. When all plans are taken together, statistical significance, based on the chi-square test ($p = .05$), is reached for all four socioeconomic measures in the expected directions. The same results are obtained for the medical record subsample, except on the income measure. The most significant difference in response between persons of upper and lower socioeconomic status is in the physician-sponsored plan. The respondents in this plan are consistently higher on all measures of social class, including the Hollingshead Two-Factor Index, which combines weighted occupation and education scores (Hollingshead, 1957). The hospital-sponsored plan is much the same, except that significance is not reached for

TABLE A-3

Figures used in the calculation of weights to correct for biases due to contract size proportions and nonresponse

Plan	Total Sample			Subsample		
	Sample (%)	Pop. (%)	Weight	Sample (%)	Pop. (%)	Weight
Large commercial						
Group size						
Large (A)	42.8	32.2	.75	42.8	32.2	.75
Medium (B)	31.6	55.1	1.74	33.8	55.1	1.63
Small (C)	25.6	12.7	.50	23.4	12.7	.54
Respondent	94.0	42.1	.45	83.5	29.0	.35
Nonrespondent	6.0	58.0	9.66	16.6	71.0	4.29
Small commercial						
Group size						
Large (A)	31.3	30.3	.97	29.7	30.3	1.02
Medium (B)	38.7	37.3	.96	38.6	37.3	.97
Small (C)	30.0	32.5	1.08	31.7	32.5	1.02
Respondent	95.1	45.4	.48	83.5	34.2	.41
Nonrespondent	4.9	54.6	11.20	16.6	65.8	3.98
Hospital-sponsored						
Group size						
Large (A)	46.0	33.0	.72	54.4	33.0	.73
Medium (B)	24.0	26.0	1.08	23.9	26.0	1.09
Small (C)	30.0	41.0	1.37	30.6	41.0	1.34
Respondent	88.6	48.5	.55	80.6	38.8	.48
Nonrespondent	11.4	51.5	4.52	19.4	61.2	3.15
Physician-sponsored						
Group size						
Large (A)	47.4	33.0	.70	45.2	33.0	.73
Medium (B)	23.9	26.0	1.09	23.5	26.0	1.11
Small (C)	28.7	41.0	1.43	31.3	41.0	1.31
Respondent	86.9	42.7	.49	74.8	31.7	.42
Nonrespondent	13.1	57.3	4.39	25.2	68.3	2.71
Large group						
Group size						
Large (A)	41.7	36.4	.87	28.6	36.4	1.27
Medium (B)	31.6	30.3	.96	27.9	30.3	1.09
Small (C)	26.7	33.2	1.24	43.6	33.2	.76
Respondent	94.4	45.4	.48	82.1	24.3	.30
Nonrespondent	5.6	54.6	9.76	17.9	75.7	4.23
Small group						
Group size						
Large (A)	24.0	38.1	1.59	43.7	38.1	.87
Medium (B)	27.5	29.3	1.07	27.0	29.3	1.08
Small (C)	48.5	32.5	.67	29.4	32.5	1.10
Respondent	93.3	59.4	.64	80.2	43.9	.55
Nonrespondent	6.7	40.6	6.06	19.8	56.1	2.83

income. The large commercial plan is significant only on income. It is interesting that the large group practice plan is the *only* one of the six in which the nonrespondents are more likely to come from families with incomes of $11,000 per year or more (53.1%). We have no ready explanation for this difference

Tests on all other variables did not reach significance.

Correcting for the biases

There are two obvious sources of bias in the sample. The first bias was created by the nature of the sampling method, since we deliberately attempted to equalize the number of consumers in the enrollment contract size strata, even though the numbers in the population were not equal across these strata. This was not entirely successful because of the shifts in estimates of contract sizes and the lack of population information for the two provider-sponsored plans. The second bias was due to nonresponse.

Statistics used for correcting these biases are provided in Table A-3.

The purpose behind the weighting procedure was to alter the sample composition so that it represented the composition of the whole population;[2] for example, to estimate the extent to which nonresponse influenced the sample, it was necessary to have some estimate of the probable behavior of the total population regarding response to the questionnaire. In the small group plan, for instance, the sample response was 59.4%. Consequently, we estimated that if all the consumers for this plan had been reached approximately 59.4% would have responded and 40.6% would not have responded, but in the sample actually used for analysis there were 609 respondents to the mail questionnaire and 44 nonrespondents. Thus the sample percentages were 93.3 and 6.7%. Therefore, in order to reduce proportionately the influence of respondents and increase the influence of nonrespondents, each respondent was counted only .64 times in the analysis (59.4/93.3). The same procedure was followed for establishing all weights listed in Table A-3.

Corrections for bias were computed by using the following formula:

$W = P/S$,

where

W = the computed weight,

---

[2] Although the sample from the small group plan was chosen at random, weights are introduced for group size to correct for errors that may have occurred because of wrong addresses, canceled policies, ineligibility due to age, etc. Group size limits used are shown in Table A-1.

P = the proportion of the attribute category in the population, or an estimate of it,

S = the proportion of the attribute category in the sample.

Finally, the weight actually applied was simply a product of the individual weights: W1 X W2, where W1 is the weight for *nonresponse* and W2 is the weight for *group size.*

Biases in the data due to more subtle influences are recognized but not corrected; for instance, we have no way of estimating the degree to which nonrespondents provided different information because they were interviewed rather than mailed a questionnaire.

Physicians

The physicians in this study were those who provided services to the consumers in the subsample and their insured family members during the 12-month period before the date on the authorization form. To the degree that the consumer sample was representative of all consumers in group enrollment contracts in Los Angeles County for the six study plans, the physicians were representative of physicians used by these consumers in these six plans. The physicians in our study were not meant to be representative of all physicians in the county.

All physicians providing services to people in the subsample during the 12-month study period were included, whether they were family physicians, specialists, consultants, or hospital house officers (interns or residents). As only medical doctors were included in the study, there were psychiatrists, but no psychologists; opthamologists, but no optometrists, etc. Place of practice was not restricted to Los Angeles County.

Names of physicians were obtained from the authorization form signed by the consumers in the subsample. Subscribers were asked to list all physicians and hospitals used by an insured member of the family during the preceding 12 months. In the group practice plans subscribers frequently could not recall the names of physicians seen, so we collected all medical records from the plans and identified physicians' signatures. For the other plans any physician or hospital listed was called on and the medical records checked to see if the care occurred during the study period. If so, all physicians whose names appeared in the medical records, as well as the physicians named on the authorization form, were sent questionnaires.

The overall response rate was 75.4%, with the best results (79.9%) coming from physicians serving the large group plan's members.

The high response from physicians was gratifying but obtained only with considerable effort. The goal was to have a questionnaire from at least one physician per family whom we identified as the "primary physician." Generally this was the doctor who provided the most medical care to the family during the 12-month study period. In order to accomplish this, we communicated with each physician, on the average, 2.2 times, but this does not reflect the number of *attempts* to reach him. In some scattered instances the physician was paid for his time and in even fewer cases, he refused to cooperate in any circumstance.

TABLE A-4
Sample size and response rates
physician study

Plan	Physicians Contacted	Response (%)	Returns (N)	Contacts/Physician All	Mail	Phone
All	1,735	75.4	1,309	2.2	1.8	0.4
Lge comm	248	73.8	183	2.3	1.8	0.5
Sm comm	347	70.3	244	2.3	1.9	0.4
Hosp-spon	244	77.0	188	2.7	2.0	0.7
Phys-spon	217	74.7	162	2.1	1.5	0.5
Lge group	443	79.9	354	1.9	1.8	0.2
Sm group	236	75.4	178	2.4	2.0	0.4

A response rate of 85% or higher is generally considered adequate to provide a representative sample and therefore would not require a nonrespondent study. Since none of the plans reached the 85% we had hoped for, we decided to code available information (published by Los Angeles County Medical Association, 1969 and 1970; Board of Medical Examiners, 1968; American Medical Association, 1965 and 1967; American Board of Medical Specialties, 1965, 1968, and 1970) on physicians who did not respond and report biases due to non-response. Recognition of possible biases is important, but we did not introduce weights to compensate for them, because the physician study represents a lesser aspect of the analysis reported in this book.

Physician characteristics on which comparisons are based are the following:

Age of physician
Years since M.D.
Specialty board status
Specialty
Location of medical school
"Inside" or "outside" physician
(group practice plans)

Characteristics of locale of practice[3]
- Social rank
- Urbanization
- Segregation
- Voting pattern

Physicians with a greater interest in health insurance were expected to respond more readily to the questionnaire. If such interest is related to length of medical experience, then we would expect recently graduated physicians to have the least interest and therefore not respond. The variable "years since M.D." proved to be significantly related to response, because the recently graduated physicians were indeed those not responding. In addition to being younger, the nonrespondents tended to be general practitioners and to have their practices in areas in which large proportions of the population were composed of ethnic minorities.

COLLECTING, ORGANIZING THE INFORMATION

Insuring Agencies

This aspect of the research involved detailed studies of each health plan's distribution of capital, operational procedures, structure of the administration, and values of the management and members of the boards of directors. As information on finances and administrative methods is rarely released because of the competitive market situation, we were unable to realize these goals completely.

---

[3] The locale of practice characteristics derived from census statistics reflecting socioeconomic and political compositions within the Los Angeles Standard Metropolitan Statistical Area (Shevky and Williams, 1949; Correl, 1965; Bell, 1953). Social rank measures the occupation, average income, dwelling rent or ownership, and education level within a census tract. Urbanization measures the density of the population. High urbanization is indicated by low fertility and single-family housing scores and high scores on women in the labor force. Segregation measures ethnic composition. Voting pattern is the average Republican vote by tract over three elections held in 1964 (presidential, senatorial, and congressional) and two in 1958 (gubernatorial and senatorial). (We are obliged to Professor Dwaine Marvick and his associates in the Department of Political Science, UCLA, for providing us with these statistics.)

Our agreement not to disclose the actual names of the participating organizations did not guarantee protection against this problem, since descriptions of structure and function provide clues to the identity of the organizations. Hence it is understandable why some health plans refused to cooperate in this phase of the research and why others agreed to limited or supervised access. Financial information, predictably, was most difficult to obtain, especially from health plans not required by law to make public financial statements.

It is interesting that the pretest of a large but very cooperative commercial health plan did not alert us to these difficulties. For this and other reasons we failed to anticipate the refusal to cooperate by the provider-sponsored plans. As we progressed, however, their main concerns became evident. They were wary of the implications that published results might have for their competitive position and were not confident that the research results would be presented in an impartial manner. The opposition to cooperation came mainly from senior members of the management and the boards of directors. Younger officials seemed enthusiastic about the study.

Lack of cooperation in some cases and unavailability of certain information in others led to problems of cross-agency comparisons. Further complications were caused by the lag time between agreements to cooperate; for instance, study on the first agency (the small group plan) began in 1967, whereas limited cooperation obtained from the hospital-sponsored plan was not cleared until 1969. As a result, the researchers put a great deal of stress on information concerning the basic concepts of sponsorship, goals, legal environment, administrative structure, and product insofar as it could be described primarily from informant interviews and printed materials. The unevenness of the questionnaire information across all six agencies limited its usefulness for this research.

Consumers

All data except for the nonrespondent interviews were collected and processed by the UCLA School of Public Health staff. Before the study was completed more than 11,000 contacts were made with consumers in the various plans.

A major obstacle to mailing questionnaires was the high mobility rate of people living in Los Angeles. To maintain the sampling proportions addresses of persons who had moved were traced whenever possible.

From the health insurance agency or the enrollment group information was gathered on date of eligibility for benefits, benefit package for each contract listing all exclusions, limitations and coinsurance features, and total premium for various family sizes.

A code manual had been developed from the consumer questionnaire pretest for the purpose of processing the data on 230 variables provided by the questionnaire for each consumer and his family. Since most of the information was in precoded form in the questionnaire (i.e., the questions were closed-end with limited choices), there was little room for subjective error on the part of the coders. The coders, who were university students, were assigned blocks of the 230 variables for which they were responsible. After a few days of coding these variables could be memorized. For the few items in which subjective judgment entered, such as assigning occupational status, coders were trained to use the Hollingshead Two-Factor Index of Social Position and the *National Opinion Research Center* ratings (Reiss, Duncan, Hatt, and North, 1961). The coders were trained and monitored by the research sociologist in charge of the consumer section of the study.

When the coding sheets were completed, the information was punched, verified, and transferred to computer tape.

For the people who authorized the release of their medical and claims records, a much more complicated procedure was used. Each physician and hospital in all plans except the group practice plans was approached separately. More than 2000 physicians and nearly 100 hospitals were named on the authorization forms and identified in the records. In the group practice plans all authorizations were verified and forwarded to plan officials. The officials called in the records and the research staff, in cooperation with the plan staff, photocopied the records.

All authorized medical records were photocopied to include a 12-month period before to the date on the form. In order to provide continuity for analysis of care, records six months before the beginning of the 12-month period and up to the date of photocopying were also obtained.

As the copies of the medical records were received they were processed by the project staff. The staff assigned to the medical records was composed of students who had experience with records and medical terminology.

A file was made for each family in the medical record study. Family members were checked for eligibility to receive benefits under the plan we were studying. Only care for eligible members was included.

All institutions and physicians listed on the authorization form were approached, and the records were checked to make sure that they were complete. The medical records were then divided into care for different family members who were eligible and that care was divided into prestudy, study, and poststudy periods. Each page was reviewed to note the date of service.

The basic unit of the medical record, the care received by one patient from a single provider on one day, including all laboratory or radiology work ordered during that contact, was termed the *medical care bit* (MCB). Medical care taking place within the study year was divided into medical care bits and arranged by date for each person in the family. Ambulatory and hospital care were treated in the same manner. When more than one provider was involved at the same time, as in an operation, each provider received a separate bit if he wrote up his activities in the medical record. The number of medical care bits identified was 11,379.

After the records had been ordered in the manner described they were reread for the purpose of finding gaps that would give clues to missing records. In all plans a number of missing records were detected. These records were traced and copied. In the group practice plans this procedure was simple, since the authorization was given for all medical care. With the other plans, reaching physicians and hospitals not listed on the authorization forms meant having to secure the subscriber's permission in each instance. These additional records were then processed as the others had been.

Another check that had to be made was comparison of the questionnaire with the authorization form for discrepancies; for instance, the questionnaire asks a person about the visits made by insured members of the family to a physician during the preceding three months. If physicians were listed on the questionnaire but not on the authorization form, the person had to be telephoned in order to clear up the discrepancy. Likewise, if expenses were indicated but no physician or hospital listed on the authorization form, further checks were made with the subscriber.

Claims information was provided by the commercial plans, the hospital-sponsored plan, and the hospital portion of the small group practice plan. When insurance claims were part of the system, plan officials assisted in matching claims information to data on the authorization forms. The claims information included names of the provider and date of service. For the physician portion of the small group practice plan and the large group practice plan there were no claiming procedures. The physician-sponsored plan refused access to the claims information.

The complete medical records folder for a family contained all the medical care bits separated by subscriber, spouse, and children. For each person prestudy and poststudy year records were included. Finally, all information received on claims from the health plan was added to the folder.

A code manual that described the operationalizing of all variables to be coded on each medical care bit was developed. Variables were defined which were summaries for the family and for the person, although many of them were computer-coded directly from the information on each medical care bit.

Variables coded were developed as indicators in three areas:[4]

Expenditures - the total value of care received, and the amount paid or covered by the health plan.[5]

Use of services - by applying the *California Relative Value Studies (CRVS)* system (California Medical Association, 1964) all medical care received was translated into CRVS units of Medicine, Surgery, Anesthesia, Radiology, and Laboratory. Hospital days were also coded.

Range of Services - major dimensions of content of the medical services received.

In addition to these three areas, various identification and control variables were coded; for instance, on each medical care bit we coded the family identification number corresponding to the consumer questionnaire identification number; identification by dependency status, age, sex; the identification number of the physician providing the medical services on that medical care bit; location of the care; whether the patient was pregnant; whether the illness was new or continuing from the perspective of the physician; and a score reflecting the level of seriousness of the illness.

Physicians

The physician information was delayed because the patient's authorization form was required before the physicians could be contacted. The listing of physicians on the authorization form

[4] Details of coding will be provided in chapters dealing with the outputs.

[5] No claims data available from physician-sponsored plan.

provided by each consumer was frequently incomplete, especially for consumers in the group practice plans. For this reason all medical records had to be photocopied and processed so that we could be sure that all physicians who provided any service during the 12-month period were included in the physician sample.

The same procedures used for coding the consumer questionnaires were followed, as much as possible, for the physician questionnaires. A different group of coders worked on coding these questionnaires. Again the questions were closed-end and required no subjective judgment.

Datasets

In order to carry out the analysis the data were arranged into the following datasets:

1. *The organization dataset.* This contained information from the organization's personnel questionnaires. Information from interviews and other sources were also compiled descriptively for each organization. (N=159)
2. *The consumer family dataset.* The families in the total sample are the units of analysis. This was the major dataset for the analysis of outputs which contained information on the subscriber and summary information on the family unit. (N=3,130)
3. *The family medical record dataset.* Families in the medical record subsample are the units of analysis. This dataset provided information on the family from the medical records. All medical record information gathered for any given family was summarized, e.g., number of CRVS units of surgery received in 12 months by all family members. (N=805)
4. *The person-medical record dataset.* Units of analysis are persons in the family who received some medical care in the 12 months studied. (N=1,215)
5. *The medical record dataset.* The unit of analysis here is the medical record bit (e.g., for ambulatory care this would be a physician visit). Datasets #3 and #4 are both derived from this one. (N=11,379)
6. *The physician dataset.* Each physician providing care to families in the medical record subsample is the unit of analysis.

REFERENCES

Bell, Wendell. "The social areas of the San Francisco bay region." *American Sociological Review,* 18, no. 1 (February 1953), 39.

Committee on Fees of the Commission on Medical Services, California Medical Association. "Relative value studies." Six Ninety Three Sutter Publications, San Francisco (1964).

Correll, Vincent. *Effect of school district size upon public interest in schools.* unpublished Ed.D. thesis, (education), University of California, Los Angeles, 1965.

Hetherington, Robert W., Rogson, Lorraine, and Buxbaum, Jessica. "Analysis of time of response to a mailed questionnaire on health insurance." *Inquiry,* 6, no. 4 (December 1969), 49-56.

Hollingshead, A. B. "Two-factor index of social position." New Haven, Connecticut, 1957. (Monograph)

Parsons, Eleanor M., *Structure, process and values in organizational goal consensus,* unpublished Ph.D. thesis (sociology), University of California, Los Angeles, 1972.

Reiss, Albert J., Duncan, O. D., Hatt, Paul K., and North, C. C. *Occupations and social status.* New York: Free Press of Glencoe, 1961, 263-275.

Shevky, Eshref and Williams, Marilyn. "The social areas of Los Angeles, analysis and typology." Berkeley and Los Angeles: University of California, 1965. (Monograph)

Vincent, Clark E. "Socioeconomic status and familial variables in mail questionnaire response." *American Journal of Sociology,* 69, no. 6 (May 1964), 647-653.

APPENDIX B

CONCEPTS AND MEASURES

THIS SECTION PROVIDES A GUIDE to indices that were developed for the study. Information is given on the meaning of each concept and how it is measured.

MEASURES ON ORGANIZATIONS

Goals: The Profit Index

Two types of goal are identified theoretically in this study: *motivating* and *legitimating*. Legitimating goals are organizational objectives developed for public consumption: they justify the existence of the organization in terms of society's needs. Motivating goals have the organization as the beneficiary rather than society. Public statements of policy and objectives stress legitimating goals. Motivating goals however, when they differ from legitimating goals, determine actual allocation of resources within the organization. In seeking to identify motivating goals, we are really asking the question "What is this organization really attempting to do?"

Motivating goals of the six health plan organizations in this study were estimated by goal rankings of three types of respondent: organization personnel, physicians and consumers. They were asked to rank a list of eight goals in order of importance for the organization in question. Organization personnel ranked their employing organization; consumers ranked the plan under which they were insured; physicians ranked the plan about which they felt they knew the most. In order of appearance in the questionnaire, the goals to be ranked were service, profit, growth, welfare of plan employees (morale), efficiency, community relations, keeping government out of the health insurance field, and keeping government out of medicine. Since the theoretical model identified *service* and *profit* as of primary interest, we were most interested in the response on these two goals.

An *average ranking* was computed for each of the two goals for all respondents. Equal weight was assigned to the three groups of respondents (organization personnel, consumers, and physicians). In this way the average ranking was influenced equally by perceptions of the three groups. The *profit index* is an expression of the relation between service and profit goals as assessed by the respondents. It is calculated by dividing the average ranking for service by the average ranking for profit. Thus the higher the resulting score (profit index), the more important the profit in comparison to service.

By this measure the small commercial plan was seen to be the most profit-oriented (profit index of 1.10) and the large group practice plan the least (index of 0.37).

Structure: Permeability

This concept reflects the degree to which an organization may be influenced by forces outside the organization. It may be thought of as a measure of potential public accountability, although a permeable organization may be influenced as well by forces in no way representative of the public interest. Our concern with the concept, however, is in the responsiveness of an organization to the people.

Two indicators were used to measure the permeability of health plans in the study. The first was amount of satisfaction expressed by consumers with actions taken by the health plan on consumer complaints. The second was the accuracy of knowledge by consumers of the terms of their benefit packages. The latter is in part a function of consumer desire and ability to learn the benefit package contents, but these factors could be taken into account by any health plan desirous of ensuring a knowledgeable clientele. Satisfaction with outcome of complaints was measured by a questionnaire item which asked those who had made a complaint in the last 12 months to indicate whether they were "completely satisfied, "somewhat satisfied," "somewhat dissatisfied," "completely dissatisfied," with action taken, or had "concluded that no action had been taken."Knowledge of benefit packages was measured by percent of respondents checking "don't know" for all nine items on a question about benefit package contents.

By these measures the provider-sponsored plans were found to be least responsive to consumers, the group practice plans the most responsive.

Product: Index of Benefit Package Comprehensiveness

Three measures were employed to estimate the comprehensiveness of benefit packages: amount of control over consumer behavior built into the package, portion of family expenses paid by the plan, and consumer-physician evaluations of coverage.

Control of consumer use of medical services was studied in terms of coverage for eight benefit package items. These items are routine physical examinations, doctors' office visits, doctors' services in the hospital, room and board in a hospital 365 days per year, maternity, doctors' house calls, care by a psychiatrist, and eye examinations for glasses. Each item is characterized by the percent of consumers in each plan with complete, nearly complete, partial, and no coverage for each item. For purposes of the comprehensiveness index the plans are ranked according to an average percent of consumers having *no coverage* for each of the eight items, with rank "1" indicating the lowest average percent hence the least controls over consumer use of medical services.

Portion of family expenses paid by the health plan was calculated from medical records, claims data, and benefit package information for a 12-month period. For the comprehensiveness index the plans are ranked in order of average percent of total bills paid. In this case rank "1" means the highest average percent paid.

Finally, both consumers and physicians were asked to evaluate the adequacy of financial benefits in each of the six plans. Consumers were asked to rate their own benefit package on a scale running from "very satisfied" to "very dissatisfied." Physicians evaluated benefit packages in response to this question: "How would you evaluate the plan you know most about on adequacy of coverage of the most usual policy sold by the plan?." Response was a checkmark in one of four categories: excellent, good, fair and poor. For the comprehensiveness index, plans were ranked according to an average percent of consumers and physicians in each plan who checked "very satisfied" and "excellent," respectively. Consumers and physicians were weighted equally. In this case rank "1" indicated the highest average percent.

The index of comprehensiveness is expressed as a sum of the rankings on the three components (control over consumers, portion of expenses paid, and consumer-physician evaluation). By this measure the large group practice plan was found to provide the most comprehensive benefits (sum of ranks equals three), whereas the hospital-sponsored plan had the least comprehensive benefits (sum of ranks equals 17).

MEASURES ON CONSUMERS

Consumer Need

This concept is meant to reflect objectively the probability that medical care should be obtained by persons with certain characteristics. It is associated closely with usual actuarial determination of "risk" of an insured population. Indicators of need used in this study are subscriber age, average age of all insured family members, presence of females of child-bearing age, family size, number of family members with chronic illnesses, and number of family members experiencing acute illness during the three months before our study. For purposes of an overall index of need we used percent figures in each plan reflecting the portion of the consumer sample in the high-risk categories. For age this was the percent 47 years and older, for average age the percent with average 40 and over, for family size the percent with three or more members, and for the other three indicators the percent of families with those characteristics (chronic and acute illness and women in the child-bearing ages). Using these percentages, we ranked plans on each indicator, with rank "1" indicating lowest need. Ranks are summed to obtain an overall need index for each plan. We found that the large group practice plan consumers had the highest need on this measure (sum of ranks 30) and that the physician-sponsored plan consumers had the lowest need (sum of ranks 11).

In the analysis of influence of consumer characteristics, consumers are divided into two categories, using four of the above six indicators. The two categories are titled *low-need families* and *high-need families*. The four indicators used are average family age (above and below 40), presence of chronic illness, presence of acute illness, and presence of females in the child-bearing years. In most instances statistics are discussed in terms of the two categories for each indicator (e.g., amount of medical care used by families with chronic illness, as compared with use by families in which no chronic illness is reported), and overall statistics presented which are averages across the four indicators.

Consumer Demand

Social factors that facilitate access to medical care and underlie a readiness to use health services are sociologically defined in this study as demand for services. Greater demand for health services is thought to be indicated by the following measures: family income of $11,000 per year or more, college education of head of household, professional and white-collar occupation of head of household, white American and high status European ethnic background, symptom-hypersensitivity (explained below), less than three of five common complaints about physicians (doctors keep patients waiting, too concerned about money, resent home visits, do not give individual attention, make you feel visits are not necessary), and recognition of the positive influence of health insurance on use of medical services.

As in the *need* measure, the plans were ranked on the above 11 characteristics, with a rank of "1" indicating the lowest demand of the six plans. The consumer demand index is calculated as a sum of these rankings. Using this measure, we found that the small group practice plan had the highest demand (sum of rankings 51) and the large commercial plan the lowest demand (sum of rankings 35).

Outcome measures are presented in terms of *high-demand* and *low-demand* families in the data analysis. Indicators of the demand concept in the analysis are two socioeconomic indicators—income and education—and three attitudinal indicators—attitude toward health insurance influence on use of services, attitude toward symptoms (symptom sensitivity), and attitude toward physicians (extent of negativity). At times data are also presented by ethnic status of the subscriber when this appears particularly interesting. As with *need*, outcome data are generally discussed in terms of differences between high-demand and low-demand categories for each indicator and overall statistics presented which are averages of outcomes for each indicator.

Symptom Sensitivity

The index of symptom sensitivity was developed by Hetherington and Hopkins (1969). It is designed to measure the respondent's inclination to seek out medical services in response to certain illness symptoms. A question in the consumer questionnaire read, "Which of the following complaints do you think are serious enough to see a doctor about?" This was followed by a checklist of 11 symptoms, each of which had been previously judged for seriousness by a panel of 10 physicians in community practice. The physicians were asked to judge each symptom on a five-point scale of seriousness, using as a basis for judgment their own experience with patients presenting those complaints. The 11 symptoms are (in order of appearance in the questionnaire) allergy, unexplained weight loss, insomnia, blood in the urine, "nerves," general fatigue, unexplained weight gain, persistent joint or muscle pains, gaseousness, pain in the chest, and frequent sore throats. As a result of the physician judgments each symptom was assigned a weight corresponding to the average rank assigned by the 10 physicians.

Guttman scaling was employed on responses to the consumer questionnaire to find out if the symptoms (or some subset of them) were scalable. The physicians' ranking was used as the criterion. Of the 11 symptoms eight were scalable at the .92 level of the coefficient of reproducibility. These eight symptoms, in order of increasing seriousness, are insomnia (least serious), "nerves," general fatigue, persistent joint and muscle pains, unexplained weight loss, pain in the chest, and blood in the urine (most serious).

For purposes of analysis the consumers were assigned to three groups on the basis of their symptom-sensitivity scores. The first group (symptom-insensitive) contains those respondents who failed to check symptoms that the panel of physicians rated on the "serious" half of the seriousness scale. The second group (symptom-sensitive) agreed with physicians about the symptoms that required medical attention. The third group (hypersensitive) constitutes those who checked symptoms that the physicians rated on the "trivial" half of the seriousness scale.

Emphasis in the analysis is on the symptom hypersensitive group. Using this measure (which is part of the demand concept), we found the highest percent of hypersensitive consumers was found in the large group practice plan and the highest percent of "insensitive" consumers in the large commercial plan.

MEASURES ON PHYSICIANS

Limiting Factors

Limiting factors are those characteristics of a physician's background that tend to restrict opportunity or "life chances" and are thought to have some effect on the kind of medical care provided by him. Indicators employed for this concept are age, years since the M.D. degree, father's socioeconomic status, location of medical school attended, and applicants per position for the medical school attended (for years of attendance). Among these measures the major discrimination was found for physician age; the small group practice physicians were significantly older on the average and the large group practice physicians were younger.

Four indicators of this concept are used in the analysis of outcomes. (Analysis of physician determinants of outcome is mainly limited to quality of care.) The categories of *low* and *high* on the limiting concept are established on the four indicators by these cutoffs: age 40 and under, upper or middle-class background (Hollingshead classes I through III), trained in the United States, Canada, Great Britain, or Scandinavia, and trained in a highly sought after medical school. Like the consumer characteristics, outcome data are discussed in terms of each of these four indicators and overall data supplied as an average of all four (to provide data for "low" and "high" limitation categories).

An additional stage in presentation of physician data is the averaging of characteristics for all physicians seen by the consumer in the 12-month study period. Thus the outcome data are presented in a form such as, "average factor quality scores for consumers visiting physicians whose average age is 40 or older are significantly lower than scores for consumers visiting younger physicians." This seemingly complex presentation results from treating the consumer as the basic unit of analysis and the average characteristics of physicians visited as consumer traits.

Qualifying Factors

This concept involves activities engaged in by the physician to qualify himself better for medical practice. These are voluntary activities beyond those required for medical practice (M.D. degree and internship). Indicators employed here are board status (certification), specialty practice (as reported by the physician), attendance at formal courses in continuing medical education, and reading of professional journals.

Analysis of the influence of qualifying factors concentrates on two indicators: certification status and continuing medical education. The *high* qualification category is indicated by board certification, and by attendance at one or more formal courses in continuing medical education during the preceding 12 months.

Facilitating Factors

There are structural and behavioral components in this concept. The structural component reflects aspects of the physician's practice that encourage good medical care. Indicators employed are number of paramedical persons available per physician, amount of time required to obtain emergency lab measures (the example used in this study is an emergency blood-sugar determination), and characteristics of hospitals used (number of beds, accreditation, occupancy). The behavioral component is measured by patient load (average number of patients seen per hour in office practice), amount of consultation with other physicians over the preceding week, number of regularly scheduled medical meetings attended per month, and "conversion factors" used to determine charges to patients.

Because of lack of variation within the group practice plans on the structural indicators, analysis concentrates on the behavioral component. Results are usually presented in terms of patient load and rates of interaction with other physicians (consultations and medical meetings).

Motivating Factors

This concept taps the influence of the attitudes of physicians toward medical care and patients. Indicators of the concept are attitude toward necessity of the annual medical examination for all people, complaints about patients, and attitudes toward medical record-keeping.

Data are presented in terms of *high* and *low* categories as before; indicators of the former are agreement with the necessity of the annual exam and fewer than three complaints about patients (five of the seven complaint items presented in the physicians' questionnaire were found to be scalable by the Guttman technique and were used in the analysis). Particular emphasis was given to analysis of the effect of the physicians' attitude that patients make visits unnecessarily, because this attitude was thought to be particularly relevant to the large group practice plan in which comprehensive benefits might encourage such visits.

The questionnaire also asked physicians to respond to seven complaints "often made by physicians about patients." The respondent was asked to check only those he *frequently* had. The items are change doctors too often, complain too much about waiting, see a doctor unnecessarily, fail to make appointments ahead of time, fail to keep appointments, expect unnecessary home and night calls, and expect too much time and attention.

MEASURES ON OUTCOME

Medical Care Bit (MCB)

Medical records copied from physician offices and hospitals were divided into medical care bits for purposes of analysis. The MCB is the portion of the record that represents a single patient-server contact and all services ordered during that contact (laboratory, radiology, and other ancillary services). We saw the MCB as the smallest discrete unit of medical care with substantive meaning. Division of the record in this manner permitted us to establish a chronological record of events in the care of one consumer. All MCBs were organized by date, and the result was a "story" of the year's medical care; if any gaps were found, they were checked out with the physicians and hospitals involved.

Each MCB was coded on aspects of the procedures performed during that contact. If there was referral to another physician, the contact with the physician to whom the patient was referred constituted another MCB.

Working definitions of each variable coded (see Chapter 4, Table 4-1) are not spelled out here because of the amount of space that would be required. For the most part variable names convey the sense of each indicator. Detailed working definitions are available from the authors on request.

The criteria for judging reliability were the following:

- 85% agreement with group coding
- errors appeared to be random and did not show consistent bias.

Quality of Care Factors

Information on the MCBs thought to be related to various aspects of the quality of medical care was factor analyzed to identify unidimensional concepts.

The factor analysis was begun by constructing an overall correlation matrix of the variables outlined in Table 4-1. Variables that accounted for cell sizes of less than 1000 were deleted as providing unstable estimates of true correlations. An initial factor analysis was run on the remaining variables by using conventional options (i.e., Varimax rotation). The analysis extracted six factors as significant, the first four of which appeared to be the theoretically predicted dimensions of range of services: *prevention, continuity,* and two aspects of the *rationality* concept.

Subsequent factor analyses were performed on different subsets of the original variables. The first of these was done on a "core" of variables derived from the first general factor analysis. Thus we began with 10 variables that had the highest loadings on (relationships to) the four interpretable factors identified by the first factor analysis. Variables were added stepwise to the analysis. It became apparent with many subsequent analyses that the four factors originally defined were stable in that their core indicators did not shift from factor to factor as other variables were added and deleted. We decided that the two dimensions predicted in the original conceptualization which did not appear in the original factor analysis would not be pursued: comprehensiveness and coordination. Indicators conceptually assigned to those dimensions either did not load significantly in the analysis or appeared in one of the four factors.

In all, 20 variables were used to define the four factors (see Table 4-2), 15 of which had high loadings significant enough (greater than .40) to be considered major contributors to the definition of the factors.

Four factors were derived from the data. These factors and their major indicators (i.e., is, those items with the biggest loadings on that factor) are as follows: (1) prevention (Pap smear, pelvic examination, annual checkup, rectal examination, physical examination); (2) rationality (physical examination, chief complaint, history, diagnosis, progress notes); (3) verification (complete blood count, urinalysis, serology, chest X ray); (4) continuity (followup visit, followup visit requested).

Each MCB is assigned a factor score based on the presence or absence of procedures such as these and on the weighting of each procedure that reflects its importance on that dimension (weights are statistically determined; they do not reflect judgmental bias). Twenty items are used to determine the factor score for any particular MCB, but the ones listed above contribute most.

In order to calculate factor scores for each of the four factors, a set of 20 factor loadings derived from the factor analysis was taken as coefficients. Then each variable was standardized as follows:

$Zi = (Xi - Mi) / Si$

where

Zi = the new standard variable

Xi = the original raw score

Mi = the mean value

Si = the standard deviation.

After the Z scores were computed, factor scores were calculated by the formula:

$Fi = \text{sum}\ (Cij \times Zj)$

where

Fi = the i th factor score

Cij = the factor loading coefficient for the i th factor and j th variable

Zj = the z value of the j th variable.

The result is a perfectly usable factor score and would normally be the final step. Certain variables, however, were included that applied only to adult women. In order to make scores between the sexes comparable, an additional procedure was employed. The highest and lowest factor scores that could be attained by men and women were computed. Then new scores were derived by subtracting the minimum from each score and dividing by the range:

$g = (f - i) / (h - i)$

where

g = new factor score

f = old factor score

i = minimum value

h = maximum value

The new score ranges from zero to one for both sexes.

For purposes of analysis factor scores are expressed as averages per person per MCB. In addition, distributions are provided to show the percent of persons with average scores in the upper 20% of the distribution ("high") and in the lower 20% ("low"). Only data on ambulatory care are presented.

Doctor Care Index

This index was designed to measure volume of services provided. Use of medical care is usually reported as doctor visits or hospital days, but these measures hide a lot of variation in the amount of work done. The doctor care index uses units of medical care assigned by the *California Relative Value Studies* and converts them into "dummy dollars" by multiplying the units by the average conversion factors reported by physicians in the study. This was necessary because the units of medical care assigned by the CRVS are not equivalent from one type of care to another, hence are not additive. From the survey of physicians we determined the following charges per unit of care: medicine $7.10, surgery $7.43, anesthesia $7.10, laboratory $5.42, radiology $5.42.

Units of the doctor care index do not represent price because the dollar values are averages across all plans. They are merely indicators of volume of service and as such are comparable across plans. For the purpose of analysis data on this index are presented as units per person.

Index